Introduction to Healthcare Information Technology

Mark Ciampa, Ph.D.
Mark Revels, Ph.D.

Australia • Brazil • Canada • Mexico • Singapore • United Kingdom • United States

Introduction to Healthcare Information Technology, **First Edition**
Mark Ciampa, Mark Revels

Vice President, Careers & Computing:
Dave Garza

Executive Editor: Stephen Helba

Managing Editor: Marah Bellegarde

Senior Product Manager:
Michelle Ruelos Cannistraci

Developmental Editor: Deb Kaufmann

Editorial Assistant: Jennifer Wheaton

Vice President, Marketing:
Jennifer Ann Baker

Marketing Director: Deborah S. Yarnell

Senior Marketing Manager:
Mark Linton

Associate Marketing Manager:
Erica Glisson

Production Director: Wendy Troeger

Production Manager: Andrew Crouth

Senior Content Project Manager:
Andrea Majot

Senior Art Director: Jack Pendleton

Library of Congress Control Number: 2012930410
Package ISBN-13: 978-1-133-78777-8
Book only ISBN-13: 978-1-133-78778-5

Cengage
200 Pier 4 Boulevard
Boston, MA 02210
USA

Cengage is a leading provider of customized learning solutions with employees residing in nearly 40 different countries and sales in more than 125 countries around the world. Find your local representative at **www.cengage.com.**

To learn more about Cengage platforms and services, register or access your online learning solution, or purchase materials for your course, visit **www.cengage.com.**

Printed in the United States of America
Print Number: 03   Print Year: 2022

Brief Contents

Table of Contents

CHAPTER 5
Medical Business Operations **143**

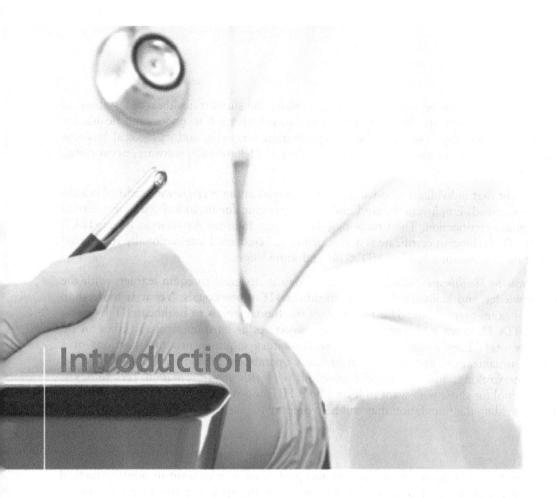

Introduction

The healthcare industry is growing at a feverish pace. In 2009, healthcare spending in the United States was almost $2.5 trillion, a 5.5 percent increase over the previous year, according to the U.S. Department of Health and Human Services Centers for Medicare and Medicaid Services (CMS). This represents almost 17 percent of all of the total economic activity in the country. Over the next decade, healthcare spending is predicted to double as the population ages and more patients visit the almost 800,000 physicians, dentists, chiropractors, optometrists, physical therapists, and podiatrists in the United States[1]

In addition to this rapid growth, the healthcare industry in the United States is undergoing some of its most significant changes in the last 100 years. The federal government is encouraging—and in some cases requiring—the healthcare industry to move from electronic medical records (EMRs), which are electronic digital versions of a patient's paper chart found in a clinician's office, to electronic health records (EHRs). EHRs focus on the total health of the patient by going beyond the standard clinical data collected in a provider's office. EHRs are designed to be shared among all the healthcare providers involved with a patient's care, such as laboratories and specialists. EHR information moves with the patient—not only between specialists, hospitals, and nursing facilities, but across the country. EHRs better support the concept of health care as a team effort that involves multiple professionals. All healthcare team members can have ready access to the latest information to provide for more coordinated and patient-centered care.

In order to support the rapid growth of health care and the movement to adopt EHRs, an increasing number of healthcare information technology (HIT) technicians will be needed.

These professionals must be able to implement, deploy, and support healthcare IT systems in a variety of clinical settings. Not only will these individuals need to understand healthcare regulatory requirements, how a healthcare organization functions, and its medical business operations, but they must also have an understanding of IT hardware, software, networking, and security.

It is important that individuals who want to be employed in the ever-growing field of healthcare IT be certified. Employers demand and pay a premium for personnel who have earned an appropriate certification. The Computing Technology Industry Association (CompTIA®) Healthcare IT Technician certificate is a vendor-neutral credential internationally recognized as validating a foundation level of HIT skills and knowledge.

Introduction to Healthcare Information Technology is designed to equip learners with the basic knowledge and skills needed to be healthcare IT professionals. Yet it is more than merely an "exam prep" book. This text teaches the fundamentals of healthcare IT by using the CompTIA Healthcare IT Technician exam objectives as its framework. It takes an in-depth view of HIT by examining healthcare regulatory requirements, the functions of a healthcare organization, and its medical business operations, in addition to IT hardware, software, networking, and security. *Introduction to Healthcare Information Technology* is a valuable tool for those who want to learn about HIT and who desire to enter this growing field by providing the foundation that will help prepare for the CompTIA certification exam.

Intended Audience

This book is designed to meet the needs of students and professionals who want to master practical healthcare IT. A basic knowledge of computers and networks is all that is required to use this book. Those seeking to pass the CompTIA Healthcare IT Technician HIT-001 certificate exam will find the text's approach and content especially helpful because all exam objectives are covered (see Appendix A and the inside cover of this book). For more information on the HIT certificate, visit CompTIA's Web site at *www.comptia.org*. However, *Introduction to Healthcare Information Technology* is much more than an examination prep book; it also covers a broad range of healthcare IT topics while satisfying the HIT exam objectives.

The book's pedagogical features are designed to provide a truly interactive learning experience to help prepare you for the challenges of HIT. In addition to the information presented in the text, each chapter includes case studies that place you in the role of problem solver, requiring you to apply concepts presented in the chapter to achieve successful solutions.

Chapter Descriptions

Here is a summary of the topics covered in each chapter of this book:

Chapter 1, "Introduction to Healthcare IT," begins by introducing the field of healthcare IT. It defines HIT, notes its benefits, and examines various regulatory agencies and regulations applicable to HIT. The chapter finishes with an overview of legal documents that HIT professionals encounter on a regular basis.

Chapter 2, "Healthcare Organizations and Operations," examines the various types of healthcare-related organizations, their operations and codes of conduct, and proper methods for managing protected health information.

Chapter 3, "Desktop IT Operations," looks at desktop IT operations in the healthcare field that support electronic records. It begins with an overview of IT, followed by how to install and troubleshoot desktop workstations and other devices, and then explores how to configure different types of devices.

Chapter 4, "Network IT Operations," examines computer networking in the healthcare field. It explores common network devices, including network servers and how to set up a network and then troubleshoot it, and then looks at the network technologies that can be used for electronic medical records and electronic health records.

Chapter 5, "Medical Business Operations," reviews the various aspects of medical business operations by covering terminology, functional departments within various organizations, clinical process and software applications, and typical medical devices.

Chapter 6, "Document Imaging and Problem Solving," explores the various aspects of document imaging, interfacing, and problem solving. It covers file types and their characteristics, scanning and indexing, medical interface components, how to diagnose interface problems, how to troubleshoot clinical software problems, and the concept of change control and why it is important.

Chapter 7, "Basic Healthcare Information Security," looks at the fundamentals of IT security as it relates to healthcare. This chapter provides a definition of information security and examines the different types of physical security that can be used to keep out data thieves. It also explores computer technology protections and how to back up data as protection against an attack or disaster.

Chapter 8, "Advanced Healthcare Information Security," examines what cryptography is and how it can be used for protection. It is followed by a study of wireless security and remote access. The chapter concludes with a look at how to securely dispose of documents.

Appendix A, "CompTIA Healthcare IT Technician Certificate Examination Objectives," provides a complete listing of the latest CompTIA Healthcare IT Technician certificate exam objectives and shows the chapters and headings in the book that cover material associated with each objective.

Appendix B, "Healthcare IT Web Sites," offers a listing of several important Web sites that contain healthcare and IT-related information.

Appendix C, "Healthcare IT Acronyms," lists the healthcare IT acronyms introduced in this book along with their meanings.

In addition, a **Glossary** compiles the chapter Key Terms and their definitions for easy reference.

Features

To aid you in fully understanding computer and network security, this book includes many features designed to enhance your learning experience.

- **Maps to CompTIA Objectives.** The material in this text covers all of the CompTIA Healthcare IT Technician exam objectives.

- **Chapter Objectives.** Each chapter begins with a detailed list of the concepts to be mastered within that chapter. This list provides you with both a quick reference to the chapter's contents and a useful study aid.

- **Healthcare IT: Challenges and Opportunities.** Each chapter opens with a vignette of a healthcare practice that helps to introduce the material covered in that chapter.

- **Illustrations and Tables.** Numerous illustrations of healthcare and IT topics help you visualize specific elements, theories, and concepts. In addition, the many tables provide details and comparisons of practical and theoretical information.

- **Chapter Summaries.** Each chapter's text is followed by a summary of the concepts introduced in that chapter. These summaries provide a helpful way to review the ideas covered in each chapter.

- **Key Terms.** All of the terms in each chapter that were introduced with bold text are gathered in a Key Terms list with definitions at the end of the chapter, providing additional review and highlighting key concepts.

- **Healthcare IT Acronyms.** A table of healthcare IT acronyms that were introduced in each chapter assists learners in recognizing and interpreting the many acronyms that are used in this field.

- **Review Questions.** The end-of-chapter assessment begins with a set of review questions that reinforce the ideas introduced in each chapter. These questions help you evaluate and apply the material you have learned. Answering these questions will ensure that you have mastered the important concepts and provide valuable practice for taking CompTIA's certificate exam.

- **Case Projects.** Located at the end of each chapter are several Case Projects. In these extensive exercises, you implement the skills and knowledge gained in the chapter through real design and implementation scenarios.

- **Healthcare IT: Challenges and Opportunities—Revisited.** A follow-up to the opening chapter vignette gives you the opportunity to apply what you have learned in the chapter to addressing a healthcare IT challenge.

Text and Graphic Conventions

Wherever appropriate, additional information and exercises have been added to this book to help you better understand the topic at hand. Icons throughout the text alert you to additional materials. The following icons are used in this textbook:

The HIT Technician Exam Objectives icon lists relevant CompTIA Healthcare IT Technician exam objectives for each major chapter heading.

The Note icon draws your attention to additional helpful material related to the subject being described.

Tips based on the authors' experience provide extra information about how to attack a problem or what to do in real-world situations.

CompTIA Healthcare IT Technician Certificate

There are five domains covered on the Healthcare IT Technician exam:

Domain	% of Examination
1.0 Regulatory Requirements	13%
2.0 Organizational Behavior	15%
3.0 IT Operations	26%
4.0 Medical Business Operations	25%
5.0 Security	21%

CertBlaster Test Prep Resources

Introduction to Healthcare Information Technology includes CertBlaster test preparation questions that mirror the look and feel of CompTIA's HIT certificate exam. For additional information on the CertBlaster test preparation questions, go to *http://www.dtipublishing.com*.

To log in and access the CertBlaster test preparation questions for *Introduction to Healthcare Information Technology*, please go to *http://www.certblaster.com/cengage.htm*.

To install CertBlaster:

1. Click the title of the CertBlaster test prep application you want to download.
2. Save the program (.EXE) file to a folder on your C: drive. (*Warning*: If you skip this step, your CertBlaster will not install correctly.)
3. Click **Start** and choose **Run**.
4. Click **Browse** and then navigate to the folder that contains the .EXE file. Select the .EXE file and click **Open**.
5. Click **OK** and then follow the onscreen instructions.
6. When the installation is complete, click **Finish**.
7. Click **Start**, choose **All programs**, and click **CertBlaster**.

To register CertBlaster:

1. Open the CertBlaster test you want by double-clicking it.
2. In the menu bar, click **File**, choose **Register Exam**, and enter the access code when prompted. Use the access code provided inside the card placed in the back of this book.

Instructor's Materials

A wide array of instructor's materials is provided with this book. The following supplemental materials are available for use in a classroom setting. All the supplements available with this book are provided to the instructor on a single CD-ROM (ISBN: 9781133787792) and online at the textbook's Web site.

Electronic Instructor's Manual. The Instructor's Manual that accompanies this textbook includes the following items: additional instructional material to assist in class preparation, including suggestions for lecture topics, syllabus, and solutions to all end-of-chapter materials.

ExamView® Test Bank. This Windows-based testing software helps instructors design and administer tests and pretests. In addition to generating tests that can be printed and administered, this full-featured program has an online testing component that allows students to take tests at the computer and have their exams automatically graded.

PowerPoint Presentations. This book comes with a set of Microsoft PowerPoint slides for each chapter. These slides are meant to be used as a teaching aid for classroom presentations, to be made available to students on the network for chapter review, or to be printed for classroom distribution. Instructors are also at liberty to add their own slides for other topics introduced.

Figure Files. All of the figures and tables in the book are reproduced on the Instructor Resources CD. Similar to PowerPoint presentations, these are included as a teaching aid for classroom presentation, to make available to students for review, or to be printed for classroom distribution.

Instructor Resources CD (ISBN: 9781133787792)

Please visit *login.cengage.com* and log in to access instructor-specific resources.

To access additional course materials, please visit *www.cengage.com*. At the *Cengage.com* home page, search for the ISBN of your title (from the back cover of your book) using the search box at the top of the page. This will take you to the product page where these resources can be found.

For those who are interested in learning more about the security topics discussed in the book, please visit the Information Security Community Site at *http://www.cengage.com/community/infosec* as an additional resource. The Information Security Community Site allows you to connect with students, professors, and professionals from around the world, download resources such as instructional videos and labs, and see up-to-date news, videos, and articles related to information security.

About the Authors

Mark Ciampa, Ph.D., Security+, is Assistant Professor of Computer Information Systems at Western Kentucky University in Bowling Green, Kentucky. Previously, he served as Associate Professor and Director of Academic Computing for 20 years at Volunteer State Community College in Gallatin, Tennessee. Dr. Ciampa has worked in the IT industry as a computer consultant for the U.S. Postal Service, the Tennessee Municipal Technical Advisory Service, and the University of Tennessee. He is also the author of many Cengage Learning textbooks, including *Security+ Guide to Network Security Fundamentals Fourth Edition*, *Security Awareness: Applying Practical Security in Your World*, *CWNA Guide to Wireless LANs*, *Second Edition*, *Guide to Wireless Communications*, and *Networking BASICS*. He holds a Ph.D. in digital communications systems from Indiana State University.

Mark Revels, Ph.D., is Assistant Professor of Computer Information Systems at Western Kentucky University in Bowling Green, Kentucky. He is a technology educator, researcher, and professional with 30 years of progressive experience, including biomedical and hospital physical plant systems management; development and management of decision support, inventory control, and logistics systems; and development and management of core manufacturing systems for multiple international manufacturers. He holds a Ph.D. in technology management from Indiana State University. He also holds three industry certifications: one in biomedical equipment management (Association for the Advancement of Medical Instrumentation), one in information systems (Institute for the Certification of Computing Professionals), and one in manufacturing and operations management (Association for Operations Management).

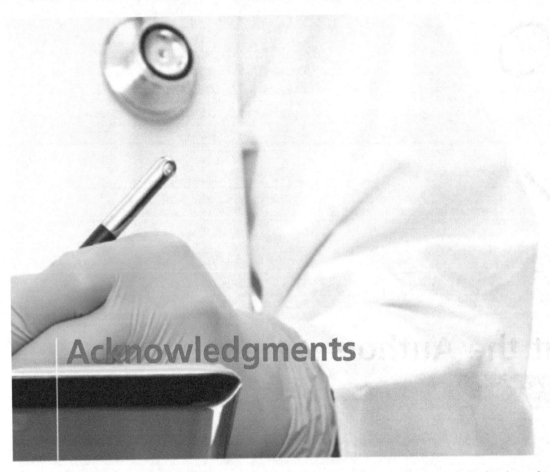

Acknowledgments

A large team of dedicated professionals all contributed to the creation of this book, and we are honored to be part of the team. Special thanks go to Executive Editor Stephen Helba for giving us the opportunity to work on this project and for providing his continual support. Also thanks to Senior Product Manager Michelle Ruelos Cannistraci, who was very supportive and helped keep this fast-moving project on track. And a big thank you to the team of peer reviewers who evaluated each chapter and provided very helpful suggestions and contributions: Betty Haar, Kirkwood Community College; Leonora Lambert, Midland College; Greer Stevenson, University of Illinois at Chicago; Nick Symiakakis, Noble Hospital; DeVonica Vaught, Indian River State College; and Lynn Ward, Montana State University – Great Falls College of Technology. And to everyone else who contributed to this book, we extend our sincere thanks.

Special recognition again goes to Developmental Editor Deb Kaufmann. Deb made many helpful suggestions, found our errors, watched every small detail, and turned it all into a book. On top of it all, Deb is a joy to work with. Without question, Deb is simply the very best there is.

Mark Revels—Thanks to my lovely wife and the love of my life, Sherry. You helped make a difficult project much less difficult. Thank you for all you do for me, for your patience and support, and for being my best friend. And to Emily and Jon, I am very proud of you both. Keep working toward your dreams.

Mark Ciampa—I want to thank my wonderful wife, Susan. Once again, she was patient and supportive of me throughout this project. I could not have written this book without her.

Reference

1. "Healthcare IT Fast Facts," CompTIA Healthcare IT Community, accessed Nov. 30, 2011, http://www.comptia.org/membership/communities/healthcareIT.aspx.

Dedication

Mark Revels—To Sherry

Mark Ciampa—To Braden, Mia, Abby, and Gabe

Introduction to Healthcare
Information Technology

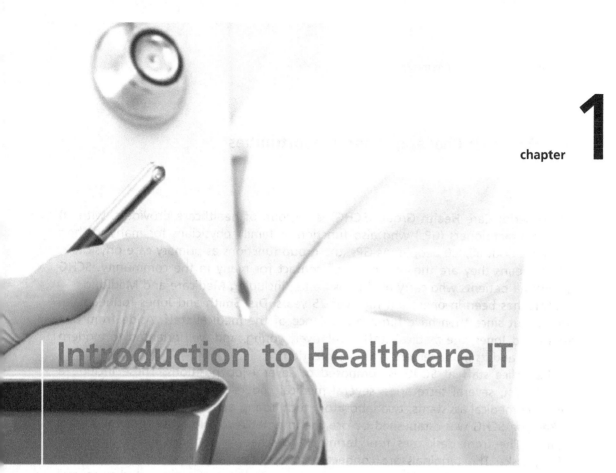

chapter 1

Introduction to Healthcare IT

After completing this chapter, you should be able to do the following:

- Define healthcare information technology

- Recognize some of the benefits of healthcare IT

- Describe the CompTIA Healthcare IT Technician Certificate

- List major healthcare regulators

- Summarize the major healthcare regulations

- Describe typical healthcare legal practices

Healthcare IT: Challenges and Opportunities

The Superior Care Health Group (SCHG) is a group of healthcare providers, with 10 general practitioners (GPs) who also function as family physicians for many in their town of about 50,000 people. As GPs, the group functions as primary care physicians, which means they are the first point of contact for many in the community. SCHG accepts all patients who carry health insurance, including Medicare and Medicaid.

SCHG has been in operation for over 25 years. Drs. Smith and Jones founded the group, but since then have hired the balance of the medical staff. Aside from Drs. Smith and Jones, the medical staff is relatively young, and well oriented to modern medicine and its management and organization.

The office staff at SCHG is composed of several job positions. These include a receptionist, several secretaries, several medical coders/billers, several transcriptionists, nine medical assistants, two laboratory technicians, and an office manager.

Because SCHG was established before the Internet revolution, use of computers is limited. The front desk uses four terminals to schedule patients and to complete billing tasks. The terminals are connected to two central personal computers that run an old version of the Linux operating system. They are also connected to several dot-matrix printers used to print billing forms and other pertinent financial information.

All patient information including the medical record is maintained by paper files. When a doctor examines a patient, all of the pertinent chart information is recorded either by the doctor writing directly in the paper chart, or by voice dictation, which is then later transcribed into the chart.

Drs. Smith and Jones developed SCHG to be as vertically integrated as possible, so they own and manage some of their medical equipment. Therefore, they have a small laboratory where routine blood tests and urinalysis can be completed on-site. As laboratory equipment becomes obsolete quickly, all the lab equipment is less than one year old. They also have a small x-ray suite for chest x-rays, broken bones, and so on. Unfortunately, x-ray equipment is very large, expensive, and hasn't really changed much for simpler examinations like those conducted by SCHG. Thus, all of the x-ray equipment is original. For cardiac concerns, they have their own EKG equipment, but only half of the machines are current; the other half are original to the group.

Drs. Smith and Jones recently learned of something new from the government called the HITECH Act. They are concerned that new government regulations will constrain their business without significant improvement in their ability to deliver quality health care.

While governments debate how to balance their budgets, these facts are clear:

- Health costs keep rising.
- Technology continues to improve while becoming less expensive.
- Information technology adoption by the healthcare industry is slower than in other industries.

The question is often raised, "Why hasn't the healthcare industry embraced information technology?" There are many reasons. Some healthcare professionals are concerned that they will not be able to recoup their investment in time and money spent to convert existing manual systems to electronic systems. Another problem is the way in which the healthcare system is fragmented. Patients are frequently required to see doctors from several different groups for the same diagnosis. This makes automation much more difficult because each group can have its own separate system. However, perhaps one of the most important obstacles is the shortage of trained healthcare technology professionals needed to implement the new technologies. As reported by the U.S. Federal Government, the need for such professionals could grow as much as 20 percent by 2018, with employment projected to grow faster than average. Even now, health information professional jobs are among the 20 fastest growing occupations in the U.S., which has driven some salaries beyond $50,000 per year.[1]

Given the demand and compensation levels for healthcare information technology professionals, it is unlikely that the need can be met using existing information technology experts. Although healthcare information technology is similar in some respects to information technology in other industries (for example, the same types of computers are used in health care as in education and manufacturing), it has many aspects that are unique. For example, healthcare providers must adhere to scores of governmental and accreditation regulations to which other industries are immune. Technologists who are employed in the implementation and maintenance of healthcare information technology must be aware of these regulations.

This chapter introduces the field of healthcare information technology. It begins by defining healthcare information technology, noting some of its benefits, and reviewing CompTIA's response to the shortage of trained healthcare information technology professionals. Then the chapter examines various regulatory agencies and regulations applicable to healthcare information technology, and finishes with an overview of legal documents that healthcare information technology professionals encounter on a regular basis.

The words *healthcare* and *health care* are not the same. When used as one word, healthcare describes an entity such as a system (as in healthcare system) or information technology (as in healthcare information technology). When used as two words, health care is a thing (as in providing health care).

What Is Healthcare Information Technology?

Healthcare information technology has been described in many ways: as a framework for managing health information, as a mechanism to improve patient care, and as an enabler of patient care coordination. All of these descriptions convey the results of using healthcare

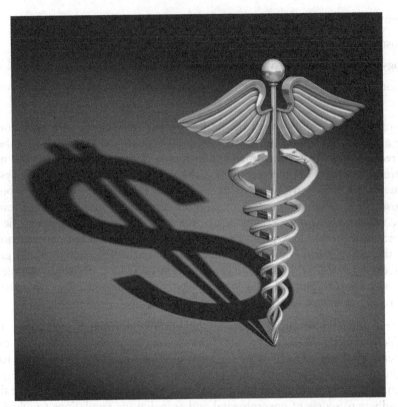

The cost of health care is a major concern for individuals and organizations
© James Stiedl/www.Shutterstock.com

information technology, but fundamentally, healthcare information technology is the application of information technology to the healthcare industry.

When defining HIT, some sources use "healthcare information technology," while others use "health information technology." They may be considered synonymous.

At the conceptual level, **information technology (IT)**, or the use of hardware and software in an effort to manage and manipulate data and information, consists of devices that input, process, and output data and information. At the physical level, these devices could include keyboards, computers, printers, and network devices, which are collectively known as **hardware**. In addition to hardware, IT consists of **software**. Software contains the logic that makes computers do what they do. Software is like a set of instructions that helps hardware process data into information. Together, hardware and software are used to manage and manipulate both data and information. Therefore, a more precise definition of **healthcare information technology (HIT)** is the use of hardware and software in an effort to manage and manipulate health data and information.

IT is composed of hardware and software

© Sergej Khakimullin/www.Shutterstock.com

 Data can be considered raw facts that have little or no meaning, while information is data with meaning. For example, hospital patient census reports are data unless they address a specific need, such as determining length-of-stay trends.

Benefits of HIT

As countries face ever-more-challenging budget crises, healthcare costs continue to be at the forefront. Headlines such as "Baby boomers worry about finances and health costs," "State employees get freeze in healthcare costs," and "Rise in healthcare costs doubles that of inflation" are common. The data behind these rising costs include the following:[2]

- In 1960, the United States spent approximately 5.2 percent of all its goods and services (also known as gross domestic product, or GDP) on healthcare. In 2007, that number had increased to 17 percent.

- The greatest share of each dollar spent (about 30 percent) goes to hospital care, while only 6 percent is allocated to nursing homes.

- The United States spent over $7400 per person for health care in 2007, up from $7026 the previous year. This represents an increase of over 5 percent, compared to the year's average inflation rate of 2.85 percent.

According to the Congressional Budget Office (CBO), advances in technology can be attributed to about half of healthcare spending increases.[3] It is clear from these statistics that the cost of health care in the United States has continued to increase over time. Although some individuals claim that the federal health care statute known as the **Patient Protection and Affordable Care Act (PPACA)** enacted in 2010 by President Barack Obama will reduce healthcare costs over time, others have proposed specific recommendations that focus on specific systemic problems.

A report from the CBO called "Evidence on the Costs and Benefits of Health Information Technology"[4] states that the use of an **electronic medical record (EMR)** for patient care would have several efficiency benefits. These include:

- Eliminating the use of medical transcription
- Reducing the need to physically retrieve patient's charts or files
- Reminding prescribers to prescribe less costly drugs
- Reducing the number of duplicated diagnostic tests

These are only a few of the benefits of using computers and other electronic technologies to manage healthcare information.

 Medical transcription is the conversion of handwritten/verbal doctor's orders and/or notes into typed or electronic format.

In order for the healthcare industry to embrace HIT, it needs professionals that understand both aspects of the industry: healthcare and information technology. As in other industries, one way professionals can differentiate themselves is by obtaining a certification.

The CompTIA Healthcare IT Technician Certificate

CompTIA is a nonprofit trade organization and advocate for the IT industry. With a 25-year history, the organization has grown to over 2000 members and 1000 business partners. This allows it to promote IT globally using a four-pronged approach:

- CompTIA provides education through various resources including webinars, forums, events, and market research.
- CompTIA provides multiple technology- and vendor-neutral certification programs for IT workers.
- CompTIA acts as an advocate for the IT industry by representing the industry in governmental settings.
- CompTIA's foundation provides IT education and training for those less fortunate.

Recently, CompTIA added a new certification program that directly addresses HIT industry needs. The **CompTIA Healthcare IT Technician Certificate** is designed to be a technology- and vendor-neutral certification program that shows a candidate has reached a certain level of proficiency in the knowledge and understanding in areas such as:

- HIT regulations
- Healthcare organization and operations
- Basic IT operations
- Network IT operations
- Document imaging
- Basic and advanced healthcare security
- Medical business operations

For a complete list of the CompTIA Healthcare IT Technician exam domains and objectives and where they are covered in this book, see Appendix A.

The program prepares students for jobs deemed critical by the U.S. Office of the National Coordinator for Health IT. These include implementation support specialists and technical and software support staff.

There are other certification bodies for HIT professionals. The American Health Information Management Association (AHIMA) has 63,000 members[5] and offers various certifications, including Health Information Management, Health Data Analysis, and Healthcare Privacy and Security.

Regulatory Compliance: Regulators

1.1 Identify standard agencies, laws, and regulations.

One of the five major areas covered by the CompTIA certification examination is HIT regulations.

A *regulation* is something that constrains or controls. For example, to regulate the flow of water, a *regulator* will compensate in high- or low-flow states in order to maintain some predetermined water flow rate. In a similar way, governmental entities regulate various aspects of citizens' lives with the purpose of providing benefits to the most people in a cost-effective manner. In this text, a **regulator** refers to a governmental entity that mandates regulations.

Regulations constrain and control
© SVLuma/www.Shutterstock.com

In the United States, regulations at the federal, state, and local level make healthcare one of the most heavily regulated industries. In addition, there are literally hundreds of private organizations with their own regulatory standards. For example, at the organizational level, the Joint Commission accredits and certifies nearly 20,000 hospitals and other healthcare organizations. At the allied health level, the American Registry of Radiologic Technicians administers certification examinations. And, of course, physicians have a large number of certification and regulatory organizations to navigate. All of these add to the complexity and cost of healthcare management.

The cost of regulation is significant. One estimate contends that the cost of healthcare regulation in the United States in 2004 was close to $1 trillion.[6]

If regulations add to the cost and complexity of healthcare, why are there so many and why do we need them? The answer to this question is complex, but at its heart is the fact that regulators are trying to ensure that patients receive adequate care that meets certain minimum standards. Furthermore, they also want patients to have broad access at a *reasonable cost.*

The major federal regulators in the United States include the Department of Health and Human Services (HHS), the Office of the National Coordinator for Health Information Technology (ONC, a staff division of HHS), the Centers for Medicare and Medicaid Services (CMS, an operating division of HHS), and the National Institute of Standards and Technology (NIST).

Table 1-1 summarizes the major regulatory agencies and their organization.

Name	Acronym	Parent Dept./Agency
Department of Health and Human Services	HHS	President
Office of the National Coordinator for Health Information Technology	ONC	HHS
Centers for Medicare and Medicaid Services	CMS	HHS
National Institute of Standards and Technology	NIST	Dept. of Commerce

Table 1-1 Primary U.S. healthcare regulatory agencies
© Cengage Learning 2013

Department of Health and Human Services

The mission of the **Department of Health and Human Services (HHS)** is fivefold: to help provide citizens with access to high-quality health care, to help people find jobs and child care, to keep food safe, to manage infectious diseases, and to extend the practice of diagnosis and treatment.

HHS is a very large organization, representing nearly 25 percent of the federal budget, and is composed of 12 operating divisions:

- *Administration for Children and Families (ACF)*—Consisting of seven subdivisions, this HHS operating division is responsible for programs that address "social well-being of families, children, individuals, and communities."

- *Administration on Aging (AoA)*—This division is responsible for administering the Older Americans Act of 1965, a law that Congress passed to address the lack of social service for older Americans.

- *Agency for Healthcare Research and Quality (AHRQ)*—The research arm of HHS, this agency supports research in major areas of health care in an effort to improve quality, lower cost, and increase safety, among others.

- *Agency for Toxic Substances and Disease Registry (ATSDR)*—This agency is responsible for the prevention of toxic substance exposure to the public.

- *Centers for Disease Control and Prevention (CDC)*—The CDC is responsible for protecting the public from diseases and other preventable conditions.

- *Centers for Medicare and Medicaid Services (CMS)*—Previously known as the Health Care Financing Administration (HCFA), CMS administers the Medicare program, the Federal portion of the Medicaid program, and State Children's Health Insurance Program (CHIP).

- *Food and Drug Administration (FDA)*—The FDA's responsibility is to ensure the quality of food, and the safety of drugs and medical devices.

- *Health Resources and Services Administration (HRSA)*—This agency makes essential primary care services accessible to the poor.

- *Indian Health Service (IHS)*—This agency makes essential health services accessible to American Indians and other native people.

- *National Institutes of Health (NIH)*—The NIH supports biomedical and behavioral research in the United States and elsewhere by doing research, training researchers, and managing information dissemination.

- *Office of the Inspector General (OIG)*—The OIG investigates and manages fraud, waste, or abuse against HHS programs.

- *Substance Abuse and Mental Health Services Administration (SAMHSA)*—This agency strives to provide reasonable care access for those with addictive or mental disorders.

In addition to the 12 HHS operating divisions, there are also 17 staff divisions. The staff division of primary importance to HIT is the **Office of the National Coordinator for Health Information Technology (ONC)**. This agency's responsibility is to coordinate the use of advanced HIT practices at the national level.

The primary HHS operational and staff divisions with which the health information technologist needs to be concerned are CMS and ONC. CMS administers the Medicare program and the federal portion of the Medicaid program. ONC provides coordination of HIT practices, but also governs the Nationwide Health Information Network (part of the HITECH Act, covered later in this chapter).

Centers for Medicare and Medicaid Services Information Technology

The **Centers for Medicare and Medicaid Services (CMS)** administers the Medicare program, the Federal portion of the Medicaid program, and the State Children's Health Insurance Program (CHIP). Medicare is health insurance for people over the age of 65, or under the age of 65 if they have certain disabilities. Medicare also covers all citizens with end-stage renal disease.

Medicare is divided into three major parts:

- *Part A*—This area of Medicare provides inpatient hospital stay insurance. Inpatient care means that care is provided while in a care facility like a hospital.

- *Part B*—Medicare Part B covers doctor's services and outpatient care. Outpatient care means that care is provided while not in a care facility like a hospital.

- *Prescription Drug Coverage*—This area of Medicare covers prescription drugs through private providers.

Medicaid is a program for low-income people whose resources do not cover certain medical expenses. Although jointly funded by the federal government and the states, it is managed by the states.

The Medicare and Medicaid programs are both very large. The Medicare program alone consumes $452 billion of the federal budget (in 2010).[7] As a result, there are significant financial incentives to increase efficiencies, particularly by using HIT. For instance, Medicare and Medicaid provide incentive programs to various providers if they adopt or implement certain certified **electronic health record (EHR)** technology. Cash incentives can be as high as $63,000, distributed over six years.

An EHR is not the same as an electronic medical record (EMR) or an electronic patient record (EPR). The EMR is an electronic record of patient care, usually in a stand-alone situation such as a doctor's office. An EHR is a collection of patient or population health information. An EPR is a synonym for EHR. A **personal health record (PHR)** is an electronic health history wherein an individual maintains their own health information.

The Office of the National Coordinator for Health Information Technology

As mentioned previously, the responsibility of the ONC is to coordinate the use of advanced HIT *practices* at the national level. The ONC's mission is to warrant the security of protected patient health information. It also works to improve health care quality while reducing health care costs, and to improve the coordination of care and the exchange of information between physicians, labs, and hospitals.

One of the major roles ONC plays in HIT is that of certifying EHR systems and providers. The purpose of this process is to help ensure that HIT systems are secure, interoperate, and can provide their purported functionalities. The three major aspects of certification include:

- *Standards and certification criteria for EHR*—ONC sets the standards and criteria for EHR technology certification.
- *Certification programs*—ONC defines the process for having EHR technologies approved.
- *Metadata standards*—ONC is currently piloting EHR metadata standards with several states.

Metadata is frequently defined as data about data. A better definition is information about content. For example, a radiologic image (content) can be described by patient, date, time, and so on. The patient, date, and time are metadata.

The National Institute of Standards and Technology

The **National Institute of Standards and Technology (NIST)**, a department of the United States Department of Commerce that sets standards for EHRs under the HITECH Act, is promoted as the country's first federally sponsored physical science research laboratory. The agency's responsibilities are many, and include such diverse activities as managing the Malcolm Baldrige National Quality Award and ensuring the proper radiation exposure level for mammograms in more than 10,000 facilities annually.

NIST's role in HIT has five main goals:

- Coordinate/harmonize standards.
- Coordinate infrastructure testing.
- Improve EHR usability.
- Extend healthcare's reach through technology.
- Perform cutting-edge research and development.

NIST, in cooperation with the Healthcare Information Technology Standards Panel (HITSP) and ONC, provides standards and specifications by which various levels of HIT system interoperability can be tested and ensured. For example, to ensure the interoperability of EHR laboratory results reporting, hardware and software developers use NIST interoperability standard IS01 V2.1, Electronic Health Record Laboratory Results Reporting, which provides specific data and communication format requirements.

 HITSP, a cooperative partnership between the public and private sectors, was formed to support the harmonizing and integrating of clinical and business standards for sharing data and information.

The overall process of HIT standards implementation process is summarized in the Table 1-2.

Standards Harmonization	Implementation	Certification	Connection
HITSP, ONC, and NIST develop and test interoperability standards	HIT software developers implement the standards	Certifying bodies test implemented software	Healthcare system users benefit from improved HIT

Table 1-2 **HIT standards implementation process**
© Cengage Learning 2013

Regulatory Compliance: Regulations

 1.2 Explain and classify HIPAA controls and compliance issues.

There are numerous regulations stemming from the regulators mentioned in the previous section, but not all address HIT. However, HIT professionals should be especially aware of the following major regulations.

HIPAA Privacy Rule

The **Health Insurance Portability and Accountability Act (HIPAA)** of 1996 is a very broad federal regulation that was developed in order to:

- Improve portability and continuity of health insurance
- Manage waste, fraud, and abuse of health care delivery
- Reduce costs and increase efficiency by standardizing the interchange of electronic data
- Protect the privacy of personal health records

As such, the act is composed of four distinct Standards or Rules. These include Privacy, Security, Identifiers, and Transactions and Code Sets. HIPAA addresses the protection and privacy of healthcare information through the **Standards for Privacy of Individually Identifiable Health Information** (also known as the **Privacy Rule,** published in 2000). As all patient information, both electronic and nonelectronic is covered, the Privacy Rule is fundamental to patient data regulation within any HIT system.

The HIPAA Privacy Rule regulates three types of entities:

- *Health care providers*—These may include individuals (like doctors) or organizations (like hospitals).
- *Health plans*—Insurance companies are exemplary health plans, but other payors are covered as well.
- *Health care clearinghouses*—These could include health information processing or billing organizations.

Collectively, these are called **Covered Entities (CE)**. The rule also extends to **Business Associates (BAs)** of Covered Entities, which are persons or other entities that perform functions for a Covered Entity as defined by HIPAA (for example, a doctor's accountant). In these circumstances, Covered Entities are required to obtain **Business Associate Agreements (BAA)**, which are contracts that ensure Business Associates of Covered Entities follow HIPAA Privacy Rule guidelines and regulations.

Any individually identifiable health information created or received by a Covered Entity or Business Associate is protected by the Privacy Rule. This includes information in verbal, paper, or electronic form. Collectively, this information is called **Protected Health Information (PHI)**, and relates to the past, present, or future health of an individual, both mental and physical. PHI also includes the provision and payment for a person's health care (for example, whether they are admitted to a hospital and who is paying). Moreover, the rule covers PHI as long as it is retained by a Covered Entity, even if the individual is deceased.

Health information is subject to many regulations
© Elnur/www.Shutterstock.com

Information that has been treated so that the individual cannot be identified (so-called deidentified information) is not considered PHI. However, this type of information must either be *certified* by a qualified statistician or expert such that there is little risk of the information identifying the individual, or the following 18 identifiers must be removed:

- Names
- All geographic subdivisions smaller than a state
- All elements of date (except year) for dates directly related to an individual, including birth date, discharge date, date of death
- Telephone numbers
- Fax numbers
- Electronic mail addresses
- Social Security numbers
- Medical record numbers
- Health plan beneficiary numbers
- Account numbers
- Certificate/license numbers
- Vehicle identifiers and serial numbers, including license plate numbers
- Device identifiers and serial numbers
- Web Universal Resource Locators (URLs)
- Internet Protocol (IP) address numbers
- Biometric identifiers, including fingerprints and voiceprints
- Full-face photographic images and any comparable images
- Any other unique identifying number, characteristic, or code

Finally, researchers and others who need health information with some personal identifiers may access it, but only after completing a *data use agreement* that specifically describes the permitted uses and disclosures of the information. The agreement must also prohibit any attempt to reidentify or contact the individuals.

In addition to the general protection of PHI data given to individuals, the Privacy Rule also provides for specific rights of individuals that Covered Entities must safeguard. These are detailed in Table 1-3.

The **Office for Civil Rights (OCR,** an office of HHS) is responsible for enforcement of the HIPAA Privacy Rule and penalties for noncompliance.

While the OCR seeks voluntary cooperation from Covered Entities, those that fail to comply may be subject to civil penalties. If the infraction occurred before February 18, 2009, the penalty amount could be up to $100 per violation with a calendar year cap at $25,000. However if the infraction occurred on or after February 18, 2009, the penalty amount could be up to $50,000 per violation with a calendar year cap at $1,500,000.

Safeguard	Covered Entity Requirements
Notice of privacy practices and written acknowledgement	Covered Entities are required to provide individuals an understandable Privacy Notice of how their PHI will be used.
Uses and disclosures of protected information	Covered Entities may use PHI in their core operations without written authorization. However, this use is to be specified in the Privacy Notice.
Minimum necessary standard	When Covered Entities use PHI, they must do so with the minimum necessary information to achieve the stated purpose.
Access	In general, individuals must be allowed access to their PHI.
Amendment	Individuals must be allowed to amend their PHI.
Accounting of disclosures	Individuals have a right to a list of PHI disclosures.
Request for restrictions	Individuals are entitled to ask a Covered Entity to restrict its uses or disclosures of PHI.
Confidential communications	Individuals are entitled to communicate with their provider by alternative means or location.
Personal representatives	Generally, a Covered Entity must treat individuals' family and other representatives the same as the individual with regard to PHI.
Deceased individuals	A Covered Entity must protect the privacy of a decedent's PHI for as long as it maintains the information.

Table 1-3 **HIPAA Privacy Rule safeguards and requirements**
© Cengage Learning 2013

In some cases, criminal prosecution could result from noncompliance with the law. For example, if an individual knowingly obtains or distributes PHI in violation of the Privacy Rule, that person could be subject to a $50,000 fine and up to one year in prison. However, these penalties increase for those who use false pretenses or try to sell, transfer, or use PHI—up to $250,000 and up to ten years imprisonment.

HIPAA Security Rule

Unlike the Privacy Rule, the **Security Rule** focuses on electronically transmitted or stored PHI (**ePHI**) used by Covered Entities. Thus, any entity that collects, maintains, uses, or transmits PHI is regulated by the rule.

Although the Security Rule has a narrower focus than the Privacy Rule because it only covers ePHI, its aim is broader. In addition to privacy of ePHI, the Security Rule seeks to ensure that Covered Entities provide certain administrative, physical, and technical safeguards for the data. These are detailed in Table 1-4.

Covered Entities must ensure that their officers and employees are complying with the Security Rule, so HIPAA training is commonplace in those organizations.

Category	Safeguard	Covered Entity Requirements
Administrative	Security management process	Must define how to prevent, detect, contain, and correct security violations
	Assigned security responsibility	Must designate a security official
	Workforce security	Must ensure that all members of the workforce have appropriate access to ePHI
	Information access management	Must address authorization and access to ePHI
	Security awareness and training	Must develop a security awareness and training program
	Security incident procedures	Must address security incidents
	Contingency plan	Must implement a contingency plan for securing ePHI (in the event of natural disaster)
	Evaluation	Must conduct a periodic security evaluation
	Business Associate contracts and other arrangements	Must develop written contracts documenting Business Associate safeguards
	Policies and procedures	Must implement reasonable and appropriate policies and procedures to comply with Security Rule
	Documentation	Must maintain documentation of policies and procedures related to compliance with the Security Rule
Physical	Facility access control	Must implement facility access controls
	Workstation use	Must address secure workstation use
	Workstation security	Must address workstation security
	Device and media controls	Must implement device and media controls
Technical	Access control	Must implement information system access controls
	Audit controls	Must implement audit controls for ePHI systems
	Integrity	Must make alteration of ePHI detectable
	Person or entity authentication	Must provide for individual person authentication
	Transmission security	Must provide for transmission security (using encryption, for example)

Table 1-4 HIPAA Security Rule categories, safeguards, and requirements
© Cengage Learning 2013

HIPAA Identifier Rule

The HIPAA Identifier Rule mandates that all Covered Entities storing or transmitting ePHI must have a standardized **National Provider Identifier (NPI)**. This identifier replaces all other identification from Medicare, Medicaid, and other government programs.

HIPAA Transaction and Code Sets Rule

The **Transaction and Code Sets Rule (TCS)** is a HIPAA regulation that mandates consistent electronic interchange of PHI for all Covered Entities. Combined with the Identifier Rule, most efficiency is expected as a result of this aspect of HIPAA.

TCS, in effect, is **electronic data interchange (EDI)** for health care. EDI can be defined as the standardized and structured exchange of electronic information between two or more parties using public and/or private networks.

Many industries already use EDI, so the technology is tested and proven. Moreover, several standards already exist. For example, the automotive industry uses the ANSI X.12 standard for electronic communications between vendors, manufacturers, and other suppliers. The TCS Rule uses several existing X.12 standards as follows:

- Health Care Claims or equivalent encounter information (X12N 837)
- Coordination of Benefits (X12N 837 or NCPDP for retail pharmacy)
- Eligibility for a Health Plan (X12N 270/271)
- Referral Certification and Authorization (X12N 278 or NCPDP for retail pharmacy)
- Enrollment and Disenrollment in a Health Plan (X12N 834)
- Health Care Claim Status (X12N 276/277)
- Health Care Payment and Remittance Advice (X12N 835)
- Health Plan Premium Payments (X12N 820)

EDI standards can define any format the parties decide to use for data exchange, such as e-mail or File Transfer Protocol (FTP).

HITECH Act

The HIT Standard Committee, the HIT Policy Committee, and the process for adoption of recommendations for standards and policies from these committees were created by the **Health Information Technology for Economic and Clinical Health Act (HITECH Act)** under Title XIII of the **American Recovery and Reinvestment Act of 2009 (ARRA)**. All of the committees and processes are overseen by the ONC.

The HITECH Act could be described as "HIPAA on steroids." This is because, among other aspects, it extends HIPAA's reach by increasing confidentiality protections for ePHI, mandating tougher penalties for confidentiality breach, and requiring public notification of organizational breaches.

One of the reasons for this increase in regulation was the lack of enforcement of the original HIPAA regulations. For example, it is reported that even though 45,000 HIPAA violation complaints were filed in 2003, fewer than 1,000 were reviewed by the Department of Justice (DOJ), and none were awarded civil damages.

The first person convicted of violating HIPAA rules was reportedly a health worker who unlawfully accessed patient records at a large university hospital while purportedly looking for celebrity files. This resulted in a four-month incarceration in 2010.[8]

There are seven major areas in which the HITECH Act strengthens HIPAA. These are as follows:

- The act provides increased resources for enforcement and increased penalties for violations.
- The act mandates that health providers cannot use patient health information without their express permission.
- The sale of private health information is severely limited as the information use must be expressly authorized by the patient.
- The act provides for increased transparency to patients as they are entitled to audit their electronic patient records.
- In addition to current Covered Entities, the act also provides that future *unanticipated* entities are also covered, thereby eliminating future privacy loopholes.
- The act mandates that all ePHI be *encrypted* either electronically or otherwise so as not to be easily intercepted.
- In the event that a breach of ePHI does occur, the act requires that patients be notified in any case of unauthorized use or disclosure of their information.

In addition to these areas, the act details specific and encompassing requirements for Business Associates and violation hierarchy.

Be careful when using e-mail for PHI communication. According to the HITECH Act, the date, time, patient identification, and user identification must be recorded when ePHI is created, modified, deleted, or printed. So, if one deletes an e-mail with PHI, a record of what was deleted and when must be maintained.

HITECH Act and Business Associates

Business Associates are those people or entities that work with a Covered Entity such that their activities require the disclosure of PHI. Examples of Business Associate functions include claims processing or administration, quality assurance, and billing. Examples of Business Associate services include accounting, data aggregation, accreditation, and so on.

The HITECH Act now encompasses Business Associates much in the same way as Covered Entities. This means that instead of being covered to the extent of a contractual agreement (as in the case of HIPAA), Business Associates are now covered by the Security Rule in the same way as Covered Entities. Thus, many of the same violation penalties apply as well.

Because e-mail is relatively insecure, many Covered Entities and Business Associates are starting to use Web portals instead. These require the users to log into an encrypted Web site. These are more secure, but not as convenient.

HITECH Act and PHI Breach In the event of a PHI breach, the Covered Entity (or Business Associate) is required to report the breach to each individual affected. In the event the breach is for PHI controlled by a Business Associate, the Business Associate is required to report the breach to the Covered Entity who then must report to the individual.

In the case where the breach involves more than 500 patients, the Covered Entity must contact HHS in addition to the individuals. The Covered Entity may also be required to contact media outlets in some cases.

HITECH Act Enforcement As the HITECH Act provides for increased enforcement, one way this is accomplished is through four levels of enforcement for both Covered Entities and Business Associates. These are detailed as follows:

- The first level of enforcement is the lowest level and is targeted at violations that are unknown, even after the Covered Entity and/or Business Associate exercised due diligence. Penalties for these violations are from $100 to a maximum of $25,000 for a given calendar year, for a given violation.

- The next level of enforcement is for reasonable cause and not for willful neglect. For these violations, the penalties range from $1000 to a maximum of $100,000 for a given calendar year, for a given violation.

- Level 3 of enforcement is for willful neglect if corrected within 30 days from knowledge of the violation. For these violations, the penalties range from $10,000 to a maximum of $250,000 for a given calendar year, for a given violation.

- Finally, the fourth level of enforcement is for willful neglect that is not corrected. For these violations, the penalties range from $50,000 to a maximum of $1,500,000 for a given calendar year, for a given violation.

It is clear from these enforcement levels that the HITECH Act Enforcement significantly increases the coverage and penalties for not complying with the Privacy Rule. It is also clear that Business Associates may need to study the act in more detail as they are now just as culpable as Covered Entities for breaching the privacy of PHI.

HITECH Act and EHRs Another function of the HITECH Act is to support providers in the adoption, implementation, and effective use of EHRs. In fact, the majority of funding for the HITECH Act goes to providing incentives (cash and otherwise) to hospitals and other healthcare professionals to stimulate the adoption of EHRs. Moreover, since Medicare expense is so great ($452 billion of the U.S. federal budget in 2010), there is significant emphasis on Medicare (and Medicaid) providers. To accomplish this, HITECH Act created:

- Workforce investments
- An HIT Extension Program
- An HIT Research Center
- HIT Regional Extension Centers (RECs)

These provide technical assistance, best practices, and grants for the purpose of assisting healthcare providers in the acceptance, employment, and effective use of EHRs. Specifically,

Part IV of the HITECH Act specifies Medicare and Medicaid incentives for HIT adoption for healthcare professionals, **prospective payment system (PPS)** hospitals, and **critical access hospitals (CAHs)**.

> PPS is a Medicare Part A system in which most of a patient's cost is reimbursed to a provider hospital based on the diagnosis, not actual cost. A CAH is a hospital that receives cost-based reimbursement from Medicare.

To qualify for HITECH Act incentives, Medicare providers must adopt the use of a *certified* EHR. In order for an EHR to be certified, it must be tested by an ONC Authorized Testing and Certification Body (ATCB).

HITECH Act and Meaningful Use

The ARRA defines the minimum requirements for EHR adoption and use, and therefore also for the associated incentives. These include the following:

- The certified EHR must be used in a meaningful manner, which could include electronic prescribing.
- The certified EHR must be used for submission of quality data and other measures.
- The certified EHR must be used for the exchange of health information that improves the quality of health care (as with care coordination).

A healthcare provider that is eligible for the Medicare EHR financial incentives under the HITECH Act is called an **Eligible Provider (EP)**. When a provider meets the preceding general guidelines and the more detailed recommendations expected to be finalized by CMS in the future, the provider is said to be meeting **meaningful use** criteria. This means the provider is eligible for the Medicare financial incentives. For example, an EP that met the meaningful use criteria in 2011 may have expected total financial incentives of $44,000. However, an EP that does not demonstrate meaningful use criteria until 2014 may only expect total financial incentives of $24,000 as detailed in Table 1-5.

Year	2011	2012	2013	2014
2011	$18,000			
2012	$12,000	$18,000		
2013	$8,000	$12,000	$15,000	
2014	$4,000	$8,000	$12,000	$12,000
2015	$2,000	$4,000	$8,000	$8,000
2016		$2,000	$4,000	$4,000
Total	$44,000	$44,000	$39,000	$24,000

Table 1-5   Maximum Medicare EHR incentive payments
© Cengage Learning 2013

There are incentives for Medicaid as well, and EPs may participate in more than one program so maximum incentives may be greater than shown. However, certain restrictions apply.

Legal Practices

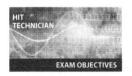

1.4 Explain and interpret legal best practices, requirements, and documentation.

There are certain healthcare legal practices that are outside the scope of the traditional regulatory environment. These include liability waivers, EHR service level agreements (SLA), and memoranda of understanding (MOU).

Health care has many related legal practices
© Oleksiy Mark/www.Shutterstock.com

Liability Waivers

Frequently, a **waiver of liability** is used by hospitals and physicians to protect them in the case that certain procedures or treatments may subject the hospital or physician to legal liability for treatment risks. A waiver of liability is a document signed by the patient that specifies the specific responsibility the hospital and physician will have should the treatment fail or cause injury.

Some states do not allow patients to negotiate this risk, nor the provider's liability.

Service Level Agreements A Service Level Agreement (SLA) is frequently used in technology applications to define the level of service a user might expect from a technology provider. In the case of HIT, SLAs usually refer to EHRs, but could also refer to other supportive technologies like telecommunication network performance.

Typically, SLAs define several performance measures. They then further define a level of service for each measure. For example, typical EHR performance measures could include the following:

- *Downtime*—Downtime refers an EHR that is nonfunctional. It may include a more detailed definition that would exclude noncontrollable factors such as telecommunication network downtime.

- *Downtime period*—This usually means how much time a service has to be nonfunctional to be defined as "down." This measure could be seconds or minutes, depending on the EHR provider.

- *Monthly uptime percentage*—This is a calculation that is the total number of minutes in a month that the EHR is down, as defined by the downtime period, divided by the total minutes in the month.

- *Schedule downtime*—Typically, EHRs, as most HIT systems, require periodic servicing. This measure defines the amount of servicing downtime the user is likely to experience. It may include a notification clause so that the user has some defined period of time to make allowances for the system outage.

- *Service credit*—This is a compensatory system for downtime. In other words, if the system is down 5 percent of the time, the provider may add a certain amount of free system time to compensate.

Memorandum of Understanding A memorandum of understanding (MOU), sometimes called a memorandum of agreement (MOA), is typically a voluntary agreement between health providers to some mutually beneficial arrangement. For example, multiple hospitals may establish an MOU regarding natural disaster preparedness so that each knows what its and the other's responsibility are in a given disaster situation.

Another example of an MOU would be between a hospital and other healthcare providers such as ambulance services, fire departments, and schools.

MOU may or may not be legally binding. Generally, a legally binding contract is expected to contain four elements as follows:

- Some form of payment or consideration must be exchanged between the parties.
- The agreement must not contain illegal activities.
- The actions of the parties must be described in the agreement.
- The agreement has to be agreed upon by all parties without threat or duress.

If an MOU has the four characteristics of a contract, it may be considered a contract and could be legally binding. Just calling an agreement an MOU does not preclude the agreement from contractual duties.

Good MOUs contain plain language, identify all parties, outline what each party is expected to do, and delineate how the agreement is terminated.

Chapter Summary

- Healthcare costs keep increasing. Even so, the healthcare industry has been a slow adopter of healthcare information technology. While there are many reasons for this, one major reason is that there are not enough healthcare information technology (HIT) professionals to implement the new technologies. HIT is the use of hardware and software in an effort to manage and manipulate health data and information. CompTIA, a nonprofit trade association, has added a certification program, Healthcare IT Technician, which directly addresses HIT industry needs.

- A regulation is something that constrains or controls. Governmental entities regulate various aspects of citizens' lives with the purpose of providing benefits to the most people in a cost-effective manner. In the United States, healthcare is one of the most heavily regulated industries. The major federal healthcare regulators in the United States include the Department of Health and Human Services (HHS), the Office of the National Coordinator for Health Information Technology (ONC, a staff division of HHS), the Centers for Medicare and Medicaid Services (CMS, an operating division of HHS), and the National Institute of Standards and Technology (NIST).

- There are numerous regulations stemming from the federal regulators. These include the Health Insurance Portability and Accountability Act (HIPAA) of 1996, which is further subdivided into Standards for Privacy of Individually Identifiable Health Information (the Privacy Rule); the Security Rule, which focuses only on electronically transmitted or stored Protected Health Information (ePHI or EHI) used by Covered Entities; the Identifier Rule, which mandates that all Covered Entities storing or transmitting ePHI must have a standardized National Provider Identifier (NPI); and the Transaction and Code Sets (TCS) Rule, which establishes regulations that mandate consistent electronic interchange of PHI for all Covered Entities. The HITECH Act extends HIPAA's reach by increasing confidentiality protections of ePHI, mandating tougher penalties for confidentiality breach, and requiring public notification of organizational breaches. The HITECH Act doesn't replace HIPAA, but it extends it, enhances penalties, and provides incentives for Electronic Health Record (EHR) adoption.

- There are certain healthcare legal practices that are outside the scope of the traditional regulatory environment. These include liability waivers, EHR Service Level Agreements (SLA), and memoranda of understanding (MOU). Waivers of liability are used by hospitals and physicians for protection in the case of certain procedures or treatments that may subject the hospital or physician to legal liability for treatment risks. SLAs usually refer to EHRs, but could also refer to other supportive technologies like telecommunication network performance. Finally, MOUs are typically voluntary agreements between health providers to some mutually beneficial arrangement.

Key Terms

American Recovery and Reinvestment Act of 2009 (ARRA)   A law enacted by the 111th United States Congress in February 2009 and signed February 17, 2009, by President Barack Obama that created the HITECH Act.

Business Associate (BA)   A person or other entity that performs functions for a Covered Entity as defined by HIPAA.

Business Associate Agreement (BAA)   Contract that ensures Business Associates of Covered Entities follow HIPAA Privacy Rule guidelines and regulations.

Centers for Medicare and Medicaid Services (CMS)   Previously known as the Health Care Financing Administration (HCFA), CMS administers the Medicare program, the Federal portion of the Medicaid program, and State Children's Health Insurance Program (CHIP).

CompTIA Healthcare IT Certificate   A technology- and vendor-neutral certificate that shows a candidate has reached a certain level of proficiency in the knowledge and skills needed to deploy and support HIT.

Covered Entities (CE)   Health care providers, health plans, and health care clearinghouses covered by HIPAA.

critical access hospital (CAH)   A hospital that receives cost-based reimbursement from Medicare.

Department of Health and Human Services (HHS)   A regulator whose purpose is to help provide people access to high-quality health care, to help people find jobs and child care, to keep food safe, to manage infectious diseases, and to extend the practice of diagnosis and treatment, among others.

electronic data interchange (EDI)   The standardized and structured exchange of electronic information between two or more parties using public and/or private networks.

electronic health record (EHR)   An electronic collection of patient or population health information.

electronic medical record (EMR)   An electronic record of patient care, usually in a stand-alone situation such as a doctor's office.

Eligible Provider (EP)   A healthcare provider that is eligible for the Medicare EHR financial incentives under the HITECH Act.

ePHI   Electronically transmitted or stored PHI.

hardware   Devices that input, process, and output data and information.

Health Information Technology for Economic and Clinical Health Act (HITECH Act)   A law created under Title XIII of the American Recovery and Reinvestment Act of 2009 (ARRA).

Health Insurance Portability and Accountability Act (HIPAA)   Broad federal regulation that was developed in order to: reduce cost and increase efficiency by standardizing the interchange of electronic data, improve portability and continuity of health insurance, manage waste, fraud, and abuse of the health care industry, and protect the privacy of personal health issues.

Healthcare information technology (HIT)   The use of hardware and software in an effort to manage and manipulate health data and information.

Information technology (IT) The use of hardware and software in an effort to manage and manipulate generic data and information.

Meaningful Use HITECH Act general guidelines used to determine financial incentives for EHR use.

memorandum of understanding (MOU) A voluntary agreement between health providers to some mutually beneficial arrangement. Sometimes called a memorandum of agreement (MOA).

National Institute of Standards and Technology (NIST) A department of the United States Department of Commerce that sets standards for EHRs under the HITECH Act.

National Provider Identifier (NPI) A HIPAA identifier replaces all other identification from Medicare, Medicaid, and other government programs.

Office for Civil Rights (OCR) An office of HHS that is responsible for enforcement and penalties for Privacy Rule noncompliance.

Office of the National Coordinator for Health Information Technology (ONC) A staff division of HHS whose responsibility is to coordinate the use of advanced HIT practices at the national level.

personal health record (PHR) An electronic health history wherein an individual maintains their own health information.

Patient Protection and Affordable Care Act (PPACA) A federal health care statute that was signed into law by President Barack Obama on March 23, 2010, and is a product of the health care reform agenda of the 111th United States Congress.

Privacy Rule A HIPAA law that regulates the protection and privacy of healthcare information; also known as Standards for Privacy of Individually Identifiable Health Information.

prospective payment system (PPS) A Medicare Part A system in which most of a patient's cost is reimbursed to a provider hospital based on the diagnosis, not actual cost.

Protected Health Information (PHI) Any individually identifiable health information created or received by a Covered Entity or Business Associate and that is protected by the HIPAA Privacy Rule.

regulator Governmental entities that mandate regulations.

Security Rule A HIPAA law that focuses on electronically transmitted or stored PHI (ePHI or EHI) used by Covered Entities.

Service Level Agreement (SLA) Agreement frequently used in technology applications to define the level of service a user might expect from a technology provider.

software Also known as computer programs, contains the logic that makes computers do what they do.

Standards for Privacy of Individually Identifiable Health Information See *Privacy Rule*.

Transaction and Code Sets Rule (TCS) A HIPAA regulation that mandates consistent electronic interchange of PHI for all Covered Entities.

waiver of liability Agreement used by providers for protection in the case of certain procedures or treatments that may subject the hospital or physician to legal liability for treatment risks.

Healthcare IT Acronyms

Table 1-6 contains healthcare IT acronyms that were introduced in this chapter. Many of these terms are listed in the CompTIA Healthcare IT Technician exam objectives, and most are also defined in the Key Terms section of this chapter. For a complete list of the healthcare acronyms used in this book, see Appendix C.

Acronym	Full Name
AHIMA	American Health Information Management Association
ARRA	American Recovery and Reinvestment Act of 2009
ATCB	Authorized Testing and Certification Body
BA	Business Associate
BAA	Business Associate Agreement
CAH	critical access hospital
CBO	Congressional Budget Office
CDC	Centers for Disease Control and Prevention
CE	Covered Entity
CMS	Center for Medicare Services
DOJ	Department of Justice
EDI	electronic data interchange
EHR	Electronic Health Record
EMR	Electronic Medical Record
EP	Eligible Provider
ePHI	Electronic Protected Health Information
HHS	Health and Human Services (U.S. Department of)
HIPAA	Health Insurance Portability and Accountability Act
HIT	healthcare information technology
HITECH	The Health Information Technology for Economic and Clinical Health Act
HITSP	Healthcare Information Technology Standards Panel
IT	information technology
MOU	Memorandum of Understanding
NIST	National Institute of Standards and Technology
NPI	National Provider Identifier

Table 1-6 Healthcare IT acronyms introduced in this chapter *(continues)*

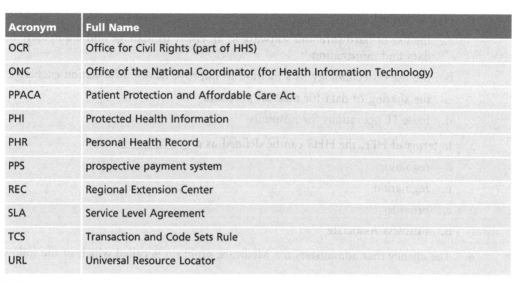

Acronym	Full Name
OCR	Office for Civil Rights (part of HHS)
ONC	Office of the National Coordinator (for Health Information Technology)
PPACA	Patient Protection and Affordable Care Act
PHI	Protected Health Information
PHR	Personal Health Record
PPS	prospective payment system
REC	Regional Extension Center
SLA	Service Level Agreement
TCS	Transaction and Code Sets Rule
URL	Universal Resource Locator

Table 1-6 Healthcare IT acronyms introduced in this chapter (*continued*)
© Cengage Learning 2013

Review Questions

1. Which of the following is true about PHI?
   a. It is electronic only.
   b. It is a major regulatory body.
   c. It does not include verbal communication.
   d. It includes verbal, paper, or electronic forms.

2. From 1960 until 2007, how much had the percentage of GDP spent on healthcare changed?
   a. Stayed about the same
   b. Increased 50 percent
   c. Increased 100 percent
   d. Increased more than 200 percent

3. According to the CBO, one advantage of EMR use is _____.
   a. increased use of medical transcriptionists
   b. better use of computer graphics
   c. reduction of duplicated diagnostics tests
   d. reduction in the use of surgical procedures

4. HIT is defined as _____.
   a. the use of hardware and software in an effort to manage and manipulate health data and information
   b. the use of technology as a method to improve health information exchange
   c. the sharing of data for medical purposes
   d. basic IT operations for hospitals

5. In terms of HIT, the HHS can be defined as a _____.
   a. regulator
   b. regulation
   c. provider
   d. Business Associate

6. The agency that administers the Medicare program is called which of the following?
   a. ONC
   b. NIST
   c. CMS
   d. HIS

7. One of the major roles of the ONC is to _____.
   a. administer the Medicare program
   b. certify EHR systems and providers
   c. develop EDI standards
   d. create EMR systems

8. Which entities does the HIPAA Privacy Rule regulate?
   a. Healthcare providers, plans, and clearinghouses
   b. Healthcare providers, hardware manufacturers, and network providers
   c. Hardware manufacturers, network providers, and clearinghouses
   d. None of the above

9. _____ are contracts that ensure Business Associates follow Privacy Rule guidelines and regulations.
   a. Covered Entity agreements
   b. Business PHI agreements
   c. Business Associate agreements
   d. Service Level Agreements

10. The agency responsible for enforcement of and penalties for Privacy Rule noncompliance is called _____.

    a.   the Office for PR Compliance

    b.   HIPAA Compliance Office

    c.   the Agency of Health Care Compliance

    d.   the Office for Civil Rights

11. The TCS Rule establishes regulations that mandate consistent _____ of PHI for all Covered Entities.

    a.   storage

    b.   electronic interchange

    c.   use

    d.   term definition

12. Which of the following is one of the seven major areas in which the HITECH Act strengthens HIPAA?

    a.   The act mandates that all ePHI be encrypted either electronically or otherwise so as not to be easily intercepted.

    b.   The act provides decreased resources for enforcement due to budget cuts.

    c.   The act sets standards for use of ePHI in infection control.

    d.   The act encourages the sale of private health information.

13. According to the HITECH Act, date, time, patient identification, and user identification must be recorded whenever _____.

    a.   legal experts mandate

    b.   the courts mandate

    c.   ePHI is used

    d.   ePHI is created, modified, deleted, or printed

14. PPS is a Medicare Part A system in which _____.

    a.   none of a patient's cost is reimbursed to a provider hospital based on the diagnosis, not actual cost

    b.   most of a patient's cost is reimbursed to a provider hospital based on the diagnosis, not actual cost

    c.   a hospital receives cost-based reimbursement from Medicare

    d.   a hospital receives cost-based reimbursement from the patient

15. Which of the following defines meaningful use?

    a. HITECH Act general guidelines used to determine financial incentive for EHR use

    b. The use of hardware and software in an effort to manage and manipulate generic data and information

    c. A voluntary agreement between health providers to some mutually beneficial use arrangement

    d. Provider use agreements used for protection in the case of certain procedures or treatments that may subject the provider to legal liability for treatment risks

16. Waivers of liability are used by hospitals and physicians for protection from _____.

    a. debt as related to patient care

    b. certain procedures or treatments that may subject a hospital or physician to legal liability for treatment risks

    c. risk due to treating indigent patients

    d. risk due to the inappropriate use of ePHI

17. As identified, which of the following is a typical SLA performance measure?

    a. Time to repair

    b. Hardware delivery time

    c. Software installation time

    d. Monthly uptime percentage

18. A good MOU _____.

    a. contains plain language, identifies all parties, outlines what each party is expected to do, and delineates how the agreement is terminated

    b. refers an EHR that is nonfunctional

    c. specifies the specific responsibility the hospital and physician will have should the treatment fail or cause injury

    d. defines the amount of servicing downtime a user is likely to experience

19. PPACA is a _____.

    a. federal health care statute that was signed into law by President Barack Obama on March 23, 2010, and is a product of the health care reform agenda of the 111th United States Congress

    b. law created under Title XIII of the American Recovery and Reinvestment Act of 2009

    c. regulator whose purpose is to help provide people access to high-quality health care

    d. health care provider, health plan, or health care clearinghouse covered by HIPAA

20. Which of the following describes an EP?

    a. The electronic portion of an EHR

    b. The electronic part of a patient's treatment record

    c. Electronic patient information as defined by the HITECH Act

    d. A provider that is eligible for the Medicare EHR financial incentives under the HITECH Act

Case Projects

Case Project 1-1: Providers and the HITECH Act

It is widely reported that healthcare providers are reluctant to adopt EHRs because they fear they may not be able to recoup the cost. Visit one or more physicians who do not have an EHR and ask them about the HITECH Act. Ask them if they know what it is, what it means to their practice, and if they plan to adopt an EHR in the future. Do you think the provider(s) you interviewed are well informed? Is their view of the HITECH Act accurate? Why or why not? Write a one-page summary of your findings.

Case Project 1-2: HIPAA versus the HITECH Act

It is said that the HITECH Act is "HIPAA on steroids." Create a table that lists the major requirements of HIPAA in one column. Then add the requirements of the HITECH Act in a second column, making sure that similar requirements are on the same rows. Finally, create a third column that notes the differences. Include a short summary that highlights the major differences between the two acts.

Case Project 1-3: Qualifications for HIT Work

Because HIT uses hardware and software in the management of health data and information, HIT professionals are required to have skills in multiple domains. Using the Internet as a resource, explore the specific requirements for HIT employment. For sources, be sure to include the CompTIA Web site, job posting services such as Monster.com, and private hiring services. Then write a one-page summary of the specific skills needed to be a HIT professional. Does the CompTIA certification address the needed skills?

Case Project 1-4: Using the HHS FAQ

Given the complex nature of HIPAA, patients and providers have many questions about the various rules. As a result, HHS compiled a frequently asked questions (FAQ) list and includes it on their Web site (*www.hhs.gov*). Go to the HHS Web site and find the FAQ in the category of health information privacy. Look up the answer to the following question: Can a laboratory e-mail test results to a physician without the express consent of the patient? Be sure to respond with the HHS answer and provided example.

Case Project 1-5: The HITECH Act and E-mail

Assume you are a personal injury lawyer specializing in car accidents. Joan Smith visits your office in a wheelchair asking you to represent her. She says her doctor will e-mail you her hospital discharge records so you can use them in court. When you receive her records, you e-mail them to your paralegal for analysis and filing. Instead of filing the electronic document on the firm's file server, your paralegal accidentally forwards the document to the defendant's attorney, who happens to be a personal friend. Did anyone violate the HITECH Act? Why or why not? If a complaint was filed, who would file it? What could the potential penalty be? Who would be penalized?

Case Project 1-6: The HITECH Act and Backups

Again, assume you are the same personal injury lawyer as in the previous case. Assume your paralegal filed the hospital discharge records on the firm's file server appropriately. Your firm excels in disaster recovery such that it has an automatic nightly backup system that saves all new files to the cloud using an Internet file backup system. However, unknown to you and your firm, a technician at the backup firm likes to look at random new files as they are being uploaded to the service's servers. As luck would have it, the technician knows Joan Smith, calls her, and asks how she is feeling since the accident. Did anyone violate the HITECH Act? If so, who, and to what extent? If not, provide a rationale. What does the HITECH Act say about transmitting ePHI?

Healthcare IT: Challenges and Opportunities—Revisited

This closing case refers to the Superior Care Health Group (SCHG) as related in the chapter opening vignette.

Assume you are the new office manager for SCHG. When hired, you were tasked with the following goals: to bring the group into the present, increase efficiency, improve healthcare delivery, and to increase net revenues. In order to accomplish these goals, you are determined to introduce an EHR. When you present the idea to the group physicians, they have the following responses:

- We don't need an EHR. Our system works fine. Why should we spend money on something we don't need?

- EHRs only increase the likelihood we will run afoul of the HITECH Act. Paper systems are inherently more secure than electronic systems.

- We already have an electronic system. What will an EHR do that our current system will not?

- Instead of meeting HHS requirements, maybe we should stop taking Medicare patients.

To complete this case, complete the following:

a. How would you respond to each physician comment? Be sure to provide a solid rationale with supporting sources.

b. Assume you must respond to the physicians' concerns in a meeting. Develop a slide presentation that addresses their concerns.

c. Assume the physicians agree with your recommendations. Create a project outline of what you recommend the group do in terms of regulators and regulations in order to meet the stated goals.

References

1. "Medical Records and Health Information Technicians," *Occupational Outlook Handbook, 2010–11 Edition*. September 29, 2010, accessed October 1, 2011, http://www.bls.gov/oco/ocos103.htm.

2. "National Healthcare Costs," *Health Guide USA*. 2011, accessed October 2, 2011, http://www.healthguideusa.org/NationalCosts.htm.

3. "Technological Change and the Growth of Health Care Spending," *Congressional Budget Office.* January, 2008, accessed October 2, 2011, http://www.cbo.gov/ftpdocs/89xx/doc8947/01-31-TechHealth.pdf.

4. "Evidence on the Costs and Benefits of Health Information Technology," *Congressional Budget Office.* May, 2008, accessed October 21, 2001, http://www.cbo.gov/ftpdocs/91xx/doc9168/05-20-healthit.pdf.

5. "AHIMA Facts," *American Health Information Management Association*, n.d., accessed November 13, 2011.

6. "Health Care Regulation: A $169 Billion Hidden Tax," CATO Institute. October 4, 2004, accessed October 2, 2011, http://www.cato.org/pub_display.php?pub_id=2466.

7. "Policy Basics: Where Do Our Federal Tax Dollars Go?" Center on Budget and Policy Priorities. April 15, 2011, accessed October 2, 2011, http://www.cbpp.org/cms/index.cfm?fa=view&id=1258.

8. "Californian Sentenced to Prison for HIPAA Violation," *Journal of American Health Information Management Association.* August 9, 2010, accessed October 21, 2011, http://journal.ahima.org/2010/04/29/californian-sentenced-to-prison-for-hipaa-violation/.

chapter 2

Healthcare Organizations and Operations

After completing this chapter, you should be able to do the following:

- Identify various healthcare organizational structures and their different methods of operation
- Explain the use of codes of conduct
- Identify EHR/EMR access roles and responsibilities for using Protected Health Information (PHI)
- Describe the proper communication methods for use in the healthcare workplace
- List best practices in handling PHI in the healthcare setting

Healthcare IT: Challenges and Opportunities

The Superior Care Health Group (SCHG) consists mainly of general practitioners (GPs). As GPs, the group functions as primary care physicians, which means they are the first point of contact for many in the community. Even though SCHG is a group of GPs, they are also a private practice because a group of single physicians provides care to individual patients.

The population is aging in their service area, and SCHG is experiencing long delays for patient appointments. This has been mainly attributed to not having enough physicians in the group. Drs. Smith and Jones, founders of the group over 25 years ago, recently decided to add two physicians to their staff. They asked their new office manager, Braden Thomas, to interview potential candidates in order to create a short list. Several doctors applied, and in the interviews the candidates asked questions like the following:

- "I've only worked in a hospital. How is practicing in this group going to be different?"
- "I guess since this isn't an acute care facility, I can be a little more relaxed here, right?"
- "Do you ever see any life-threatening cases here?"
- "Do I have to make hospital visits if I work here?"
- "Since I'm fresh from my hospital internship, what kind of patients will I be dealing with here?"

As Braden continued to screen candidates, it became clear that he needed to know more about the differences between private practice and hospitals in order to answer their questions.

The delivery of health care to a large population requires large and complex organizations, both in breadth and depth. For example, many people think of hospitals when they think of health care. However, hospitals are usually not the first organizations to see the *patient*. In the case of emergency patients, *first responders* like police, firefighters, and emergency medical technicians usually see the patient at the outset. Moreover, there are numerous organizations that frequently play supporting roles in hospital operation. These can include material suppliers, drug companies, diagnostic companies, and even power providers. In this chapter, you will explore the various types of healthcare-related organizations, their operations, codes of conduct, and proper methods for managing protected health information, or PHI.

Healthcare Organizational Structures and Operation

 2.4 Identify organizational structures and different methods of operation.

Organizational structure can be thought of as the framework through which a group of like-minded people work on tasks for a common goal. Organizational structure defines the authority, responsibilities, lines of communication, rights, and duties of the group. In health care, there are several basic types of organizational structure, each with different methods of operations.

Organizational Structures

With regard to organizational structure, healthcare organizations are no different from other organizations. However, because of the nature of their common goal, they present many challenges and a unique organizational culture. For example, in what other organization is the common goal to save lives, reduce suffering and pain, and eliminate disease? Because of these goals, healthcare organizations can be very stressful and demanding environments. One place where this is especially true is the hospital.

Hospitals

Hospitals have unique goals and organizational cultures
© Stephen Mahar/www.Shutterstock.com

Hospitals are healthcare organizations that treat patients for injury or disease and usually provide *inpatient* or long-term care. Inpatient care refers to treatment the patient receives while *admitted* to the hospital and physically residing there for one or more nights. Hospitals also provide *outpatient* care, which means the patient is not admitted and does not reside overnight.

There are various types of hospitals and each type has its own goals. For example, while teaching hospitals share the goal of treating patients for injury or disease, they also have the goal of teaching medical students, nursing students, and other healthcare practitioners. Teaching hospitals are frequently linked organizationally to large universities. Other types of hospitals may include:

- *General hospitals*—This type of hospital is most common. Typically, a general hospital has radiology, surgical, maternity, isolation, psychiatric, burn, and laboratory facilities. Because they admit patients for overnight stays, such hospitals are frequently categorized by their bed count. A large metropolitan hospital may have 1,000 beds, whereas a small rural hospital may have 15.

- *Contagious disease hospitals*—In some cases, a hospital may only treat patients who have infectious, contagious, or otherwise communicable diseases. They may have many of the facilities of a general hospital, but have specialized facilities for isolation.

- *Nursing homes (also convalescent hospitals)*—For patients with *chronic* disease or disability, or for patients who require a long time period for recovery, convalescent hospitals provide a subset of facilities provided by general hospitals. As a result, the cost is usually lower and the hospital is better equipped for long-term care.

- *Psychiatric hospitals*—Psychiatric hospitals are specifically designed to exclusively treat patients with mental disorders. As a result, they have few of the facilities found at general hospitals.

- *Orthopedic hospitals*—*Orthopedic* disorders are disorders of the musculoskeletal system. This includes bones, nerves, joints, muscles, ligaments, and tendons. These hospitals have many of the facilities of general hospitals, but have specialized staff and facilities for the care of orthopedic disorders.

- *Pediatric hospitals*—*Pediatrics* is defined as childhood medicine. These hospitals have many of the facilities of general hospitals, but have specialized staff and facilities for the care of children.

As organizations, hospitals usually divide functionality into departments. The number and types of departments depend greatly on hospital type and size. For example, a mental hospital will not likely have a burn unit, nor would a convalescent hospital be equipped for acute care. Also, a 15-bed hospital may not have a laboratory or other facilities found in a 1,000-bed hospital.

 In health care, *chronic* refers to something that is prolonged. For example, chronic pain is pain that continues for a long time. The opposite would be *acute* pain, which is pain that happens suddenly.

Hospital departments can be categorized into those that provide health care, those that directly support healthcare-providing departments, and those that indirectly support heathcare-providing departments. While medical departments will be discussed in more depth in Chapter 5, typical healthcare departments found in general hospitals are included the following nonexhaustive list:

- *Cardiac care unit (CCU)*—The term *cardiac* means related to the heart. CCUs care for patients who have severe cardiac conditions such as damage due to a heart attack (lack of blood flow to the cardiac muscle), cardiac swelling, irregular rhythms, and so forth. In some hospitals, cardiac patients are also treated in ICUs.

- *Emergency room (ER)*—The ER receives patients with acute conditions that may be life threatening or need immediate treatment.

Emergency rooms (ER) are a specialized department of a hospital where patients with acute conditions that may be life threatening or need immediate treatment and are categorized into five levels. Level 1 is the highest level and requires that surgical specialists and subspecialists like surgeons and anesthesiologists be available at all times. Lower-level ERs mainly stabilize patients for travel to higher-level ERs.

- *Gynecology (GYN)*—Gynecology is the study of the female reproductive system. As a matter of practice, many if not most gynecologists (doctors who specialize in gynecology) also specialize in obstetrics. As a result, the two functions are frequently combined into one department called OB/GYN.

- *Intensive care unit (ICU)*—Patients with life-threatening diseases or *trauma* frequently need specialized care. This can include intensive monitoring using specialized electronic monitoring equipment. In some cases, the patient's breathing must be supported through mechanical devices known as ventilators. In comatose patients, feeding tubes are used to maintain the proper dietary nutrition levels. ICUs maintain the equipment, systems, and staffing to support these patients. Some ICUs also care for cardiac patients, but usually this is accomplished in the CCU.

- *Medical/Surgical (Med/Surg)*—This department primarily cares for adult patients before and after surgery. However, it also sees patients after an illness or injury, and sees those on medication who need nursing care. It is frequently one of the largest healthcare departments.

- *Neurology*—The *nervous system* is composed of the brain, spinal cord, and retina. Illness or trauma to the nervous system is managed by this department.

- *Obstetrics (OB)*—Obstetrics is the medical specialty that manages female reproduction, specifically pregnancy, childbirth, and the postnatal period following childbirth. The gynecology function is frequently combined with obstetrics into one department called OB/GYN.

- *Oncology*—The study of cancer is called oncology. This branch of medicine addresses the diagnosis, treatment, and follow-up of patients with cancer. An oncology department may be staffed with specialists and have specialized diagnostic and treatment equipment.

- *Pediatrics (Peds)*—Because infants, children, and adolescents have specialized needs, they are generally not treated within the general patient population. Instead, special departments are maintained with staff appropriate for the children's age, size, and disease or trauma type.

- *Physical therapy (PT)*—A goal of physical therapy is the improvement or maintenance of patient movement. This is accomplished using specialized staff and equipment.

- *Psychiatry (Psych)*—Psychiatry is the study and treatment of mental disorders. Thus, a psychiatry department will have psychiatrists and other specialized staff for that purpose.

- *Surgery (OR)*—The surgery department is where surgical operations are conducted. In a surgical operation (or procedure) the patient's body is penetrated or opened in order to allow access for the purpose of assessing or correcting a disease or injury. Surgery can also be affiliated with a recovery room, where post surgical patients are moved directly after surgery until *anesthesia* wears off.

Typical departments that directly support the departments that provide health care in general hospitals can include the following:

- *Laboratory (Lab)*—Laboratories are departments that provide various chemical, microbial, microscopic, and other studies in order to diagnose and treat disease or injury.
- *Pathology (Path)*—Pathology refers to the study and diagnosis of disease. A pathology department provides the staff and equipment used to help make clinical diagnostic decisions. For example, samples removed during surgery (biopsies) will be analyzed microscopically by pathology for disease.
- *Pharmacy*—Pharmaceuticals are chemical compounds used for the treatment of disease and injury. As a department, the pharmacy provides both traditional over-the-counter pharmaceuticals, but also specially prepared compounds and medications as needed.
- *Radiology (Xray)*—The radiology department provides imaging equipment that may use x-rays, ultrasound, or nuclear isotopes as a method to detect and diagnose disease or injury.

Table 2-1 lists the departments typically found in a hospital with their abbreviations and abbreviation pronunciations.

Department	Department Abbreviation	Abbreviation Pronunciation
Cardiac Care Unit	CCU	See-See-You
Emergency Room	ER	Eee-Are
Gynecology	GYN	Gee-Y-En
Intensive Care Unit	ICU	Eye-See-You
Medical/Surgical	Med/Surg	Med Surge
Neurology	[no abbreviation]	
Obstetrics	OB	Oh-Bee
Oncology	[no abbreviation]	
Pediatrics	Peds	Peads
Physical Therapy	PT	Pea-Tee
Psychiatry	Psych	Psych
Surgery	OR (operating room)	Oh-Are

Table 2-1 **Selected departments typically found in hospitals**
© Cengage Learning 2013

Typical indirect-support departments (or *ancillary services*) found in general hospitals include:

- Health information management (medical records)
- Information technology (IT)
- Clinical (or biomedical) engineering
- Facilities management (maintenance/operations)
- Administration
- Food and nutrition services
- Security
- Material management

Private Practices Physicians are professionals who diagnose, prescribe, and treat disease and injury. When doing this, they are said to be medical practitioners or practicing medicine. Medical practitioners are usually licensed by a governing body to practice medicine without supervision from others, which categorizes them as professionals.

It is important to distinguish between the term *medical practitioner* and *medical provider*. Practitioners practice medicine without direct supervision. Medical or health providers cover a broader cross section of supervised professionals. For example, registered nurses are medical providers but are always supervised. Nurse practitioners also provide nursing care but are unsupervised.

The way in which physicians organize themselves in order to provide care generally falls into three categories: private practice, group/partnership, or system.

In **private practice**, a single physician provides care to individual patients. This can be in a private office, a clinic, or other setting. Essentially, it is a business-like transaction between the single doctor and a single patient.

A physician can also work with a group of other physicians, thereby reducing overhead for staff and facilities. The physician may or may not be in private practice in the group setting. If the group is physician owned, then it can still be considered private. However, if the group is very large, like a non-physician-owned healthcare system, then the practice is no longer private.

The trend today is for younger physicians to join large healthcare systems instead of going into private practice. In fact, in 2002, approximately 20 percent of hospitals owned medical practices. However, by 2008, that percentage had more than doubled.[1] The reasons are numerous, but one reason is the challenges that small practices face in negotiating with *third-party payer* systems (health insurance) for service reimbursement.

Nursing Homes (Convalescent Hospitals) Some patients have long-term disease or disability or require a long time period for recovery. Nursing homes are equipped for these patients with these needs.

Nursing homes are similar to hospitals as they mainly address the needs of inpatients. However, unlike hospitals, they typically do not have acute care functions like emergency, intensive care,

Nursing homes meet the needs of patients with chronic disease or long recovery periods
© Alexander Raths/www.Shutterstock.com

obstetrics, and surgery. Moreover, there are usually fewer if any direct support functions like radiology, pharmacy, pathology, and laboratory as these services are sourced from external providers on an as-needed basis.

To be reimbursed by Medicare, a nursing home must meet Medicare's criteria for designation as a *Skilled Nursing Facility (SNF)*, which consists primarily of having the appropriate *skilled nursing staff*. Examples include registered, licensed practical and vocational nurses; physical and/or occupational therapists; and audiologists, among others.

 It is a frequent misconception that Medicare will pay for a patient's long-term care in a nursing home. Medicare will only pay for necessary skilled care for up to 100 days. Stays beyond 100 days are the responsibility of the patient. For specific information on this, see *http://www.medicare.gov/longtermcare/static/home.asp.*

A facility must also meet Medicaid's criteria for designation as a *Nursing Facility (NF)* in order to be reimbursed by Medicaid for patient expenses. However, patient criteria are more stringent as some patients may need care for multiple years. For example, patients must:

- Have a need for skilled nursing care
- Have income below a defined level
- Have assets below a defined level
- Be a citizen of the United States (by birth or naturalization)
- Be a resident of the state in which the nursing home is located

Typically, a caseworker from the state will coordinate communication between the patient, Medicaid, and the nursing home.

Assisted Living Facility An assisted living facility (ALF) also provides for overnight stays. However, instead of addressing the needs of people with disease or injury, ALFs are primarily designed for elderly people or others who need some degree of assistance with *activities of daily living (ADL)*. Thus, ALFs do not have patients, but residents. Also, ALFs typically do not have skilled nursing care staff but use trained professionals who supervise their residents' ADLs, including medication supervision, bathing, dressing, and so on.

Medicare and Medicaid do not reimburse ALFs. Therefore, ALF expense is the responsibility of the resident.

Home Health Care In some cases, patients may be able to receive **home health care**. Rather than have the patient come to a hospital, clinic, or physician's office, home health professionals go to the patient.

For example, in treatment of some disease or injury it may be necessary to have bandages changed on a routine basis, do certain types of physical therapy (PT), or maintain a regimen of *intravenous (IV)* fluids. Rather than have the patient come to a hospital, clinic, or physician's office, home health professionals go to the patient.

Home health care may be staffed by both nonmedical and skilled nursing professionals, depending on the need. Some patients may only need help bathing, dressing, or preparing meals and not require skilled care. Conversely, patients needing IV management or PT will need skilled care. If so, the skilled care provided will be certified by a physician.

Medicare and Medicaid will reimburse certain home health care costs, depending on eligibility criteria and type of illness or injury.

Hospice The term **hospice** refers to the care of terminally ill patients either at home or in dedicated facilities. These patients usually require *palliative care*, which means the relief and prevention of suffering. Although there are dedicated centers that specialize in caring for the terminally ill, hospice care is often given in-home, much like home health care.

Hospice care can include treating all aspects of the terminally ill such as the following:

- Skilled care for the patient on a 24-hour, seven-day-per-week basis
- Pharmaceuticals necessary to provide patient comfort
- Necessary medical equipment like hospital beds, oxygen generators, and IV equipment

Generally, Medicare and Medicaid will reimburse most hospice costs, depending on eligibility criteria.

Surgical Centers and ASCs In some cases, surgical procedures can be accomplished without the patient needing an overnight stay. This is known as *outpatient surgery* or *same-day surgery*. Although these surgical procedures are frequently done in hospital outpatient **surgical centers**, there are also healthcare facilities known as *ambulatory surgical centers (ASC)* that specialize in this type of surgery (the word **ambulatory** refers to walking, so ambulatory surgery refers to surgery on patients who are able to walk—or be wheeled—away).

Frequently, the surgical procedures performed by ASCs are less complex than those performed on an inpatient basis. Examples may include:

- *Minor surgeries*—These include surgeries to treat bone spurs, bugling or herniated discs, or partial vertebrae removal.
- *Pain management*—These include insertion, removal, or management of neurostimulators used for pain control.
- *Diagnostics procedures*—These include laparoscopies, which use a small scope to examine internal organs such as the liver or reproductive organs.

In many cases, ASCs are totally or partially owned by the physicians who perform the procedures.

Methods of Operation

Healthcare organizations have different methods of operation based on their different operational characteristics. A *method of operation* can be defined as the customs or practices normally used to achieve the common goal of the organization. Three specific operational characteristics used to differentiate healthcare organizations include the scope of work, availability of resources, and formality of procedures.

Differences in Scope of Work The scope of work (the tasks involved in accomplishing a goal or objective) is very dissimilar in different healthcare organizations. For example, general hospitals usually have the broadest scope in that they try to save life, reduce suffering and pain, and eliminate disease of any patient presented for treatment. Comparatively, a nursing home is only equipped to treat patients with chronic disease or disability, or for patients who require a long period for recovery. So, as an example, patients experiencing acute chest pain would not be well served at a nursing home. Table 2-2 summarizes the various levels of scope for each identified healthcare organization.

Healthcare Organization	Type of Disease/Injury/Activity	Residency
General hospital	Any	Inpatient/outpatient
Contagious disease hospital	Contagious disease only	Inpatient
Nursing home	Chronic disease or disability	Inpatient
Psychiatric hospital	Mental disorders only	Inpatient/outpatient
Orthopedic hospital	Musculoskeletal disorders only	Inpatient/outpatient
Pediatric hospital	Any disorder, but only for children	Inpatient/outpatient
Private practice	Any non-life-threatening disorder	Outpatient
Assisted living facility	Assistance with activities of daily living only	Inpatient
Home health care	Assistance with certain treatments	Outpatient
Hospice	Assistance with terminal disease or injury	Inpatient/outpatient
Surgical center	Less complex surgeries	Outpatient

Table 2-2 **Scope of work for identified healthcare organizations**
© Cengage Learning 2013

In some cases the size of the organization may make a difference in the scope of the work. For example, a small rural hospital will have a more narrow scope than a large general hospital. Likewise, a small home health organization may offer fewer services than a large home health organization.

There are many types of healthcare resources
Created by the author with Wordle/www.wordle.net

Availability of Resources Resources are the means by which organizations achieve their collective goals. Frequently, these are divided into four types: financial, human, physical, and information.

- *Financial resources* refer to the economic or monetary resources needed for the organization to function. This is a major area of concern in most every healthcare organization because the way financial resources are developed is very different from other industries. As opposed to being paid for service by the person receiving the service, healthcare organizations are frequently paid by *third-party payers* like insurance companies or the government. As a result, the healthcare organization may not receive the billed amount and may even lose money on the service.

- *Human resources* refer to people. As in many industries, there can be a wide range of human resource needs in a healthcare organization. For example, hospitals staff a variety of positions, from low skilled to very high skilled. However, at other healthcare organizations, the breadth of staffing may be less significant. As an example, a nursing home may be operated with registered nurses, but usually does not have physicians on staff.

- *Physical resources* are the places and equipment needed to achieve the common goal in healthcare organizations. Large general hospitals may have numerous physical resources. Conversely, home health care organizations usually have few physical resources as their work is mainly accomplished in the patient's home.

- *Information* is also an organizational resource. Having the right information in the right place at the right time is very important to most healthcare organizations. In some cases, it can be the difference between life and death.

Table 2-3 summarizes financial resource availability for identified healthcare organizations.

Healthcare Organization	Financial Resource Availability	Comments
General hospital	High	Numerous payers, gifts, endowments
Contagious disease hospital	Medium	Fewer payers than general hospitals
Nursing home	Low	Largely government prospective payment system
Psychiatric hospital	Medium	Fewer payers than general hospitals
Orthopedic hospital	Medium	Fewer payers than general hospitals
Pediatric hospital	High	Numerous payers, gifts, endowments
Private practice	Low	Comparatively low overhead, low cost
Assisted living facility	Low	Largely private pay
Home health care	Low	Comparatively low overhead, low cost
Hospice	Low	Supported by government or gifts
Surgical center	Medium	Numerous payers, lower overhead than hospitals

Table 2-3 **Availability of financial resources for identified healthcare organizations**
© Cengage Learning 2013

In many cases, if financial resources are readily available, other resources like human and physical resources are more easily acquired. Thus, knowing how the healthcare organization is compensated for service is foundational to understanding general resource availability.

Formality of Procedures Formality refers to a set of established behaviors. Thus, with reference to healthcare organizations, **formality of procedure** refers to the set of established behaviors for collectively achieving the organization's goal. In this context, high formality means there is little deviation from set procedures. Low formality means higher deviation from set procedures.

Typically, formality increases when risk to the patient increases. For example, when a patient enters a hospital emergency room with heart attack symptoms, they are treated in a very programmatic way, using a predetermined set of protocols. This is because the risk to a patient's life for deviating from the set of established behaviors is great.

Table 2-4 identifies and summarizes the formality of procedures for identified healthcare organizations.

Healthcare Organization	Formality	Comments
General hospital	High	High-risk acute care
Contagious disease hospital	High	High-risk care
Nursing home	Medium	Low-risk chronic care
Psychiatric hospital	Medium	Low-risk chronic care
Orthopedic hospital	High	High-risk care
Pediatric hospital	High	High-risk acute care
Private practice	Medium	Low-risk diagnostic/treatment
Assisted living facility	Low	Low-risk assistance
Home health care	Low	Low-risk assistance
Hospice	Low	Low-risk assistance
Surgical center	High	High-risk care

Table 2-4 **Formality of procedures for identified healthcare organizations**
© Cengage Learning 2013

Frequently, acute care organizations also happen to be high-formality organizations. This is because many acute disorders are life threatening.

Codes of Conduct

2.5 Given a scenario, execute daily activities following a code of conduct.

A **code of conduct** refers to rules for behavior to which a group of people adhere. In the case of healthcare organizations, the groups are organizations of healthcare professionals. Codes of conduct are similar to formality of procedure, in that both spell out rules for behavior. However, formal procedures tend to be more rigid and are governed by strict rules. Codes of conduct are governed by a consensus of professionals.

Many healthcare organizations have specific written codes of conduct. However, codes of conduct are often similar for the same type of organization or organizational function. For example, the written code of conduct for one hospital is likely to be very similar to the code of conduct for another hospital. Similarly, the code of conduct for nurses will probably be very similar to the code of conduct for radiology technicians.

Codes of conduct frequently address numerous behaviors, but in healthcare organizations the core issues include communication, procedural behavior, social behavior, and sanitation.

For an example of a code of conduct, see the code of conduct for the Johns Hopkins Hospital at http://dcs.jhmi.edu/cvo/CodeofConduct.pdf (requires Adobe Acrobat Reader).

Communication

Codes of conduct often specify how and what healthcare professionals should communicate

© Sukhonosova Anastasia/www.Shutterstock.com

Because of the general nature of healthcare, and because it is very personal to the end user (the patient), communication is very important, not only in the sense of accuracy, but also in the sense of professionalism. The question becomes: What is professional communication?

There are two major aspects to the definition of **professional communication** (the use of written, aural, or other information exchange methods). The first is the style of communication, or *how* it is said. In a high-formality healthcare organization or setting, it is important to use a formal communication style. This means avoiding the use of contractions (like *don't* or *isn't*), slang, vulgarities, or other speech practices that may interfere with the delivery of the message. When a patient's life is in the balance, the healthcare team must be able to communicate efficiently and effectively.

The second aspect applies to the content of the communication, or *what* is said. This means only talking about topics that have bearing on the situation at hand, especially in the presence of patients. It is considered highly inappropriate to talk about outside activities, relationships, or other staff members in front of patients.

Adapting Procedural Behavior

Even in healthcare organizations where the formality of procedure is low, staff members always have to consider the setting in order to know the correct **procedural behavior**, which is the level of procedural formality based on the type of treatment or diagnostics being administered. As an example, each setting within a hospital has its own procedures based on its organizational function. Staff should be familiar with each setting so they can exhibit the proper procedural behavior when in that particular environment. The following list summarizes typical examples:

- *Imaging room*—**Imaging rooms** can be intimidating to patients because they are rooms used for diagnostics and contain large, unfamiliar machines used for x-ray, ultrasound, or other electronic technology-based procedures. In these surroundings, patients may be in pain, uncomfortable, unconscious, and in various states of being disrobed. Therefore, procedures and communications in these situations are very formal and professional.

- *Procedure room*—In some cases patients require minor procedures that require privacy or specialized equipment that may not be widely available. **Procedure rooms** are settings wherein patients who require minor procedures and privacy or specialized equipment may be treated. In these settings, patients may also be in pain, uncomfortable, unconscious, and in various states of being disrobed. As a result, procedures and communications in these situations are very formal and professional.

- *Recovery room*—Post surgical patients are moved to **recovery rooms** directly after surgery until anesthesia wears off and their vital signs stabilize. Typically, post surgical patients may be in pain and semiconscious. Procedures and communications in these situations are less formal, but still professional as many patients are awake and fully recovered.

- *Examination room*—Some physical examinations can be very intimate and embarrassing. As a result, **examination rooms** provide a private place where the patient can be examined without embarrassment. In some cases examination rooms are really just beds with curtains drawn around them for visual privacy. Procedures and communications in these situations are less formal, but still professional since staff are still in direct patient contact.

- *Emergency room*—Patients with acute conditions that may be life threatening or need immediate treatment are treated in the emergency room. Because of the emergent status of the patient, procedures and communications are usually very formal and professional. In addition, as the ER takes in all types of diseases and injuries, it can frequently be chaotic, which makes professionalism even more important.

Based on these examples, it is clear that functional areas in healthcare organizations have different procedural behavior requirements. This is mainly based on the level of interaction with the patient, and the patient's state of health, mind, and physical presentation.

Sanitation

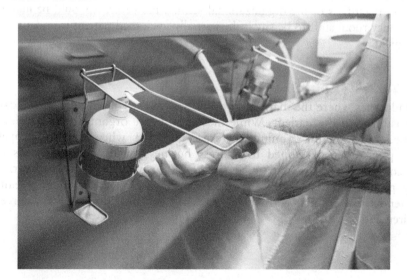

Sanitation is extremely important in healthcare organizations
© Tyler Olson/www.Shutterstock.com

One area of procedural behavior that is extremely important in healthcare organizations is **sanitation**. The delivery of health care frequently involves physical hazards as a result of close proximity to, or contact with, biological or chemical disease components. As a result, there is a focus on sanitation, which includes the sterilization of facilities and instruments, and proper disposal of contaminated wastes such as used hypodermic needles, bandages, gauze, and other medical supplies.

Infection control among patients is also of paramount importance in the healthcare setting. Contagions that originate in a hospital (or other healthcare setting) are called *nosocomial infections* and are strictly monitored and managed through specific procedures. Typical infection control procedures may include the following:

- Hand washing
- Cleaning and sterilization
- Use of antimicrobials
- Use of protective equipment

As a further protection against nosocomial infections, healthcare workers are sometimes required to be vaccinated for various pathogens such as influenza, diphtheria, mumps, and others.

Social Behavior and Sensitivity of the Environment

In addition to differences in procedural behavior, **social behavior**, or the conduct caused by or affecting other people, also has to be considered. Specific types of social behavior include shyness, aggression, competitiveness, and deception.

In the healthcare environment, certain social behaviors are considered acceptable while others are not. This is usually a result of the **sensitivity of the environment**. In this context, sensitivity usually means the condition of the patient. For example, it may be appropriate for a maintenance worker to express a state of shyness if accidentally exposed to a partially unclothed patient, regardless of the organizational setting. However, it would be inappropriate for an emergency room staff to be shy if the partially unclothed patient is under their care and needs treatment.

Conforming to Management Requirements

Unlike other industries where the main responsibility is to the shareholder, healthcare has a major responsibility to the patient. While most healthcare organizations develop their operating procedures with this in mind, there are occasions when **managerial operating procedures**, or procedures developed to address business or operational needs of the organization, conflict with patient care. For example, private hospitals can turn away nonemergency patients for lack of insurance or other means of payment. Healthcare professionals tend to be trained with the patient in mind and don't always agree with business requirements.

Protecting Healthcare Information

2.2 Identify EHR/EMR access roles and responsibilities.

Individually identifiable health information created or received by a Covered Entity or Business Associate is protected by the HIPAA Privacy Rule. This Protected Health Information (PHI) includes information in verbal, paper, or electronic form and relates to the past, present, or future health of an individual, both mental and physical. PHI also includes the provision and payment for a person's health care (for example, whether they are admitted to a hospital and who is paying). Moreover, PHI is protected as long as it is retained by a Covered Entity, even if the individual is deceased.

Access Roles and Responsibilities

Depending on their roles, healthcare team members and Business Associates have varying levels of access to PHI.

Healthcare Team Access Each healthcare team member, both medical and technical, has a unique responsibility in terms of, access to, and the maintenance of PHI in the electronic health record/electronic medical record (EHR/EMR). Table 2-5 summarizes these roles.

Entity	Create	Read	Modify
Medical Doctor (MD)	Yes (2)	Yes (2)	Yes (2)
Doctor of Osteopathic Medicine (DO)	Yes (2)	Yes (2)	Yes (2)
Nurse Practitioner (NP)	Yes (2)	Yes (2)	Yes (2)
Advanced Registered Nurse Practitioner (ARNP)	Yes (2)	Yes (2)	Yes (2)
Registered Nurse (RN)	Yes (2)	Yes (2)	Yes (2)
Certified Registered Nurse Anesthetist (CRNA)	Yes (2)	Yes (2)	Yes (2)
Physician Assistant (PA)	Yes (3)	Yes (3)	Yes (3)
Doctor's Assistant (DA)	Yes (3)	Yes (3)	Yes (3)
Patient Care Technician (PCT)	Yes (3)	Yes (3)	Yes (3)
Medical Assistant (MA)	No	Yes (4)	No
Nursing Unit Clerk (NUC)	No (4)	Yes (4)	Yes (4)
Licensed Practical Nurse (LPN)	Yes (2)	Yes (2)	Yes (2)
Practice Manager (PM)	Yes (2)	Yes (2)	Yes (2)

Table 2-5 **Protected Health Information access roles** *(continues)*

Entity	Create	Read	Modify
Office manager	No	Yes (4)	No
Staff	No (4)	No (4)	No (4)
Security administrator	No (4)	No (4)	No (4)
Network administrator	No (4)	No (4)	No (4)
System administrator	No (4)	No (4)	No (4)
Desktop support	No (4)	No (4)	No (4)
Database administrator	No (4)	No (4)	No (4)

Table Notes:
1. There are specific protocols for making entries or changes to the patient chart.
2. Some paraprofessionals like PAs and DAs may make PHI changes under direct supervision.
3. Covered Entities must use PHI with the minimum necessary information to achieve the stated purpose. While nonmedical personnel may have technical access, they have no authority to create, read, or modify PHI unless it is necessary to achieve the stated purpose.

Table 2-5 Protected Health Information access roles *(continued)*
© Cengage Learning 2013

Business Associate Access Business Associates are those entities that work with a Covered Entity such that their activities require the disclosure of PHI. Examples of Business Associate functions include claims processing or administration, quality assurance, billing, and so on. Examples of Business Associate services include accounting, data aggregation, and accreditation, among others.

The HITECH Act now encompasses Business Associates much in the same way as Covered Entities. This means that instead of being covered to the extent of a contractual agreement (as in the case of HIPAA), Business Associates are now covered by the HIPAA Security Rule in the same way as Covered Entities.

Access Limitations Based on Role and Exceptions

During normal circumstances the access roles and responsibilities previously identified are generally in effect. However, due to the irregular nature of the healthcare environment, there may be times in which traditional access roles may have to be superseded. For example, while a database administrator would not normally read PHI, this standard procedure could be overridden temporarily in an emergency situation.

Access to Sensitive Patient Data

While Covered Entities are required to follow HIPAA guidelines for general PHI, some information may have more stringent guidelines. For example, individuals are entitled to ask a Covered Entity to restrict its use or disclosures of their PHI. Thus, this information must be identified as controlled and access roles must be modified appropriately.

Proper Communication

2.3 Apply proper communication methods in the workplace.

The HIPAA Privacy Rule requires that Covered Entities provide patients the right to privacy and confidentiality for their PHI. The HIPAA Security Rule further protects electronic PHI by requiring Covered Entities to prevent loss or unauthorized access. As a result, there are procedures that must be followed for various types of communication.

While the Security Rule has a narrower focus than the Privacy Rule as it only covers ePHI, its aim is broader. In addition to privacy of ePHI, the Security Rule seeks to ensure that Covered Entities provide certain physical and technical safeguards for communication of the data. These are as follows:

- *Backups*—This means that a permanent copy of all ePHI is maintained.
- *Unique identifiers*—Unique usernames and passwords are to be used for all distinct user accounts.
- *Emergency access*—Procedures must be maintained for obtaining necessary ePHI during an emergency.
- *Timeout*—Procedures must be maintained that terminate an electronic communication session after a period of inactivity.
- *Encryption*—All ePHI must be encrypted such that communications will be undecipherable except to authorized recipients.
- *Audit trails*—Mechanisms must be present that record activity in information systems that contain or use ePHI. For example, if PHI is deleted or changed, a mechanism exists in order to determine who made the changes and when.
- *Integrity*—Mechanisms must be present that prevent unauthorized destruction or alteration of ePHI.
- *Authentication*—Procedures must be in place to ensure those seeking access to ePHI are authentic.
- *Disposal*—Procedures must be in place to address the final disposition of ePHI.

The identified safeguards are to be applied to all forms of communication. This may include any or all of the following:

- *E-mail*—**E-mail** (or electronic mail) is the system of electronic message exchange over the Internet or other computer networks.
- *Instant messaging*—Like e-mail, **instant messaging** (IM) is a method of sending electronic messages, but is closer to real time. IM messages tend to be shorter than e-mail and can be likened to electronic chatting.
- *Fax*—The transmission of an electronic representation of printed material is called a **fax** (or facsimile).

- *File transfer protocol*—A method by which computer files can be transferred from one system to another over the Internet or other computer network is called **File Transfer Protocol (FTP)**.
- *Telephone*—**Telephones (phones)** are handset devices used to transmit electronic representations of the human voice from one phone to another.
- *Voice over IP*—The use of the Internet and IP networks to route and carry telephone calls is called **Voice over IP (VoIP)**.

Table 2-6 summarizes the application of safeguards for various methods of electronic communication, including e-mail, IM, fax, FTP, telephone, and VoIP.

Safeguard	E-mail	IM	Fax	FTP	Phone	VoIP
Backups	1	1	10	1	17	1
Unique identifiers	2	2	11	2	12	2
Emergency access	3	3	12	2	12	3
Timeout	4	4	12	4	12	4
Encryption	5	9	13	5	18	5
Audit trails	6	6	14	6	17	6
Integrity	7	7	13	7	12	7
Authentication	2,7	2	15	2,7	12	2,7
Disposal	8	10	16	8	19	8

Table Notes:
1. Use off-site backups
2. Use unique usernames and passwords
3. Provide for authorized administrative access
4. Use timed screensavers to log out users
5. Use PGP or TLS protocols
6. Use system-level logging tools
7. Use cryptographic protocols such as SSL, TLS, PGP
8. Set backups to expire after specific duration
9. Use encrypted applications such as X-IM

10. Not generally available for this method
11. Verify phone numbers of intended recipients
12. Not applicable
13. Use encrypted fax service
14. Use fax machine history
15. Control physical access to fax machine
16. Destroy paper after specific duration
17. Record conversation
18. Voice encryption does exist, but is not widely used
19. Destroy recorded conversation after specific period

Table 2-6   Safeguards for various electronic communication methods
© Cengage Learning 2013

Encryption protocols like PGP, SSL, and TLS are covered in Chapter 8. Also, for more information on e-mail encryption protocols, see http://www.internet-computer-security.com/Spam/E-mail-Encryption.html.

Data Handling Procedures

2.1 Use best practices for handling PHI in the workplace.

In addition to specific safeguards for differing types of communication methods, there are best practices for the general use of technology that help ensure PHI is protected.

Personal computers (PCs), printers, and other electronic devices can be used to gain access to PHI, either because PHI is stored on the device, or because the device is connected by a *network connection* to the PHI. Therefore, access to these devices should be controlled.

There are usually two methods of data access: physical and electronic. Physical access means that an individual can physically use a device. Electronic access means that an individual can access the device or data without being physically present. Managing control of physical and electronic access requires very different measures.

One method of physical access control includes managing physical **placement,** which is a method by which an electronic device that can be used to access PHI is located so as to minimize authorized access. For example, the PC or printer can be placed in a locked room or in a location where access is supervised by authorized individuals.

Data protection is essential to safeguard PHI
© Lukas Radavicius/www.Shutterstock.com

For PCs, **privacy screens** may also be used. A privacy screen is a device that is attached to a computer monitor that prevents anyone not sitting in front of the monitor from reading its contents. These are frequently found in areas where PHI is displayed on a monitor, but not all individuals in the area are authorized to have access to the data (a hospital admissions area, for example).

Another method to control visibility of computer screens is the use of **screensavers**. These are programs that lock out computer screens after a predetermined period of time. Then, when a user wishes to see the screen again, they have to enter a password.

Another way to control physical access is the use of **time lockouts** (or timeouts). In this case, just as with a screensaver, the program that is being used locks out users after a certain period of time. Thus, if an authorized user walks away from the system, another unauthorized user cannot use it until they are validated with the correct username and password.

Chapter Summary

- There are various healthcare organizational structures, each with different methods of operation. Organizational structures can be thought of as a framework on which a group of like-minded people work on tasks for a common goal. In health care, most often this goal is to save life, reduce suffering and pain, and eliminate disease. However, the way in which each organization approaches this goal is different. For example, hospitals treat patients for acute injury or disease and usually provide inpatient or short-term care. Contrast this to a nursing home wherein the goal is to care for patients with chronic disease or disability, or care for patients who require a long time period for recovery.

- A code of conduct refers to behavior rules to which a group of people adhere. Even though different healthcare organizations approach their common goal using different methods, each has a similar code of conduct. For example, the written code of conduct for one hospital is likely to be very similar to that of another hospital, even if they are different types of hospitals. This is because all healthcare organizations exist for the benefit of the patient.

- PHI includes information in verbal, paper, or electronic form, and relates to the past, present, or future health of an individual, both mental and physical. There are numerous EHR/EMR access roles and responsibilities for using PHI. In general, the best approach to managing PHI is to remember that Covered Entities must use PHI with the minimum necessary information to achieve the stated purpose. While non-medical personnel may have technical access, they have no authority to create, read, or update PHI unless it is necessary to achieve the stated purpose of the organization. Moreover, in terms of ePHI, date, time, patient identification, and user identification must be recorded when ePHI is created, modified, or printed.

- Various communication methods are used in the healthcare setting. These can include e-mail, IM, fax, FTP, telephone, and VoIP. For each of these methods, there are safeguards that can be deployed to protect the information being transmitted or received. These include backups, unique identifiers, emergency access protocols, timeouts, encryption, audit trails, integrity mechanisms, authentication, and ePHI disposal protocols.

- Some of the best practices in handling PHI in the healthcare setting include controlling physical access to PCs and printers whenever possible. Examples include managing physical placement, using privacy screens, engaging screensavers, and using time lockouts.

Key Terms

ambulatory Refers to walking. So ambulatory surgery refers to surgery on patients who are able to "walk"—or be wheeled—away.

assisted living facility (ALF) A facility primarily designed for elderly people or others who need some degree of assistance with activities of daily living (ADL).

code of conduct Rules for behavior to which a group of people adhere. There are other codes of conduct, but in the case of healthcare organizations, this is similar to formality of procedure, but more rigid.

e-mail A system of electronic message exchange over the Internet or other computer network.

emergency room (ER) A specialized department of a hospital where patients with acute conditions that may be life threatening or need immediate treatment are treated.

examination room A private place in a healthcare setting where patients can be examined.

fax The transmission of an electronic representation of printed material.

File Transfer Protocol (FTP) A method by which computer files can be transferred from one system to another over the Internet or other computer network.

formality of procedure Refers to the set of established behaviors for collectively achieving the organization's goal.

home health care Rather than have the patient come to a hospital, clinic, or physician's office, home health care professionals go to the patient's home.

hospice Care is for terminally ill patients either at home or in dedicated facilities.

hospitals Healthcare organizations that treat patients for injury or disease and usually provide *inpatient* or long-term care.

instant messaging (IM) A method of sending electronic messages, but closer to real time. IM messages tend to be shorter than e-mail and can be likened to electronic chatting.

imaging rooms Imaging rooms are used for diagnostics such as x-ray, ultrasound, or other electronic technology-based procedures.

managerial operating procedures Procedures developed to address business or operational needs of the organization.

personal computer (PC) An electronic device that can be used to gain access to PHI, either because PHI is stored on the device, or because the device is connected by a network connection to the PHI.

placement A method by which an electronic device that can be used to gain access to PHI is located so as to minimize unauthorized access.

printer An electronic device that can be used to gain access to PHI.

privacy screen A device that is attached to a computer monitor that prevents anyone not sitting in front of the monitor from reading its contents.

private practice In private practice, a single physician provides care to individual patients. This can be in a private office, a clinic, or other setting.

procedural behavior Procedural behavior refers to the level of procedural formality based on the type of treatment or diagnostics being administered.

procedure rooms Procedure rooms are settings wherein patients who require minor procedures and privacy or specialized equipment may be treated.

professional communication Communication is professional if that communication does not have to be managed or monitored. This includes both style and content.

recovery room Postsurgical patients are moved to recovery rooms directly after surgery until anesthesia wears off and their vital signs stabilize.

resources The means by which organizations achieve their collective goals. Frequently, these are divided into four types: financial, human, physical, and information.

sanitation The focus on the sterilization of facilities and instruments, and proper disposal of contaminated wastes such as used hypodermic needles, bandages, gauze, and other medical supplies.

scope of work Defines the range of activities accomplished in an organization. General hospitals usually have the broadest scope in that they will try to save life, reduce suffering and pain, and eliminate disease of any patient who is presented for treatment.

screensaver Program that locks out a computer screen after a predetermined period of time.

sensitivity of the environment Sensitivity in a healthcare context usually means the condition of the patient.

social behavior Refers to conduct caused by or affecting other people.

surgical center Center for outpatient surgery. Also known as ambulatory surgical center (ASC).

telephone (phone) Handset device used to transmit electronic representations of the human voice from one phone to another.

time lockout Refers to the automatic logout of a computer program after a predetermined period of time so that unauthorized users cannot use the system until they are validated with the correct username and password.

voice over IP (VoIP) The use of the Internet and IP networks to route and carry telephone calls.

Healthcare IT Acronyms

Table 2-7 contains healthcare IT acronyms that were introduced in this chapter. Many of these terms are listed in the CompTIA Healthcare IT Technician exam objectives, and most are also defined in the Key Terms section of this chapter. For a complete list of the healthcare acronyms used in this book, see Appendix C.

Acronym	Full Name
ADL	Activities of Daily Living
ALF	Assisted Living Facility
ARNP	Advanced Registered Nurse Practitioner
ASC	Ambulatory Surgical Center
CCU	Cardiac Care Unit
CRNA	Certified Registered Nurse Anesthetist
DA	Doctor's Assistant
DO	Doctor of Osteopathic Medicine
ER	Emergency Room
FTP	File Transfer Protocol
ICU	Intensive Care Unit
IM	instant messaging
IV	intravenous
LAB	Laboratory
LPN	Licensed Practical Nurse
MA	Medical Assistant
MD	Medical Doctor
MED/SURG	Medical/Surgical
NF	Nursing Facility
NP	Nurse Practitioner
NUC	Nursing Unit Clerk
OB/GYN	Obstetrics/Gynecology
OR	Operating Room
PA	Physician Assistant
PATH	Pathology

Table 2-7 **Healthcare IT acronyms introduced in this chapter** *(continues)*

Acronym	Full Name
PC	Personal computer
PCT	Patient Care Technician
PEDS	Pediatrics
PM	Practice Manager or Physical Medicine
PSYCH	Psychiatry
PT	Physical Therapy or Physical Therapist
RN	Registered Nurse
SNF	Skilled Nursing Facility
VoIP	Voice over Internet Protocol
XRAY	Radiology

Table 2-7   Healthcare IT acronyms introduced in this chapter (*continued*)
© Cengage Learning 2013

Review Questions

1. Which of the following is true about hospitals?
    a. They are only for terminally ill patients.
    b. They mainly treat chronically ill patients.
    c. They treat patients for injury or disease and usually provide inpatient or short-term care.
    d. They treat patients for injury or disease and usually only provide outpatient care.

2. The type of patients treated at nursing homes usually includes _____.
    a. those with chronic disease or disability, or who require a long time period for recovery
    b. those with acute disease or disability, or patients who require a short time period for recovery
    c. children
    d. those with disorders of the musculoskeletal system

3. Patients with life-threatening diseases or trauma frequently need specialized care in _____.
    a. CCU
    b. OB/GYN
    c. ICU
    d. CCU

4. A pathology department provides the staff and equipment used to _____.

   a. provide various chemical, microbial, microscopic, and other studies in order to diagnose and treat disease or injury

   b. help make clinical diagnostic decisions

   c. provide traditional over-the-shelf pharmaceuticals and specially prepared compounds and medications as needed

   d. provide imaging equipment that may use x-rays, ultrasound, or nuclear isotopes as a method to detect and diagnose disease or injury

5. Nursing homes are similar to hospitals as they mainly address the needs of inpatients. However, unlike hospitals, _____.

   a. they typically do not have acute care functions like emergency, intensive care, obstetrics, and surgery

   b. they typically have more regulation

   c. they are typically larger

   d. they only treat children

6. What is another name for outpatient surgical centers?

   a. Chronic care surgical centers

   b. Hospitals

   c. Ambulatory surgical centers

   d. Covered Entities

7. Hospitals usually have the broadest scope of work because _____.

   a. they can be very complex

   b. they try to save life, reduce suffering and pain, and eliminate disease of any patient who is presented for treatment

   c. they have complex managerial procedures

   d. they are reimbursed by CMS

8. What type of organizational resource is PHI?

   a. Financial

   b. Human

   c. Physical

   d. Information

9. Low formality of procedure means _____.

   a. lower deviation from set procedures

   b. no procedures

   c. higher deviation from set procedures

   d. none of the above

10. Many _____ happen to also be high-formality organizations.

    a. acute care organizations

    b. chronic care organizations

    c. ambulatory organizations

    d. outpatient organizations

11. Codes of conduct frequently address numerous behaviors, but in healthcare organizations, the core issues include _____.

    a. communication, VoIP, and FTP

    b. communication, procedural behavior, social behavior, and sanitation

    c. communication, PC, and printer placement

    d. communication and behavior

12. In a high-formality healthcare organization or setting, what communication style should be used?

    a. Electronic

    b. Paper

    c. English

    d. None of the above

13. What procedural behavior should be adopted in imaging rooms?

    a. Informal

    b. Formal

    c. Relaxed

    d. None of the above

14. Nosocomial infections are _____.

    a. quickly cured

    b. hospital originated

    c. treated as an acute disease

    d. chronic in nature

15. Hand washing, cleaning and sterilization, use of antimicrobials, and the use of protective equipment are all examples of _____.

    a. formal behavior

    b. outpatient care procedures

    c. informal care procedures

    d. infection control procedures

16. According to the HITECH Act, date, time, patient identification, and user identification must be recorded when electronic PHI (ePHI) is _____.

    a. communicated

    b. created, modified, or printed

    c. transmitted

    d. encrypted

17. Unique identifiers are a _____ for ePHI.

    a. technical safeguard

    b. control mechanism

    c. timeout device

    d. none of the above

18. To transmit telephone calls over the Internet, one could use _____.

    a. VoIP

    b. Fax

    c. Encrypted ePHI

    d. FTP

19. A _____ is a device used to prevent unauthorized individuals from seeing a computer monitor.

    a. blinder

    b. screensaver

    c. privacy screen

    d. time lockout program

20. Can a fax be encrypted?

    a. No, because it is on paper

    b. Yes, but it can't be read until it is decrypted

    c. No, fax signals are already encrypted

    d. Yes, using an encrypted fax service

Case Projects

Case Project 2-1: Healthcare Organizational Structures

Visit your local hospital and ask for a tour. When completed, write a one-page paper that describes what you learned. How did your hospital compare to those listed in this chapter?

Case Project 2-2: Codes of Conduct

Use the Internet as a research resource and find codes of conduct for three different healthcare organizations. Then develop a chart that compares what they say about communication, procedural behavior, social behavior, and sanitation.

Case Project 2-3: EHR/EMR Access Roles for Using PHI

Covered Entities must use PHI with the minimum necessary information to achieve the stated purpose. While nonmedical personnel may have technical access, they have no authority to create, read, or update PHI unless it is necessary to achieve the stated purpose. Research various nonmedical roles and outline how they may come in contact with PHI or ePHI. Write a one-page paper on your research.

Case Project 2-4: Proper Communication Methods

There are two major aspects to the definition of professional communication. The first is the style of communication (how it is said). The second aspect is the content of the communication (what is said). Develop a scenario for a sensitive environment. In one case, create an example of unprofessional communication for that environment. In another case, create an example of professional communication for that environment.

Case Project 2-5: PHI Best Practices I

Research privacy screens. What options are available? How difficult are they to use? Write a one-page paper on your research.

Case Project 2-6: PHI Best Practices II

Using the Internet or other sources, conduct research on physical access security for electronic devices. Create a table that lists and compares the characteristics of each approach. Which would you recommend for healthcare? Why? Write a one-page paper on your findings.

Healthcare IT: Challenges and Opportunities—Revisited

Refer to the Superior Care Health Group (SCHG) case as related in the chapter opening section, "Healthcare IT: Challenges and Opportunities." Assume you are in Braden's position and are conducting the interviews.

For this case, answer the following:

a. What do you (as Braden) need to know about healthcare organizations in order to answer the interviewees' questions? Develop a one-page discussion.

b. Which interviewee questions are about procedural behavior and which are about social behavior? Do research to determine the difference. Develop a one-page discussion.

c. In an acute setting like a hospital, sensitivity of the environment can be high. Is SCHG likely to be the same? Why? Under what conditions would this answer be different?

References

1. "More Doctors Giving Up Private Practices," *The New York Times*. March 25, 2010, accessed October 3, 2011, http://www.nytimes.com/2010/03/26/health/policy/26docs.html?pagewanted=all.

chapter 3

Desktop IT Operations

After completing this chapter, you should be able to do the following:

- List the different types of computing resources and computer languages

- Explain how to set up a desktop workstation

- List the steps in troubleshooting hardware and software

- Describe how to configure devices

Healthcare IT: Challenges and Opportunities

Most of the Superior Care Health Group (SCHG) staff is relatively young and oriented to modern medicine and its management and organization. However, the use of technology in SCHG is limited. All patient information, including medical records, is maintained in paper files. The front desk uses four terminals to schedule patients and to complete billing tasks, and the terminals are connected to two personal computers that run an old version of the Linux operating system. The terminals are also connected to several older printers used to print billing forms and other pertinent financial information. This system was installed almost 10 years ago by a local computer business that has since closed.

With the impending changes in healthcare management, SCHG is aware that it needs to modernize and expand its use of information technology (IT) in the front office as well as for enhancing the heath care provided to its patients. However, SCHG is unsure where exactly to begin. Two different value-added resellers (VARs) have called on SCHG in the last six months and offered to install an entire "turnkey" system that would provide all of the latest "bells and whistles." However, after examining the proposals, SCHG determined not to pursue using VARs. They decided that the cost is excessive at this time, and because both VARs are not located in their immediate area, they are concerned about receiving prompt support. Also, because their previous computer business consultant closed and left them without any support, SCHG is wary of contracting with a similar organization.

SCHG has decided to hire a certified healthcare IT professional who can determine what their needs are and gradually introduce new technology instead of installing an entire new system all at once. SCHG has decided to hire Abby Wesley, an instructor from the local college, as a consultant to assist them in the process. Abby teaches in the Department of Health Services and is very knowledgeable in IT as it relates to health care.

A meeting has been set up between Abby and Braden Thomas, the SCHG office manager. Braden begins by telling Abby that although their office technology is currently meeting their needs, he knows that changes are needed. He wonders what kinds of changes Abby will recommend, and why. What will Abby say?

When electronic computers were introduced almost 70 years ago, the U.S. federal government was among the first organizations to adopt this technology. The task of collecting, organizing, and processing millions of "data points" such as tax records, census data, military service records, research, and other types of data could be easily streamlined using technology. As computers became smaller but more powerful and more affordable, the business sector eagerly embraced the opportunity to replace paper copies of documents—that were read, sorted, and filed by an army of employees—with computing devices that were faster, cheaper, and more accurate. Other economic sectors, such as banking, manufacturing, sales, transportation, and education, quickly followed suit.

However, one sector that has been slower to embrace the benefits of computers has been the healthcare industry. Although hospitals routinely use computers for managing patient information, billing, inventory, and, more recently, supporting innovations such as electronic digital imaging, it is recognized industry that an even broader use of technology by hospitals would be beneficial. One specific subset of the healthcare industry that has not been eager to use technology has been physicians in small private practices. It is not uncommon to visit your doctor's office and see thousands of folders holding paper patient records behind the office receptionist. During an examination a nurse practitioner may scribble notes on a piece of paper while the doctor writes out a drug prescription on a pad of paper. For a variety of reasons, including cost and the lack of standards, the use of computers and handheld mobile devices has not widely penetrated the local doctor's office.

This is now poised to change significantly. U. S. federal laws are accelerating the shift to electronic health records (EHR) by all healthcare providers by setting target dates for widespread adoption. Hospitals and healthcare providers can even receive incentive payments when they adopt the "meaningful use" of electronic health records. With the increased use of EHR, the need for healthcare information technology (IT) professionals will likewise dramatically increase.

In this chapter, you will learn about desktop IT operations in the healthcare field that support electronic records. First, an overview of IT will be presented, followed by how to install and troubleshoot desktop workstations and other devices. Finally, you will explore how to configure different types of devices.

IT Overview

3.1 Identify commonly used IT terms and technologies.

Although the terms electronic *medical* records and electronic *health* records are often used synonymously, there is a significant difference in their definitions. An *electronic medical record (EMR)* is an electronic digital version of a patient's paper chart found in a clinician's office. A patient's EMR would contain the medical and treatment history of the patient in that practice. There are several advantages of EMRs over paper records to monitor and improve the overall quality of care within the practice. These include:

- Easily track data over time
- Quickly identify which patients are due for preventive screenings or checkups
- Efficiently monitor how large numbers of patients are performing by evaluating blood pressure readings, vaccinations, weight control, and so forth

A significant disadvantage to EMRs is that it they cannot be easily and accurately electronically distributed. In many practices, EMRs are still created in handwritten form. This makes it difficult to fax or even mail a legible copy to specialists or other members of a healthcare team. The handwritten format also makes it difficult—if not impossible—to electronically scan the paper EMR to create an electronic copy. This forces the office staff to retype the information on the computer, taking valuable time away from other more urgent tasks. In addition, this can also lead to transcription errors if the material is difficult for a clerical person without a medical background to interpret.

Paper records have drawbacks for both office staff and medical personnel
© Claires/www.Shutterstock.com

In contrast, an *electronic health record (EHR)* focuses more on the *total* health of the patient by going beyond the standard clinical data collected in a provider's office. EHRs are designed to be shared among all the healthcare providers involved with a patient's care, such as laboratories and specialists. EHR information moves with the patient—not only between specialists, hospitals, and nursing facilities but also across the country. EHRs better support the concept of health care as a team effort that involves multiple professionals. All healthcare team members can have ready access to the latest information to provide for more coordinated and patient-centered care.

Due to the lack of flexibility in sharing EMRs, some healthcare IT professionals regard EMRs as no better than a paper record and feel EMRs may have even contributed to the slow adoption of EHRs by private practices.

The advantages of EHRs include:

- Data collected by the primary care provider can inform an emergency department clinician about the patient's life-threatening allergy so that correct care can be appropriately administered, even if the patient is unconscious.

- A patient can log in to his or her own record through the Internet and see the trend of lab results over time. This may help provide motivation to take medications and keep up with recommended lifestyle changes.

- The lab results conducted by the primary care physician previously can be used by a specialist without running duplicate tests.

- A clinician's notes from the patient's recent hospital stay can be used to create more accurate discharge instructions and follow-up care.

In order to support EHRs, a healthcare IT professional must have an understanding of the types of computing resources that are used in storing, processing, and transmitting EHRs, as well as a knowledge of the different computer programming languages used in the processing.

Types of Computing Resources

The computing resources used in managing EHRs can be grouped into four broad categories. These include mainframe computers, terminal services, client-server computing, and cloud computing.

Mainframe Computer

Mainframe computers are expensive computers designed to process massive amounts of data quickly. These computers are large (they require a dedicated room), powerful (their speed is measured in millions of instructions performed per second), and expensive (up to several million dollars in cost). Mainframe computers can support hundreds of users simultaneously through a process known as *time-sharing*. Each user is connected to the mainframe through a *dumb computer terminal*, which is essentially a computer monitor, mouse, and keyboard that has no processing capabilities. The mainframe computer gives a tiny fraction of its processing power to each user on a rotating basis. Because of its high speed, the mainframe is able to service all users without any noticeable delay.

NOTE

The term *mainframe* is derived from the way in which the machines were originally built. All of its different units, such as processing, communication, and so forth. were actually hung onto a large metal frame, so that the *main* computer was built into a *frame*.

Due to their high cost, mainframe computers are most frequently used in government, financial services, retail, and manufacturing industries. Although mainframes may be found in a chain of large hospitals all sharing the same mainframe computer, they would not be used in a local physician's office.

Client-Server Computing

Consider a single piece of rope. By itself it cannot trap a fish or a soccer ball. Yet if several individual pieces of rope are all woven together at regular intervals to form a *net*, they can ensnare fish and balls. The difference is that when they are connected together the pieces of rope can do much more than if they are alone.

A *network* is defined as anything that resembles a net in how it looks or functions. A network of politicians has more power than just one elected official. A network of roads can move more traffic than a single street. Just as with a net, much more can be accomplished through a network by connecting the individual parts together instead of working alone.

The same is true with computers. By itself, one computer can perform many functions, such as create a document, calculate a complex formula, or draw an image. Yet the power of one stand-alone computer is limited to the processing power of its hardware, the software that is installed on that computer, and any devices that are directly connected to it. But the capabilities of that computer can be dramatically increased when it is connected to other computers and devices to form a computer network. A *computer network* is defined as multiple interconnected computers and devices. Connecting the computers together increases the capabilities of each computer so that the user can accomplish more tasks.

The purpose of a computer network can be summarized in a single word: sharing. Just as the individual pieces of rope share the load of the net by trapping a ball or a fish, a computer network is likewise designed for sharing resources such as files, information, or printers.

The most common type of computer networking is **client-server computing**. A client-server network is controlled by at least one special high-powered computer called a *server*, while the individual computers on the network are called *clients*. A server-based network is illustrated in Figure 3-1. Servers are usually dedicated to running the network and do not function as clients; rather, the sole function of a server is to service the requests received from the network clients. Today's servers are typically smaller units that slide into a rack that can accommodate multiple servers, as illustrated in Figure 3-2.

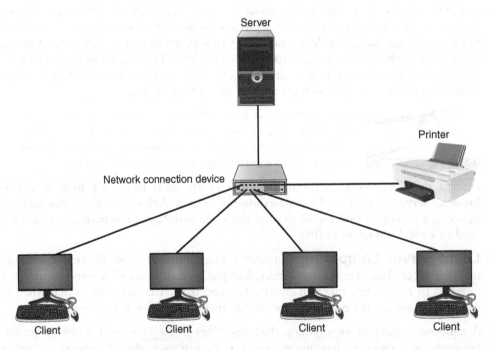

Figure 3-1 Client-server computing
© Cengage Learning 2013

Figure 3-2 Servers in a rack
© corepics/www.Shutterstock.com

 Like a mainframe computer, a server uses a type of time-sharing so that all users on the network can be accommodated without any perceptible delays. However, servers are much smaller and less expensive than mainframes.

Traditionally, different servers (such as a Web server or an e-mail server) running different software would each be installed on a separate physical computer. However, the number of servers in today's organizations has grown exponentially, and it has become expensive to purchase, install, and maintain hundreds of physical servers. One recent enhancement to client-server computing is **virtualization,** in which more than one server can run on the same physical piece of equipment. Virtualization creates one or more *virtual* (electronic) instances of a server that can then be run with other software or virtual instances on one *actual* server. Virtualization allows multiple virtual servers (even running different software) to function on a single physical server, thus significantly reducing costs. Server virtualization is shown in Figure 3-3.

Before virtualization

After virtualization

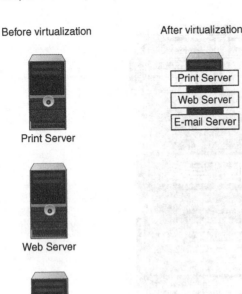

Print Server

Web Server

E-mail Server

Figure 3-3 Virtualization
© Cengage Learning 2013

In addition to reducing costs associated with purchasing and maintaining multiple servers, virtualization can likewise reduce electrical expenses. The cost of electricity to run servers as well as keep a server room cool doubles about every five to six years, and for every $1 spent on computing equipment in data centers, an additional $0.50 is spent to power and cool them. Because a typical server utilizes only about 10% of its capacity, virtualization can dramatically reduce energy costs by configuring one physical server to support multiple virtual instances.[1]

Terminal Services A variation of client-server computing is **terminal services**, in which software that allows for applications are installed on servers and then accessed and executed through desktop clients, instead of installing applications on each individual client computer. This results in a significant cost and time savings in installing, configuring, managing, and maintaining the applications, which now can be done centrally on a smaller number of servers instead of on every desktop client. Because the processing is carried out on the server instead of the client computer, older desktop computers can be used as clients with terminal services, reducing the need to purchase the latest high-performance desktops. Microsoft offers a popular Terminal Services package for Windows servers, and similar products are available from other vendors and for other operating systems.

In many ways, a desktop client running terminal services is similar to a dumb computer terminal.

Cloud Computing Cloud computing is a "pay-per-use" model in which customers pay only for the computing resources that they need at the present time. It also is a relatively recent way for users to access computing resources online such as storage or computing power without having to purchase extra hardware or software. The term *cloud* refers to the fact that the resources are accessed "in the cloud," that is, through the Internet. Apple iCloud is an example of cloud computing for individuals. With iCloud, instead of storing music, photos, and other files on your own computer, you keep them "in the cloud" so they are available whenever and wherever you want them. Many businesses and other organizations are also turning to cloud computing.

Although various definitions of cloud computing have been proposed, the definition from the National Institute of Standards and Technology (NIST) may be the most comprehensive: *Cloud computing is a model for enabling convenient, on-demand network access to a shared pool of configurable computing resources (e.g., networks, servers, storage, applications, and services) that can be rapidly provisioned and released with minimal management effort or service provider interaction.*[2]

Cloud computing can perhaps be best understood when it is compared to a similar model known as *hosted services*. In hosted services, servers, storage, and the supporting networking infrastructure are shared by multiple "tenants" (users and organizations). Using a network connection purchased from an organization that provides Internet connectivity called an **Internet Service Provider (ISP)**, the tenant contracts the hosted service for a specific period of time. As more resources are needed (such as additional storage space or computing power) the tenant must contact the hosted service and negotiate an additional fee as well as sign a new contract for those new services.

Cloud computing, on the other hand, is a "pay-per-use" model in which customers pay only for the computing resources that they need at the present time. As computing needs increase or decrease, the cloud computing resources can be quickly (and automatically) scaled up or down. Table 3-1 lists the characteristics of cloud computing.

Characteristic	Explanation
On-demand self-service	The consumer can automatically increase or decrease computing resources without requiring any human interaction from the service provider.
Universal client support	Virtually any networked device (desktop, laptop, smartphone, tablet, and so forth) can access the cloud computing resources.
Invisible resource pooling	The physical and virtual computing resources are pooled together to serve multiple simultaneous consumers that are dynamically assigned or reassigned according to the consumers' needs; the customer has little or no control or knowledge of the physical location of the resources.
Immediate elasticity	Computing resources are "elastic" in that they can be increased or decreased quickly to meet demands.
Metered services	Fees are based on the computing resources used.

Table 3-1 Cloud computing characteristics
© Cengage Learning 2013

There are three service models in cloud computing:

- *Cloud Software as a Service (SaaS)*—In this model, the cloud computing vendor provides access to the vendor's software applications running on a cloud infrastructure. These applications, which can be accessed through a Web browser, do not require any installation, configuration, upgrading, or management from the user.

- *Cloud Platform as a Service (PaaS)*—Unlike SaaS, in which the application software belonging to the cloud computing vendor is used, in PaaS the consumer can install and run their own specialized applications on the cloud computing network. Although the customer has control over the deployed applications, they do not manage or configure any of the underlying cloud infrastructure (network, servers, operating systems, storage, and so forth).

- *Cloud Infrastructure as a Service (IaaS)*—In this model, the customer has the highest level of control. The cloud computing vendor allows the customer to deploy and run the customer's own software, including operating systems and applications. The consumer has some control over the operating systems, storage, and their installed applications, yet they do not manage or control the underlying cloud infrastructure.

Programming Languages

Just as individuals use a natural language like English or Italian to communicate, a *computer programming language* is used to communicate instructions to the computer hardware. Programming languages are used to create programs that a computer executes. For example, a programming language can be used to create a calendar program. When a user executes or *launches* the calendar program, this software instructs the computer hardware about the tasks that it must perform (accept keyboard input, display characters on the screen, direct output to the printer, and so forth). In addition, when one program needs to communicate with another program, a set of specifications known as an **application programming interface (API)** is used. This serves as a set of standardized requests between the different software programs and makes it easier for computer programmers to write programs.

Although estimates vary widely, there may be as many as 8,500 different computer programming languages. Many of these are highly specialized, while others are more general in nature. The programming languages most often associated with Web development include:

- *Hypertext Markup Language (HTML)*—The **Hypertext Markup Language (HTML)** is the common language for creating Web page contents. A *markup language* is a method for adding annotations to the text so that the additions can be distinguished from the text itself. HTML is a markup language that uses specific words (*tags*) embedded in brackets (< and >) that a Web browser then uses to display the contents in a specific format.

- *Extensible Markup Language (XML)*—Another markup language is **Extensible Markup Language (XML)**. There are several significant differences between XML and HTML. First, XML is designed to *carry* data instead of indicating how to display it, as with HTML. Also, XML does not have a predefined set of tags; instead, the user defines her own tags.

- *PHP*—**PHP** is a programming language that is used to create Web content that will change (is *dynamic*) instead of remaining the same (*static*). The code that is created through the PHP language is embedded into the HTML document on the Web server and then is displayed through the user's Web browser. PHP stands for *PHP: Hypertext Preprocessor.*

- *Active Server Pages (ASP)*—An alternative to PHP is **Active Server Pages (ASP)**. Like PHP, the ASP programming language is used to create dynamic Web pages on a Web server.

- *Flash*—**Flash** is a multimedia platform that can be used to add special effects, such as animation, video, and interactivity to Web pages. Flash runs in a local Web browser instead of on a Web server.

- *Structured Query Language (SQL)*—The **Structured Query Language (SQL)** is a programming language used to view and manipulate data that is stored in a database. Web pages that allow users to enter data (such as a product number) and receive information (such as the item's cost) typically use SQL.

Setting Up a Desktop Workstation

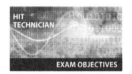

3.2 Demonstrate the ability to set up a basic PC workstation within an EHR/EMR environment.

Desktop computer workstations remain the "workhorses" of computing, particularly in a healthcare setting. It is important for a healthcare IT professional to have an understanding of how the key hardware components as well as the software of a modern computer function. This knowledge is important when properly installing and configuring a desktop workstation and in troubleshooting problems.

Parts of a Desktop System

The basic parts of a desktop computer are broken down into two categories. These are the hardware and the software of the system.

Desktop Hardware A standard desktop computer system is shown in Figure 3-4. The hardware can be divided into three areas. The first is *processing hardware*, or the components that actually perform the necessary computations. The *central processing unit (CPU)* is the "brains" of the computer. The CPU rests in a *socket* that is connected to the computer's *motherboard*, which is a printed circuit board that contains the primary components of the computer. The motherboard allows these components to communicate with each other and itself and is located in the large case called the *system unit*. A motherboard with a CPU is illustrated in Figure 3-5.

The second category of hardware is *input hardware*, which are the devices through which data is entered into the computer. **Keyboards**, the most common type of input hardware, have evolved from a flat panel with keys to specially sculptured models that are designed to be less stressful on hands by providing a higher degree of comfort, also known as *ergonomics*. An ergonomic keyboard is shown in Figure 3-6. Devices like tablets and smartphones that use touch screens often have *soft keyboards*, or keyboards that show on-screen and operate by touch. A pointing device such as a **mouse** or touch pad is used to rapidly position a pointer at specific location.

Figure 3-4 Standard desktop computer system

© Dmitry Melnikov/www.Shutterstock.com

Figure 3-5 Motherboard with CPU

© Norman Chan/www.Shutterstock.com

Figure 3-6 Ergonomic keyboard
© Realinemedia/www.Shutterstock.com

The final category is *output hardware*. Output hardware consists of devices that provide the results of the computer's processing, such as a **monitor** that displays the results, a *printer* that records on paper, or *speakers* that transmit sounds. Output hardware is often a separate external device and today is connected to the main computer through a physical interface known as a **universal serial bus (USB)** connection.

Desktop Software Software found on a desktop computer typically falls into one of three different categories. **Operating system (OS)** software serves as the "intermediary" between the user and the computer hardware. For example, a user who wants to print a document may drag an icon representing a file and then drop it onto a printer icon. The underlying OS then allocates memory, assigns processes, communicates with the printer, and monitors the progress, all without requiring any technical instructions from the user. This means that users do not have to possess an advanced knowledge or skill set for using the hardware; instead, they can focus on tasks to be performed (*what*) instead of the detailed mechanics (*how*). Common desktop operating systems include Microsoft Windows, Apple Mac OS, and Linux.

Desktop operating systems are credited with the rapid and widespread growth of personal computers.

A second category of desktop software is *utility software*. Utility software supports the OS by providing additional functionality that may not be found in the core OS. For example, operating systems allow users to copy files from one device (such as an internal hard drive) to another device (such as a network file server). However, many OSs do not have the capability of *synchronizing* the files between devices by comparing the files on one device with the other device so that only the most recently updated files are copied (instead of copying all files). A separate utility program that does perform synchronization between devices can be installed on the computer to perform this task more quickly. The user then launches the synchronization utility software program through the OS.

Desktop operating systems are constantly evolving by adding what once was utility software to the core OS. This has resulted in complaints by many utility software developers that their programs are no longer in demand because the functionality is included for free in operating systems.

Application software is the final category of desktop software. Application software is "general" software that can be used for a variety of different tasks. Unlike utility software that may perform a single task (such as synchronizing files between devices), application software such as a *word-processing* program can be used to create a memo, write a report, or design a flyer. Other types of application software include *spreadsheets* (used to manipulate numbers), *database programs* (software that can store and easily retrieve information in a variety of ways), and *presentation software* (used to display text and figures to an audience). When several of these application programs are "bundled" into one group, it is called a *suite*. The best-known bundled suite of application software is the Microsoft Office suite.

Since its introduction, the current version of Microsoft Office has been installed on average once every second on a desktop computer somewhere around the world.

Installing and Configuring a Workstation

One of the primary duties of a healthcare IT professional is to properly install and configure a computer system. Although today's computers vary in size and hardware configuration, a standard set of tasks apply to any installation:

- *Select the proper location*—Before unpacking the new computer, the first step is to determine the best location for the system. It should be within easy reach of an electrical outlet or *surge protector* as well as the network connection (for a wired network). There should be adequate space for the computer, its cables, any peripheral devices, and workspace for the user to lay out materials while using the system. The monitor should be positioned away from light sources that could produce a reflective glare (such as in front of a window with no blinds or directly beneath a fluorescent ceiling light).

The monitor should be positioned about one arm's length away from the user when they are seated comfortably in front of it to avoid eyestrain.

- *Unpack the components*—After removing the contents from the box the desktop system came in, it is important to check off each item against the packing list of included items to ensure that nothing is missing. The next step is to unwrap all the different parts. For desktop systems, remove any protective plastic covers from the front of the system unit and monitor. After unpacking any cables, the keyboard, mouse, and other components should be arranged on the desk area.

- *Connect the components to the system unit*—Following the manufacturer's instructions, the next step is to connect the keyboard, mouse, monitor, and printer to the system unit by inserting the cables of each part into the proper connection. Figure 3-7 illustrates some of the different connection types found on computers, and Table 3-2 lists the components that connect to them.

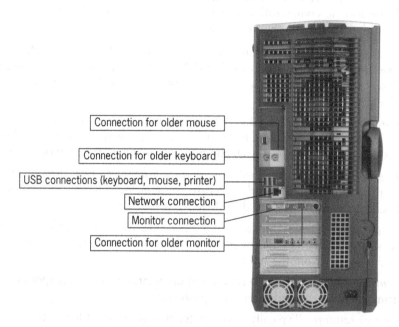

Connection for older mouse

Connection for older keyboard

USB connections (keyboard, mouse, printer)

Network connection

Monitor connection

Connection for older monitor

Figure 3-7 Computer connections
© Carolina K. Smith, M.D./www.Shutterstock.com

Component	Connection
Keyboard	Keyboards today use a USB connection, while older keyboards may require a separate keyboard connector that is colored purple.
Mouse	Like keyboards, a mouse is typically connected to any available USB connection; an older mouse may require a separate mouse connector that is colored green. A mouse can also be wireless, using a USB connection transmitter.
Monitor	Monitors are connected to the white connector; older monitors are connected to the blue connector.
Printer	Modern printers use a USB connection.
Network	Network connections are typically not colored, yet they resemble a larger telephone jack connector. These network connections are called *RJ-45* (telephone connections are *RJ-11*).

Table 3-2 Computer components and connections
© Cengage Learning 2013

Older computers do not rely as heavily on USB connections to connect components as today's computers do. Older printers had special connections known as *DB-9* and *DB-25*.

NOTE

Once the computer is installed, it is then turned on and the basic operating system setup is initiated, at which time the user is asked to enter the proper time zone and registration information. Following the basic operating system setup, the workstation should be properly configured. Although the specific configuration will vary depending upon the user's needs, the general configuration options include the following:

- *Create user accounts*—An administrator account should first be created with a unique password. Next, different user accounts should be created for each person using the computer. Users should not share the same account, nor should they be given administrative capabilities.

- *Run hardware diagnostic tests*—Because the computer hardware could have been damaged in transport, it is a good idea to run a diagnostic test first to determine if there are any problems that need to be solved while the computer is still protected under warranty.

- *Install updated drivers*—A **driver** is software that the computer's operating system uses to interact with specific hardware. Although drivers are included in the operating system, updated drivers often are available to download from the Internet.

- *Update the operating system*—Updates to the operating system are made available to address new security vulnerabilities or provide additional functionality. These are available as downloads from the Internet.

- *Turn on security protections*—Based on the requirements of the office, specific security settings may be enabled to provide protection.

- *Configure power settings*—Typically, a computer that is not used for a set period of time will be set to "sleep" to conserve power. It is important to configure these settings based on the requirements of the office.

- *Install software*—Specific software that is required for the office should be installed and if necessary, updated.

- *Create a backup image*—After all of the updates and installations are complete, a backup of the system should be performed.

Maintaining the computer after it has been installed and configured is also important. This includes installing software updates, removing programs that are no longer used, and checking the security settings.

Troubleshooting

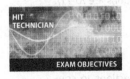

3.3 Given a scenario, troubleshoot and solve common PC problems.

Troubleshooting, or tracing and correcting problems, is an essential skill for a healthcare IT technician. Troubleshooting does not always require that a technician be able to physically overhaul a device, such as using tools to open and fix a monitor or a printer. Instead, troubleshooting often involves *identifying* the problem and then *assessing* the different options for solving the problem. Troubleshooting involves solving both hardware and software problems, as well as consulting documentation available from the hardware or software vendor.

 One of the best troubleshooting tools is the documentation that accompanies the hardware or software. Although printed manuals are a thing of the past, updated information can be obtained from the vendor's Web site.

Hardware

Due to the modular nature and low cost of today's computer electronics, rarely is time spent attempting to repair faulty hardware. Instead, a healthcare IT technician is usually tasked with quickly identifying the problem and deciding if it can be quickly corrected; if not, then the item is usually replaced with a functionally similar item.

Whereas at one time computer monitors were large and heavy box-like items that resembled older television sets, today's monitors are thin and relatively light, as shown in Figure 3-8. For a monitor that does not function properly, there are no repairable components for a healthcare IT technician to inspect or replace; instead, a technician should determine if the problem is the result of a connection or setting. Table 3-3 lists the problems, power light settings on the monitor, and troubleshooting questions to be asked when looking for a solution for a faulty computer monitor.

Figure 3-8 Computer monitor
© Kitch Bain/www.Shutterstock.com

Problem	Power Light Settings	Troubleshooting Questions
Screen is blank	Power light is off	Is the monitor plugged into an electrical outlet? Is the outlet or power supply on? Is the power cord connection tight?
Screen is blank	Power light is on	Are the contrast and brightness settings correct? Is the monitor cable connected to the computer? Is the video card inside the computer seated properly?
Image flickers	Power light is on	Is the cable to the computer connected and tight? Is there outside interference from speakers, lights, or fans?
Screen goes blank if not used	Power light is off or blinking	Is the computer set to go into sleep mode? Does pressing a keyboard key bring back the screen?

Table 3-3 Troubleshooting a computer monitor
© Cengage Learning 2013

Troubleshooting printers can be more involved, because printing problems are typically a result of either the printer hardware or the software that manages the printer. Some typical troubleshooting tips for printers include:

- *The printer will not print*—Be sure the printer is powered on and properly connected to the computer with a tight cable connection. Also, the printer driver may need to be updated.

- *A print spooler error message appears or the printer is printing more slowly than usual*—A *print spooler* is software that temporarily stores print jobs on the computer hard disk or in memory (called *random access memory*, or *RAM*) until the printer is ready to print them. An error message usually indicates a problem with the print spooler or its resources. It may be necessary to reboot the computer to restart the print spooler services.

- *The printer only prints part of a page, prints a blurry or faded image, or prints using inaccurate colors*—The printer ink or toner cartridge may need to be replaced. The healthcare IT professional should check the printer status information on the computer, or if the printer has a status display area it may indicate a low ink or toner condition.

- *One or more blank pages are ejected*—If a new printer ink cartridge or laser toner cartridge has been installed, the transparent protective tape may not have been removed. It may be necessary to "fan" the edges of the paper before inserting it into the printer, and store the paper in a cool, dry place.

 If paper jams in the printer, do not try to pull the paper out backward. Instead, turn the printer off and gently pull the paper in the direction of the normal paper path.

Although problems with a computer mouse are relatively rare, Table 3-4 lists troubleshooting tips for a mouse.

Symptom	Probable Causes	Solutions
Pointer on screen does not move as mouse moves	Dirt buildup on mouse trackball	Remove ball and clean
Pointer on screen moves too slow or too fast	Operating system configuration settings for mouse are disabled or set too low	Adjust settings
Wired mouse does not work when computer is started	Cable is disconnected	Turn off computer and reseat cables; restart computer
Wireless mouse does not work or functions erratically	Several	Move mouse closer to transmitter, plug transmitter into different USB port, replace batteries

Table 3-4 Troubleshooting a computer mouse
© Cengage Learning 2013

When any external device does not function properly, the cause is often a bad cable connection, or the power cord itself is not properly seated. In such cases, power off the device, reseat all connections, and turn it back on.

Software

One area of software troubleshooting involves installing periodic security updates to software. As more features and *graphical user interfaces (GUIs)* were added to operating systems over time, they have become much more complex. Because of this increasing complexity, software conflicts, performance issues, and even security vulnerabilities were often unintentionally introduced. To address these operating systems problems that are uncovered after the software has been released, software vendors usually deploy a software update to address the vulnerabilities. These fixes can come in a variety of formats. A security **patch** is a general software security update intended to cover vulnerabilities that have been discovered. Whereas an **update** is a universal software enhancement for all customers, a **hotfix** is software that addresses a specific customer situation and often may not be distributed outside that customer's organization. A **service pack** is software that is a cumulative package of all security updates plus additional features.

There is no universal agreement on the definition of these terms. For example, whereas most vendors and users refer to a general software security update as a patch, Microsoft calls it a *security update*.

Due to the quantity of patches, it is important to have a mechanism to ensure that patches are installed in a timely fashion. Modern operating systems, such as Mac OS and Microsoft Windows, have the ability to perform automatic updates. The desktop system interacts with the vendor's online update service and can automatically download and install patches or alert the user to their presence, depending on the configuration option that is chosen. The automatic update configuration options for most operating systems are similar to those for Windows 7, seen in Figure 3-9. It is important that computers be set to automatically download and install these patches whenever they become available.

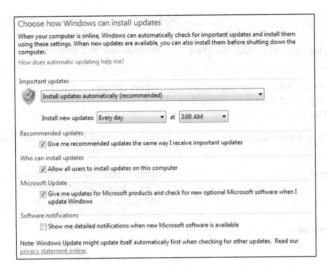

Figure 3-9 Microsoft Windows 7 automatic update options
© Cengage Learning 2013

Microsoft releases its security updates regularly on the second Tuesday of each month, called "Patch Tuesday."

Another area of software troubleshooting is to update drivers. Hardware vendors will sometimes update their drivers to take advantage of new hardware or provide additional functionality. Updating drivers involves downloading the driver from the vendor's Web site and then installing it through the operating system.

On a Windows computer, click **Start** and **Control Panel** and **System and Security** and finally **Device Manager** to update a driver.

Configuring Devices

3.4 Install and configure hardware drivers and devices.

Another important skill of a healthcare IT technician is the ability to properly configure devices that connect to a personal computer. These types of devices include mobile storage devices, mobile computing devices, and imaging devices. First, however, an understanding of the types of physical interfaces commonly found on devices and computers is important.

Physical Interfaces

The word *interface* was used as far back as the 1880s to refer to a surface forming a common boundary between regions, such as a river that separated two adjacent cities. However, with the introduction of computers, the term was adopted to refer to the point of interaction between a computer and another device (like a printer or keyboard). A computer interface (more commonly, the term *port* is used) refers to the connection on a microcomputer to which an external device is attached. Figure 3-8 displayed earlier in the chapter illustrates some of the common connections on a microcomputer.

Due to the rapid change of technology, some interfaces once common on microcomputers are rarely used today. These legacy interfaces include a **serial port,** which sent one bit of information at a time from the computer to the connected device, a *parallel port* that sent multiple bits simultaneously in a side-by-side configuration, and a **small computer systems interface (SCSI).** SCSI is an older set of standards that can transmit information at relatively high speeds.

More recently, these interfaces have been replaced with a universal serial bus (USB) interface. USB is usually characterized by a flat end-connector, as shown in Figure 3-10. This industry standard, developed in the mid-1990s, defines the cables, connectors and protocols used for connection, communication, and power supply between computers and devices. There currently are three versions of USBs:

Figure 3-10 USB connector
© David Good/www.Shutterstock.com

- *USB 1.0*—This version was first released in early 1996 and specified data rates of transmission between 1.5 and 12 million bits per second (Mbps). Due to several problems, this version was updated and replaced with USB 1.1 in mid-1998 and become the first widely adopted USB version.
- *USB 2.0*—Released in 2000, this version of USB gained wide acceptance by adding a higher transmission speed of 480 Mbps.
- *USB 3.0*—USB 3.0 devices can transmit up to 5 billion bits per second (gigabits per second or Gbps). This standard was released in late 2008.

Because serial and parallel ports have been replaced by USB interfaces to accommodate external devices, many desktop computers have as many as 10 USB ports.

An interface known as **IEEE 1394** transfers bits one at a time like an older serial bus yet at much faster speeds (800 Mbps). IEEE 1394 is frequently used for high-speed communications and data transfer between personal computers and digital audio, digital video, and even automotive applications. IEEE 1394 has replaced SCSI interfaces.

The IEEE 1394 interface is also known by the brand names FireWire (Apple), i.LINK (Sony), and Lynx (Texas Instruments).

IEEE stands for the *Institute of Electrical and Electronics Engineers*, a professional organization that sets standards for electronic communications.

Bluetooth is the name given to a wireless technology that uses short-range *radio frequency (RF)* transmissions and provides for rapid ad hoc device pairings. Originally designed in 1994 by the cellular telephone company Ericsson as a way to replace wires with radio-based technology, Bluetooth has moved well beyond its original design. Bluetooth technology enables users to connect wirelessly to a wide range of computing and telecommunications devices. It provides for rapid "on the fly" connections between a Bluetooth-enabled device such as a cellular smartphone or a laptop computer and a set of Bluetooth headphones or a mouse. Several of these Bluetooth-enabled product pairings are listed in Table 3-5.

Category	Bluetooth Pairing	Usage
Automobile	Hands-free car system with cell phone	Users can speak commands to browse the cell phone's contact list, make hands-free phone calls, or use its navigation system.
Home entertainment	Stereo headphones with portable music player	Users can create a playlist on a portable music player and listen through a set of wireless headphones or speakers.
Photographs	Digital camera with printer	Digital photos can be sent directly to a photo printer or from pictures taken on one cell phone to another phone.
Computer accessories	Computer with keyboard and mouse	Small travel mouse can be linked to a laptop or a full-size mouse and keyboard that can be connected to a desktop computer.
Gaming	Video game system with controller or headset	Gaming devices and video game systems can support multiple controllers, while Bluetooth headsets allow gamers to chat as they play.
Sports and fitness	Heart-rate monitor with wristwatch	Athletes can track heart rates while exercising by glancing at their watches.
Medical and health	Blood pressure monitors with smartphones	Patient information can be sent to a smartphone, which can then send an emergency phone message if necessary.

Table 3-5 **Bluetooth products**

Bluetooth is named after the tenth-century Danish King Harald "Bluetooth" Gormsson, who was responsible for unifying Scandinavia.

Bluetooth is designed for data communication over short distances (up to 33 feet/10 meters). The current version is Bluetooth v4.0 (a subset is known as Bluetooth Low Energy), but all Bluetooth devices are backward compatible with previous versions. The rate of transmission is 1 Mbps (megabit per second).

A bit is the smallest piece of digital electronic data. A byte is equal to 8 bits. A *megabit (Mb)* is 1 million bits. A *megabyte (MB)* is 1 million *bytes*. A *gigabit (Gb)* is 1 billion bits, and a *gigabyte (GB)* is 1 billion bytes. A *kilobit (Kb)* is 1000 bits, while a *kilobyte (KB)* is 1000 bytes. A *terabyte (TB)* is 1 trillion bytes.

Mobile Storage Devices

Mobile storage devices are external devices that provide additional storage capabilities to that found in the computer itself. These common devices are often used to back up the data on the computer's hard drive or transfer data from one computer to another. Mobile storage devices can be divided into those that utilize magnetic storage, optical storage, or electronic storage.

Magnetic Storage The oldest storage technology is *magnetic storage*. The surface of the storage medium is covered with a magnetic substance that stores data as a series of magnetic patterns. These patterns can be easily erased and rewritten, giving the magnetic storage device the ability to continually change its contents.

An **external hard drive** is similar to an internal hard disk drive (HDD) found inside the computer, except that it can be portable and is connected to the system with a USB or IEEE 1394 interface. All magnetic hard disk drives contain one or more *disks* (also called *platters*) that are stacked atop each other and enclosed in a sealed housing. The disks are coated with the magnetic substance, and special *read/write heads* move across the disks to sense the presence or absence of a magnetic pattern.

External hard drives generally come in two sizes. Portable external hard drives are smaller but very portable, as illustrated in Figure 3-11. These drives have a smaller capacity and are typically used to transfer data from one device to another device using a USB interface. Desktop external hard drives, seen in Figure 3-12, are larger in both physical size (about 6.5 × 5 inches or 16.5 × 12.7 cm) as well as storage capacity. These devices are less portable, designed to be set in a location and not frequently moved. They often serve as backup storage to a computer's internal hard drive and may use a USB or faster IEEE 1394 interface.

Desktop external hard drives have a separate power connection, while portable external hard drives receive their power through the USB cable.

Figure 3-11 Portable external hard drive
© Ruslan Ivantsov/www.Shutterstock.com

Figure 3-12 Desktop external hard drive
© Igor Grochev/www.Shutterstock.com

Another type of magnetic storage uses **magnetic tape**. As its name implies, magnetic tape is a long, narrow strip of plastic whose surface is covered with a magnetic substance. A device that stores computer data on magnetic tape is a *tape drive*. Although magnetic tape is still an alternative to a magnetic disk for backups due to its low cost and high capacity, magnetic tape is being replaced by other types of storage.

Optical Storage Instead of using a disk or tape covered with a magnetic substance, *optical storage* takes an entirely different approach to storing data. Data is recorded on the surface of a disc by burning marks into the surface in a specific pattern that can then be read back with the aid of light, which often consists of a precisely focused laser beam. The **compact disc (CD)** is an optical storage medium that was originally developed in 1982 for audio systems and was later used for recording computer data. Measuring 4.75 inches (120 millimeters), a standard disc can store 700 MB of data or 80 minutes of audio. Because nothing touches the encoded portion, the CD will not degrade as with other types of media.

Besides the standard size CD, there are also mini-CDs that can hold about 200 MB of data and business card CDs that store up to 65 MB.

Although the same physical size as a CD, a **Digital Versatile Disc (DVD)** has a much higher storage capacity, ranging from 1.46 GB to over 17 GB. Two additional optical formats, known as *HD DVD* and *Blu-ray Disc (BD)*, were released in 2006 as successors to DVD. Today Blu-ray is the preferred medium and can hold up to 50 GB.

DVDs were originally known as Digital Video Discs because they were intended for playing movies. As these discs were later used for computer data, the name changed to Digital Versatile Discs.

Solid-State Storage The solid-state or electronic memory inside a computer is *volatile*, meaning that it requires a constant electrical power source for the data to be retained; if the power goes off, everything in memory is lost. However, a special type of electronic storage does not require a constant power source. Known as *flash memory*, it can be used to store and electrically erase data. One of the most common applications for flash memory is a **USB flash drive**, which is a small, often thumb-sized portable storage medium that utilizes flash (solid-state) storage (not to be confused with the Flash multimedia platform), as illustrated in Figure 3-13. Compared to magnetic hard drives, flash drives use little power, have no fragile moving parts, are inexpensive, and have a relatively large storage capacity, yet they are small enough to easily carry in a pocket.

The primary disadvantage of USB flash drives is that due to their small size, they can be easily misplaced or otherwise lost. If the data stored on the flash drive is sensitive, this can become a serious security risk. Many organizations prohibit employees from copying specific types of data onto a flash drive or ban using them altogether.

Another type of electronic storage that also uses flash memory is a **Secure Digital (SD)** card, which is a small form factor card used for storage in handheld devices, as illustrated in Figure 3-14. This small form factor (32 mm × 24 mm × 2.1 mm) started as a portable storage device for digital cameras and handheld devices. Now there is an even smaller micro SD card, often used for extra smartphone storage.

Figure 3-13 USB flash drive
© vkoshkarov/www.Shutterstock.com

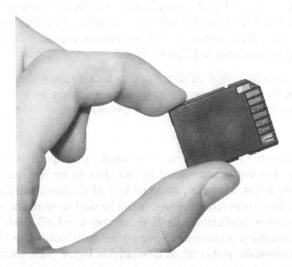

Figure 3-14 SD card
© Tuit Vlad/www.Shutterstock.com

A variation of an SD card is Secure Digital Input Output (SDIO), which is a combination of an SD card and an input/output (I/O) device such as a wireless *network interface card (NIC)* used to communicate with a wireless network. One type of SDIO card is a combination of a wireless adapter and storage. Once inserted into a digital camera, pictures can be wirelessly transmitted across the network to a desktop or laptop's hard disk drive, or to a wireless printer.

Mobile Devices

One of the defining characteristics of modern computing is mobility. The ability to carry a computing device in a backpack, purse, or even pocket was unimaginable even to science fiction writers 100 years ago. And yesterday's mobile devices—portable *laptop* computers and smaller *netbook* devices—are being replaced with even more portable devices today.

Leading the charge today of new mobile devices are *tablets*. Early model **tablet PCs** were enhanced laptop computers with screens that could rotate and be written on using a stylus. Tablet PCs are being replaced today by newer **tablet** devices that are lightweight touch-screen computing devices like the Apple iPad and Samsung Galaxy. These tablets are smaller than the typical laptop and usually do not run the standard operating systems found on desktop computers; instead, they have specialized mobile operating systems that are similar to those used on smartphones. Tablets use a touch screen that can be manipulated through finger swipes and generally do not have a separate keyboard. Figure 3-15 illustrates a tablet.

Figure 3-15 Tablet devices are becoming very popular
© Frank Gaertner/www.Shutterstock.com

Like tablets, cellular telephones have evolved from large "bricks" that could only make phone calls into today's sophisticated **smartphones** that can also surf the Web, receive e-mail, provide driving instructions, display photos, play music, and much more. Users can also easily download *apps* (application software) that provide even more functionality.

Although a **portable media player** like the Apple iPod or Sony Walkman is sometimes considered to be capable of only playing music, portable media players can also be used to store other types of data. These players store songs and data using flash memory. Some players have a small screen that allows the user to view images, videos, and documents.

Imaging Devices

Imaging devices are used to capture information and convert it to an electronic format. For example, an imaging device can digitize a paper memo so that it can be stored electronically on a hard drive. Different types of imaging devices are commonly found in a healthcare office. A **document scanner** is used to create an electronic image of a paper document. A **fax printer** is a combination of a printer and a facsimile (fax) machine, which can capture and then transmit an electronic image of a document over standard telephone lines to a receiving fax machine.

Card/badge scanners are scanners that process employees' ID cards or badges for entry into a sensitive area or for access to restricted areas. Each employee is assigned an ID card or badge that is read when it is "swiped" through a scanner at the entrance to a restricted area. The scanner allows only approved employees to enter, and can restrict certain employees from entering at specific times, while allowing others to pass through. These systems can also capture the date and time that each employee enters.

A *barcode* is an optical machine-readable representation of data that uses parallel lines of different widths and spacing. At one time, barcodes could only be read by special optical scanners called **barcode scanners**, but special readers and interpretive software now allow barcodes to be read by other devices such as smartphones.

A **signature pad** is a device that is used to capture a handwritten signature and store a digitized image of the signature for later validation if needed. A **digital camera** can be used to create a digital image of virtually any object.

Installation and Configuration

Installing and configuring mobile storage devices, imaging devices, and other types of computer-related devices is a relatively basic process:

1. First, the proper interface port to be used must be identified. A device is connected to the computer by plugging it into an available USB or IEEE 1394 interface port. If the operating system does not immediately recognize the device, it could mean that the specific port has been disabled. The computer's *Basic Input Output System (BIOS)* is responsible for enabling or disabling ports. The BIOS can be accessed when the computer is first turned on before the operating system loads.

2. Once the proper interface port is identified and it is verified that it is enabled, the next step is to install the correct drivers. Recall that a driver is software that the computer's operating system uses to interact with specific hardware. Although some drivers are included in the operating system, updated drivers often are available to download from the Internet, or drivers may be included on a CD or DVD that comes with the hardware device. Sometimes the instructions that come with the hardware device will specify that the drivers on the CD should be used instead of the operating system drivers. If this is the case, a special setup program must be run *before* the device is connected to the interface port, so be sure to read the documentation that comes with the device before connecting it to any port. If no special setup program is included, then the drivers contained in the operating system can be used.

3. Next, the device is to be connected to the proper interface port (after the interface port has been enabled or when prompted by the special setup program). Sometimes drivers are installed automatically when you plug a device into the proper interface port, in a process called plug and play. Once the device has been recognized and the drivers loaded, the operating system will display a message that the device is ready for use.

4. Finally, the device should be configured for how it will be used. This is usually accomplished by running the software that accompanies the device.

Chapter Summary

- An electronic medical record (EMR) is an electronic digital version of the paper charts found in a clinician's office. A patient's EMR would contain the medical and treatment history of the patient in that particular practice. In contrast, an electronic health record (EHR) goes beyond the standard clinical data collected in one provider's office. EHRs are designed to share information with other healthcare providers, such as laboratories and specialists. To support EHRs, a healthcare IT professional must have an understanding of computing resources and how they are used in a healthcare setting.

- Mainframe computers are designed to process massive amounts of data quickly. Although mainframes may be found in a chain of large hospitals all sharing the same mainframe computer, they would not be used in a local physician's office. A computer network is defined as multiple computers and devices that are interconnected. The most common type of computer network involves client-server computing, in which at least one special high-powered computer called a server provides resources to the individual computers on the network called clients. One enhancement to client-server computing is virtualization, which allows several "virtual instances" of servers to reside on one physical server. A variation of client-server computing is Microsoft Terminal Services, which allows for applications to be installed on servers and then executed through desktop clients. Cloud computing is a "pay-per-use" model in which customers access computing resources online and pay only for the resources that they need at any given time. As computing needs increase or decrease, cloud computing resources can be quickly (and automatically) scaled up or down.

- A computer programming language is an artificial language that is used to communicate instructions to computer hardware. Programming languages are used to create programs that a computer executes. When one program needs to communicate with another program, a set of specifications known as an application programming interface (API) is used. This serves as a set of standardized requests between the different software programs and makes it easier for computer programmers to write programs.

- Desktop computers are broken down into two basic elements. Hardware is the physical device itself. Hardware is classified by function (processing hardware, input hardware, and output hardware). Software is the programs that run on the hardware. Software found on a desktop computer typically falls into one of three categories. Operating system (OS) software serves as the interface between the user and the computer hardware. Utility software supports the OS by providing additional functionality that may not be found in the core OS. Application software is "general" software that can be used for a variety of different tasks.

- Troubleshooting is tracing and correcting problems. Troubleshooting computer equipment today often involves identifying the problem and then assessing the different options for solving the problem or replacing the hardware.

- A security patch is a general software security update intended to cover vulnerabilities that have been discovered. An update is a universal software enhancement for all customers. A hotfix is software that addresses a specific customer situation and often may not be distributed outside that customer's organization. A service pack is software that is a cumulative package of all security updates plus additional features.

- A computer interface or port refers to the connection on a computer to which an external device is attached. Due to the rapid change of technology, some interfaces once common on microcomputers are rarely used today. These legacy interfaces include serial ports, parallel ports, and small computer systems interface (SCSI) interfaces. More recent interfaces include the universal serial bus (USB) interface and IEEE 1394. Bluetooth is a wireless technology that uses short-range radio frequency (RF) transmissions and provides for rapid device pairings.

- An external hard drive functions in a similar fashion to an internal hard disk drive, but is removable. There are two basic sizes of external hard drives. Portable hard drives are smaller in size and storage capacity, while desktop external drives are larger in size and storage capacity. Tape drives are older storage devices that use magnetic tape to store data. Optical storage devices use laser beams to store data on a disc. Compact disc (CD) and Digital Versatile Disc (DVD) are the two most common types of optical storage. A completely electronic type of storage known as flash memory can be used to store and erase data. Unlike magnetic and optical storage, flash storage involves no moving parts. The most common applications for flash memory are USB flash drives and Secure Digital (SD) cards. Some laptops also use internal flash drives.

- Tablet PCs are enhanced laptop computers with screens that can rotate and be written on using a stylus. Newer tablet devices, such as the Apple iPad, are significantly different. These tablets have operating systems similar to those on smartphones. Tablets are manipulated through finger swipes on a touch screen. Cellular telephones have evolved into today's sophisticated smartphones that can perform a variety of tasks. Portable media players can also be used to store data as well as audio. These players generally use flash memory, and some even have a small screen that allows the user to view images, videos, and documents.

- Imaging devices are used to capture information and convert it to an electronic format. A document scanner is used to create an electronic image of a paper document. A fax printer is a combination of a printer and a facsimile (fax) machine. Card/badge scanners are used areas in which access is restricted. Each employee is assigned an ID card or badge that is read when it is "swiped" through a scanner. Barcode scanners can "read" barcode symbols, while a signature pad is a device that is used to capture a handwritten signature and store a digitized image of the signature for later verification.

- Installing and configuring computer devices involves four basic steps: (1) identify the proper interface port for the device, (2) install the correct driver for the device, if necessary, (3) connect the device to the proper interface port, and (4) complete any additional configuration of the device by running the software that accompanies the device.

Key Terms

Active Server Pages (ASP) A programming language alternative to PHP that is used to create dynamic Web pages on a Web server.

application programming interface (API) A set of specifications that allows one program to communicate with another program.

application software "General" software that can be used for a variety of different tasks.

barcode scanner An optical scanner that can read a bar code.

Bluetooth A wireless technology that uses short-range radio frequency (RF) transmissions and provides for rapid ad hoc device pairings.

card/badge scanner A scanner that processes employee ID cards or badges for entry into a sensitive area.

client-server computing The most common type of computer networking in which at least one special high-powered computer called a server services requests from other (usually less powerful) computers on the network called clients.

cloud computing A "pay-per-use" model in which customers pay only for the computing resources that they need at the present time.

compact disc (CD) An optical storage medium that was originally developed in 1982 for audio systems and was later used for recording computer data.

digital camera A device that can be used to create a digital image of virtually any object.

Digital Versatile Disc (DVD) An optical storage medium that has a high storage capacity ranging from 1.46 GB to over 17 GB; also called Digital Video Disc.

document scanner A device used to create an electronic image of a paper document.

driver Software that the computer's operating system uses to interact with specific hardware.

Extensible Markup Language (XML) A markup language often used in creating Web pages that is designed to carry data instead of just indicating how to display it, as with HTML.

external hard drive A hard drive that functions in a similar fashion to an internal hard disk drive found inside the computer, except that it can be portable and is connected to the system with a USB or IEEE 1394 interface.

fax printer A combination of a printer and a facsimile (fax) machine.

Flash A multimedia platform that can be used to add special effects, such as animation, video, and interactivity to Web pages.

hotfix Software that addresses a specific customer situation and often may not be distributed outside that customer's organization.

Hypertext Markup Language (HTML) The common language for displaying Web page contents.

IEEE 1394 An interface that transfers bits one at a time like an older serial bus yet at much faster speeds (800 Mbps).

Internet Service Provider (ISP) An organization that provides Internet connectivity.

keyboard The most common type of input hardware.

magnetic tape A long, narrow strip of plastic whose surface is covered with a magnetic substance, used in tape drives to back up data. Tape drives are an older technology.

mainframe computer A large, expensive computer designed to process massive amounts of data quickly.

monitor An output device that that displays the results of processing on a screen.

mouse A pointing device used to rapidly position a pointer at a specific location.

operating system (OS) Software that serves as the "intermediary" between the user and the computer hardware.

patch A general software security update intended to cover vulnerabilities that have been discovered.

PHP A programming language that is used to create Web content that will change (is dynamic) instead of remaining the same (static).

portable media player A device that can play music, store data, and display images and videos.

Secure Digital (SD) card A small form factor card used for storage in handheld devices.

serial port A legacy interface that sends one bit of information at a time from the computer to the connected device.

service pack Software that is a cumulative package of all security updates plus additional features.

signature pad A device that is used to capture a handwritten signature and store a digitized image of the signature for later verification if needed.

small computer systems interface (SCSI) An older set of standards that can transmit information at relatively high speeds.

smartphone Sophisticated cellular telephone that can also surf the Web, receive e-mail, provide driving instructions, display photos, play music, and use other applications (apps).

Structured Query Language (SQL) A programming language used to view and manipulate data that is stored in a database.

tablet Lightweight touchscreen computing device like the Apple iPad or Samsung Galaxy that uses a specialized mobile operating system to perform many functions common to larger computers, such as media playing, Web browsing, e-mail, and video chat. Most do not have a separate keyboard.

tablet PC Enhanced laptop computer with a screen that rotates and can be written on using a stylus.

Terminal Services Software that allows for applications to be installed on servers and then executed through desktop clients, instead of installing applications on each individual client computer.

universal serial bus (USB) The most common type of physical interface for connecting an external device to a computer.

update A universal software enhancement for all customers.

USB flash drive A small, often thumb-sized portable storage medium that utilizes flash (solid-state) storage.

virtualization The means of creating and using one or more virtual instances of a server on one physical server.

Healthcare IT Acronyms

Table 3-6 contains healthcare IT acronyms that were introduced in this chapter. Many of these terms are listed in the CompTIA Healthcare IT Technician exam objectives, and most are also defined in the Key Terms section of this chapter. For a complete list of the healthcare acronyms used in this book, see Appendix C.

Acronym	Full Name
API	application programming interface
ASP	Active Server Pages
BIOS	Basic Input Output System
CD	Compact Disc
CD-ROM	Compact Disc-Read Only Memory
CD-RW	Compact Disc-Rewritable
CPU	central processing unit
DB-9	serial communications D-shell connector, 9 pins
DB-25	serial communications D-shell connector, 25 pins
DVD	Digital Video Disc or Digital Versatile Disc
DVD-R	Digital Video Disc-Recordable
DVD-RAM	Digital Video Disc-Random Access Memory
DVD-ROM	Digital Video Disc-Read Only Memory
DVD-RW	Digital Video Disc-Rewritable
Gb	gigabit
GB	gigabyte
GUI	graphical user interface
HDD	hard disk drive
HTML	Hypertext Markup Language
IEEE	Institute of Electrical and Electronics Engineers
ISP	Internet Service Provider
Kb	kilobit
KB	kilobyte
Mb	megabit
MB	megabyte
NIC	network interface card

Table 3-6 **Healthcare IT acronyms introduced in this chapter** *(continues)*

Acronym	Full Name
OS	operating system
PHP	PHP: Hypertext Preprocessor
RAM	random access memory
RF	radio frequency
RJ-11	registered jack function 11
RJ-45	registered jack function 45
SCSI	small computer system interface
SD card	Secure Digital card
SQL	Structured Query Language
TB	terabyte
USB	universal serial bus
XML	Extensible Markup Language

Table 3-6 **Healthcare IT acronyms introduced in this chapter (*continued*)**
© Cengage Learning 2013

Review Questions

1. The electronic digital versions of the paper charts found in a clinician's office are called _____.
   a. electronic health records (EHR)
   b. electronic medical records (EMR)
   c. electronic healthcare reports
   d. office electronic data (OED)

2. A _____ is a very large computer and is designed to process massive amounts of data very quickly.
   a. mainframe
   b. server
   c. client
   d. tablet

3. The most common type of computer networking is _____.
   a. mainframe-server
   b. client-server
   c. cloud-server
   d. load balancer

4. _____ is a means of creating and using one or more *virtual* instances of a server on one *actual* physical server.

   a. Compression

   b. Resource management

   c. Server optimization

   d. Virtualization

5. _____ allows for applications to be installed on servers and then executed through desktop clients.

   a. Terminal Services

   b. Active Server Pages (ASP)

   c. Smart Terminals

   d. Dumb Servers

6. Which of the following is not a cloud computing model?

   a. Cloud Software as a Service (SaaS)

   b. Cloud Platform as a Service (PaaS)

   c. Cloud Infrastructure as a Service (IaaS)

   d. Cloud Server as a Service (CSaaS)

7. Each of the following is a language associated with Web development except _____.

   a. Hypertext Markup Language (HTML)

   b. Extensible Markup Language (XML)

   c. Flash

   d. DoS

8. What software serves as an intermediary between the user and the computer hardware?

   a. Application Interface (AI)

   b. Operating system (OS)

   c. Synchronizing Software (SS)

   d. Graphical User Software (GUS)

9. An example of an application is _____.

   a. Microsoft Windows

   b. a word processor

   c. a file synchronization program

   d. drivers

10. Which of the following is not a step in installing a new computer?

    a. Select the proper location.

    b. Check off each item against the packing list.

    c. Configure the proxy server.

    d. Connect the components to the system unit.

11. A backup image of a new computer should be made _____.

    a. as soon as it is taken out of the box

    b. so that no backups on new computers are necessary

    c. before any software or updates are installed

    d. after the system has been properly configured

12. Which of the following is not a troubleshooting question when examining a computer monitor that has a blank screen and the power light is off?

    a. Is the monitor is plugged into an electrical outlet?

    b. Is the electrical outlet or power supply on?

    c. Are contrast and brightness settings correct?

    d. Is the power cord connection tight?

13. Why is troubleshooting a printer more difficult than troubleshooting other devices?

    a. Printing problems are often a result of either the printer hardware or the software that manages the printer.

    b. Printers are notoriously difficult to troubleshoot because they have so many moving parts.

    c. Because printers rarely have problems, there is no good strategy for troubleshooting them.

    d. It is impossible to troubleshoot a modern printer, so any faulty printer must be disposed of and replaced.

14. A _____ is software that is a cumulative package of all security updates plus additional features.

    a. service pack

    b. hotfix

    c. patch

    d. rollout

15. Which of the following is not a legacy interface that is rarely found on desktop computers today?

    a. Universal serial bus (USB)

    b. Serial port

    c. Parallel port

    d. Small Computer Systems Interface (SCSI)

16. Each of the following is a brand name for the IEEE 1394 interface except _____.

    a. i.LINK

    b. USB

    c. Lynx

    d. FireWire

17. Bluetooth is a(n) _____ technology.

    a. wireless

    b. wired

    c. remote distance

    d. outdated

18. Which type of device is most likely to be used for storing an entire backup of a desktop computer?

    a. External portable hard drive

    b. External desktop hard drive

    c. Magnetic tape backup

    d. CD-ROM

19. Which of the following is considered optical storage?

    a. Digital Versatile Disc (DVD)

    b. External portable hard drive

    c. USB flash drive

    d. Tape drive

20. A portable media player _____.

    a. can only play music

    b. can store data and images

    c. cannot be connected to a desktop computer

    d. cannot have a screen for viewing documents

Case Projects

CASE PROJECTS

Case Project 3-1: How Healthcare Technology Is Being Used

Schedule a visit with the office manager for a local physician or the Public Relations officer at a hospital to determine what information technology they are currently using. In the interview process, inquire how long the technology has been in place, what its advantages are, if it is meeting the current needs of the organization, what future changes are being planned, and so on. Write a one-page summary of your findings.

Case Project 3-2: Virtualization

Use the Internet to research file server virtualization. What are its advantages? What are its disadvantages? What are some of the most popular technology tools that are being used to create and manage virtual environments? What are the security risks with virtualization? Write a one-page paper on your research.

Case Project 3-3: Cloud Computing Security

Can confidential patient information be securely stored in "the cloud"? Use the Internet to research cloud computing security. What do the experts say regarding the security of data that is stored on a remote server? What protections would a physician or hospital need to keep their data secure? Are these requirements different from those of a non-health care organization? Based on your research, would you recommend that cloud computing be used for storing patient information? Why or why not? Write a one-page paper on your research and opinions.

Case Project 3-4: Ergonomics

When setting up a new workstation, it is important to know and apply the basic rules of ergonomics to ensure the safety of the user. What ergonomic considerations should be considered when setting up a workstation? Use the Internet to identify how a workstation should be correctly installed with consideration given to seating, lighting, desk height, mouse and keyboard layout, and so forth. Then create a one-page checklist of the different recommendations that could be used when setting up a new workstation.

Case Project 3-5: Troubleshooting

Suppose that a computer is powered on but nothing happens. What troubleshooting steps should be taken? Use the Internet or other books to create a table similar to those in this chapter regarding the steps to take when a computer is turned on but nothing appears on the screen.

Case Project 3-6: USB 3

The latest version of USB is USB 3. What are its advantages? Is it backward compatible with previous versions of USB? What types of devices will support USB 3? When is it anticipated that this version will become commonplace? Use the Internet to research USB 3 and write a one-page paper on your findings.

Healthcare IT: Challenges and Opportunities—Revisited

Refer to the Superior Care Health Group (SCHG) case as related in the chapter opening section entitled "Healthcare IT: Challenges and Opportunities." Assume you are in Abby's position and Braden Thomas asks these questions:

- Why should we upgrade our technology? It is working fine for us now.
- How can we measure the cost of our investment? Will it reduce the number of employees that we need or permit us to see more patients per hour? Is there a way to quantitatively measure the effectiveness?
- Which of the following would you recommend for a doctor's office of our size: client-server networking or terminal services? Why?
- What is a list of questions that should be asked of applicants if we advertise for a healthcare IT professional?

For this case, complete the following:

1. How would you respond to each question? Be sure to give reasons for your answers.
2. Assume you must respond to Braden's questions in a meeting with the physicians. Develop a slide presentation that addresses these questions. The presentation should be at least seven slides in length.
3. Pretend that Braden and the physicians agree with your recommendations. Create a project outline and timeline of what you recommend for hiring a healthcare IT professional and for researching the needs of SCHG.

References

1. "IBM Energy Efficiency," IBM Systems. Accessed Nov. 15, 2011, http://www-03.ibm.com/systems/x/solutions/infrastructure/energy/overview.html.

2. Mell, Peter and Grance, Tim, "The NIST Definition of Cloud Computing," NIST Computer Security Division Computer Security Resource Center. Oct. 7, 2009, accessed Apr. 2, 2011, http://csrc.nist.gov/groups/SNS/cloud-computing/.

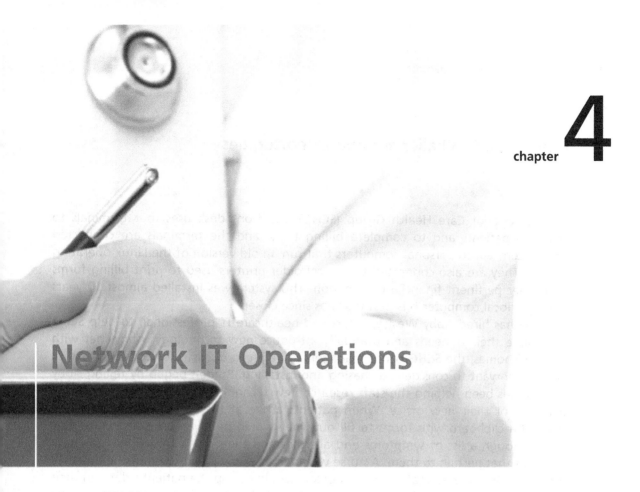

chapter 4

Network IT Operations

After completing this chapter, you should be able to do the following:

- List and describe standard networking devices

- Explain the function of servers

- Explain how to set up basic networking

- List the steps for troubleshooting a network

- Describe different options for EHR/EMR network technologies

Healthcare IT: Challenges and Opportunities

At the Superior Care Health Group (SCHG), the front desk uses four terminals to schedule patients and to complete billing tasks, and the terminals are connected to two centralized personal computers that run an old version of the Linux operating system. They are also connected to several older printers used to print billing forms and other pertinent financial information. This system was installed almost 10 years ago by a local computer business that has since closed.

SCHG has hired Abby Wesley, a certified healthcare IT professional, to help SCHG determine their IT needs and gradually introduce new technology. Abby met with Braden Thomas, the SCHG office manager, to begin to discuss the technologies that SCHG may want to consider purchasing and installing. Braden began by telling Abby that he has been helping the staff research new technologies and they have created a vision for their new office. When patients arrive at the office, instead of being handed a clipboard with forms to fill out, they would be given an iPad, where they scroll through a list of symptoms and allergies and then tap with a finger to check the ones that pertain to them. A nurse would use her own iPad to enter the patient's vital signs. In the examination room, doctors would call up the patient's data on their own tablets, which would also provide a list of the most likely diagnoses for the patient's symptoms. After the visit, doctors would dictate notes straight into their tablets, where the notes would be instantly transcribed and stored with other data about the patient.

Abby tells Braden that these are certainly ambitious goals, though well within the reach of today's technology. However, the first step is to replace the aging terminals and centralized personal computers with a modern and more efficient computer network. Braden asks, "So what type of network does SCHG need to implement this technology?"

The underlying foundation of computing technology in an office is the computer network. Without a network in place, a computer is limited to only the software installed on it and the devices directly connected to it. E-mail, file sharing, Web surfing, and a wide array of other common functions cannot occur unless a computer network is in place.

In this chapter, you will learn about network IT operations in the healthcare field that support electronic health records. First, you will explore common network devices, and then you will look at network servers. Next, you will examine how to set up a network and then troubleshoot it. Finally, you will study the network technologies that can be used for electronic medical records and electronic health records.

Standard Network Devices

3.1 Identify commonly used IT terms and technologies.

"Any sufficiently advanced technology is indistinguishable from magic." This quotation is attributed to Sir Arthur C. Clarke, the famous British science fiction author and futurist. Although networks might seem to fit into this category of "magic" as they transmit files to remote printers and access Web pages stored halfway around the world—all within fractions of a second—in reality networks use some relatively straightforward technology.

Usually, the problem with understanding networking stems from the fact that there are a variety of different elements (clients, servers, network operating systems, and so on) functioning on various levels (hardware, software, communication technology). In order to address this confusion, in 1978 the *International Organization for Standardization (ISO)* released a set of specifications that was intended to describe how dissimilar computers could be connected together on a network. The ISO demonstrated that what happens on a network device when sending or receiving traffic can be best understood by portraying this transfer as a series of related steps. Looking at what happens during each step and how it relates to the previous or next steps can help compartmentalize computer networking and make it easier to understand. The ISO called its work the *Open Systems Interconnection (OSI)* reference model, and the 1983 version of the OSI model is still used today. The OSI model illustrates how a network device prepares data for delivery over the network to another device, and how data is to be handled when it is received.

NOTE Started in 1947, the goal of the ISO is to promote international cooperation and standards in the areas of science, technology, and economics. Today, groups from 162 countries belong to this organization that is headquartered in Geneva, Switzerland. Their Web site is www.iso.org.

The key to the OSI model is *layers*. The model breaks networking steps down into a series of seven layers. Within each layer, different networking tasks are performed. In addition, each layer cooperates with the layer immediately above and below it. The OSI model gives a conceptual representation of how a computer prepares data for transmission and how it receives data from the network, and illustrates how each layer provides specific services and shares with the layers above and below it. Figure 4-1 lists the seven layers, and Table 4-1 describes these OSI layers.

TIP There are several different mnemonics that can be used to memorize the layers of the OSI model. These include *All People Seem To Need Data Processing* (for Layers 7–1) and *Please Do Not Throw Sausage Pizza Away* (for Layers 1–7).

At one time, there were several competing standards for different *local area network (LAN)* technologies. However, today the most common LAN technology is called *Ethernet*. One of the characteristics of Ethernet is that it divides the data to be transported across the network

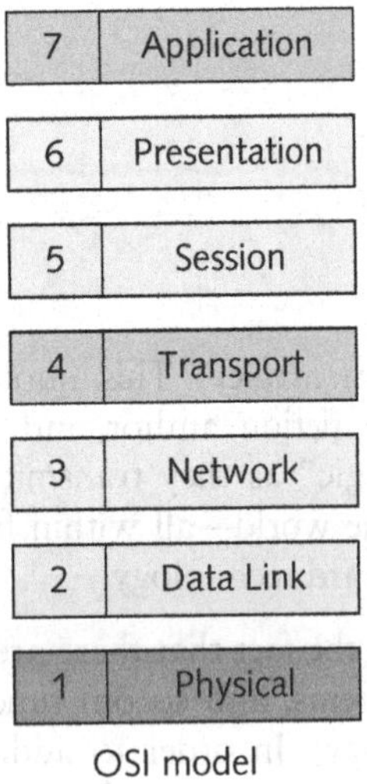

OSI model

Figure 4-1 OSI layers
© Cengage Learning 2013

Layer Number	Layer Name	Description	Function
Layer 7	Application Layer	The top layer, Application, provides the user interface to allow network services.	Provides services for user applications.
Layer 6	Presentation Layer	The Presentation Layer is concerned with how the data is represented and formatted for the user.	Is used for translation, compression, and encryption.
Layer 5	Session Layer	This layer has the responsibility of permitting the two parties on the network to hold ongoing communications across the network.	Allows devices to establish and manage sessions.
Layer 4	Transport Layer	The Transport Layer is responsible for ensuring that error-free data is given to the user.	Provides connection establishment, management, and termination as well as acknowledgments and retransmissions.
Layer 3	Network Layer	The Network Layer picks the route the packet is to take and handles the addressing of the packets for delivery.	Makes logical addressing, routing, fragmentation and reassembly available.
Layer 2	Data Link Layer	The Data Link Layer is responsible for dividing the data into packets. Some additional duties of the Data Link Layer include error detection and correction (for example, if the data is not received properly, the Data Link Layer would request that it be retransmitted).	Performs physical addressing, data framing, error detection and handling.
Layer 1	Physical Layer	The job of this layer is to send the signal to the network or receive the signal from the network.	Involved with encoding and signaling, data transmission, and reception.

Table 4-1 OSI reference model
© Cengage Learning 2013

into smaller units called *packets*. As you learned in Chapter 3, the most common form of computer networking is called *client-server computing*. This type of network is controlled by at least one high-powered computer—a *server*—while the individual computers on the network are called *clients*. Other standard network devices can be classified by the OSI layer at which they function. These devices include hubs, switches, routers, and domain controllers.

Hubs

A *hub* is an older device for connecting multiple Ethernet devices on a network, typically by using *shielded twisted-pair (STP)* copper cables to make them function as a single network segment. Hubs work at the Physical Layer (Layer 1) of the OSI model. This means that they do not read any of the data passing through them and are ignorant of the source and destination of the frames. A hub will only receive incoming frames, regenerate the electrical signal, and then send the frames out to all other devices connected to the hub. A hub is illustrated in Figure 4-2.

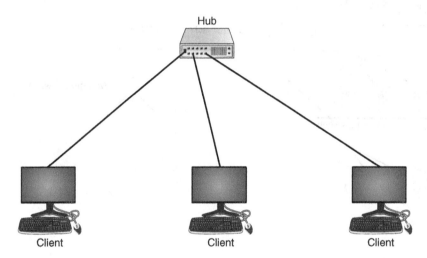

Figure 4-2 A hub is an older type of network device; today hubs have largely been replaced by switches
© Cengage Learning 2013

Because a hub repeats all frames to all of its attached network devices, it not only increases network traffic but also can be a security risk. Hubs are rarely used today, and many organizations restrict or even prohibit their use.

Switches

A network **switch** is similar to a hub in that it is a device that connects network segments together. However, unlike a hub, a switch has a degree of "intelligence." Operating at the Data Link Layer (Layer 2), a switch can learn which device is connected to each of its ports, and forward only frames intended for that specific device (*unicast*) or frames sent to all devices (*broadcast*). Each device connected to the switch has a unique *media access control (MAC)* address (also called the hardware address). A switch learns by examining the MAC address that is included in the frames that it receives and then associates its port with that

MAC address of the device connected to that port. This improves network performance and provides better security.

In most network environments, networks are divided or segmented by using switches to divide the network into a hierarchy. *Core switches* reside at the top of the hierarchy and carry traffic between switches, while *workgroup switches* are connected directly to the devices on the network. This is illustrated in Figure 4-3.

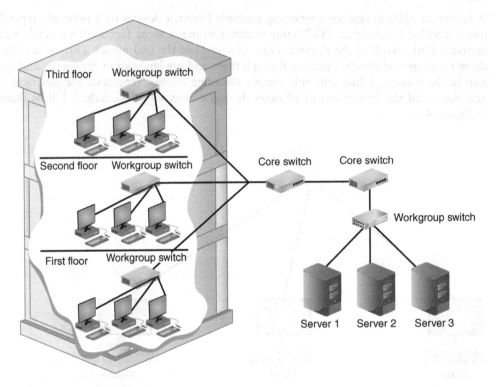

Figure 4-3 Core and workgroup switches

© Cengage Learning 2013

Core switches must work faster than workgroup switches because core switches must handle the traffic of several workgroup switches.

Routers

Operating at the Network Layer (Layer 3), a **router** is a network device that can forward packets across computer networks. When a router receives an incoming packet, it reads the destination address and then, using information in its routing table, sends the packet to the next network toward its destination. Routers can also perform a security function. A router can be configured to filter out specific types of network traffic. For example, a router can be set to disallow incoming packets that have invalid addresses or to disallow packets from specific addresses.

Domain Controllers

In a network using Microsoft Windows software, a *domain* is collection of devices that all share a central directory database. This central database contains accounts and security information for the resources in that domain. A **domain controller** is a server that manages the security-related elements on the network for the user. This allows for the security to be centralized and more easily managed.

A Windows domain controller is generally suited for organizations when more than 10 client computers are being used.

Servers

3.1 Identify commonly used IT terms and technologies.

3.5 Compare and contrast basic client networks and tools.

3.9 Classify different server types, environments, features, and limitations.

Servers play a crucial role in a client-server computing environment. There are several different types of services and servers along with different protocols. In addition, servers must be properly managed to be effective.

Services and Servers

There are a variety of "provisions" that servers provide for users on the network. The most common are:

- *Print services*—Print services allow multiple users to share printers across a network. Instead of purchasing, installing, and maintaining multiple printers—each directly connected to a user's computer—print services allow for a single centrally located higher-speed (and more feature-rich) printer to serve the printing needs of all users in an office or a computer lab. This results in a significant cost savings.

- *File services*—The ability to share user-created files (such as a report created by a word processor or a departmental budget developed using a spreadsheet program) by storing them in a central location where they can be accessed by other users who have the correct permissions is known as file services. Having a single copy of a file available to any approved users helps to conserve storage space as well as prevent different versions of the same file circulating (with one user updating one version while another user updates another version).

- *Application services*—**Application services** are processes that run software for network clients and thus enable clients to share processing power across a network. These application services serve as an *interface* for a service-related architecture so that network-based applications can dynamically interact with other applications.

- *Communication services*—Networks can help users communicate using a variety of tools, such as e-mail, telephony, and instant messaging. This is called communication services.

These different network services can be provided through a server dedicated to that function. A **print server** is a server exclusively dedicated to managing printing functions across the network, while a *file server* can be responsible for managing file services. A **database server** is a server that provides services to a *database* of stored data. This data can be easily stored and then retrieved from one central location. An **application server** can be used to centrally store applications (such as a multiuser version of a word processor) that are accessible and run across the network on client computers, instead of installing the software separately on each client. One of the reasons an application server can function is because of the **operating system and application interoperability**, which allows for the applications to run on either the network's operating system or on the local client.

Server Management

There are several tasks associated with managing servers. Two of the most common are load balancing and allocating storage space.

Load Balancing Consider the checkout lines at a typical grocery store. Which checkout line should be chosen? A customer who has finished shopping usually selects the line that is the shortest so as to check out quickly. However, the shortest line at a given point in time does not always mean that it is the quickest line; if a customer at the front of the line has trouble with a payment or if the scanner malfunctions, the other longer lines may actually check out customers more quickly. An impatient customer may become agitated and must then decide if it is worth moving to another line (and starting at the end of that line) or to stay where they are. In order to address this problem, some stores at peak periods will have a single line where customers line up with a manager at the front of the line. The manager directs the customer to the next available line and prevents customers from entering a line where there is a scanner malfunction. In short, the manager balances the load of customers checking out.

In a similar way, network *load balancing* is a technology that can help to evenly distribute work across a network. Requests that are received can be allocated across multiple devices such as servers. To the user, this distribution is transparent and appears as if a single server is providing the resources. Load-balancing technology provides these advantages:

- The probability of overloading a single server is reduced.
- Each networked computer can benefit from having optimized resources.
- Network downtime can be reduced.

Load balancing can either be performed through software running on a computer or as a dedicated hardware device known as a *load balancer*. A hardware load balancer is sometimes called a *Layer 4–7 router*. This is because the hardware device can direct requests to different servers based on a variety of factors, such as the number of server connections, the server's processor utilization, and overall performance of the server.

Managing Storage One of the most challenging tasks in managing a file server is to provide adequate storage for electronic records, documents, memos, e-mails, and similar types of data. This is because the number of documents stored in recent years has skyrocketed, making it difficult to predict and manage the amount of storage space needed. Organizations today store virtually all electronic documents because of the Federal Rules of

Civil Procedures, which were amended in late 2006. These rules made Electronically Stored Information (ESI) subject to legal discovery called E-Discovery. (*Discovery* is the pretrial phase in a civil lawsuit in which both plaintiffs and defendants can request documents and similar evidence from other parties and can even compel them to produce the evidence by a subpoena.) E-Discovery imposes new institutional obligations on organizations so that they must preserve historical and prospective ESI from destruction, and when requested produce it (if it is relevant, not privileged, and reasonably accessible) in its original format. Failure to produce documents (called *spoliation of evidence*) can result in sanctions (monetary fines or penalties), adverse inference instruction to the jury, a reversal of the burdens of proof, and even dismissal of the claims or defenses. In order to protect themselves, most organizations now save all electronic documents.

In one case the courts found that an organization deliberately failed to turn over e-mails in a discovery. As a result, the court shifted the burden of proof and awarded $1.45 billion in damages to the opposing party, $850 million of which were punitive damages.[1]

There are now several different technologies available that can provide enhanced storage capabilities for documents. One of the most promising is *storage virtualization*, which hides the physical resources of storage (such as a specific hard drive) from the user. All storage devices are "pooled" and appear as a large repository of storage. Additional storage capabilities such as hard drives can easily be added to the pool.

Protocols

In the world of international politics, *protocols* can be defined as the forms of ceremony and etiquette. These rules of conduct and communication are to be observed by foreign diplomats and heads of state while working in a different country. If they were to ignore these protocols, they would risk offending the citizens of the host country, which might lead to a diplomatic incident or, even worse, a war.

Computer networks also have protocols, or rules for communication. These protocols are essential for proper communication to take place between network devices. Three common protocols are Transmission Control Protocol/Internet Protocol (TCP/IP), wireless protocols, and Remote Desktop Protocol (RDP).

Transmission Control Protocol/Internet Protocol (TCP/IP) The most common protocol suite used today for local area networks (LANs) as well as the Internet is **Transmission Control Protocol/Internet Protocol (TCP/IP)**. TCP/IP is not one single protocol; instead, it is several protocols that all function together. This combination of protocols is known as a *protocol suite*. Although the TCP/IP suite is composed of different protocols, the two major protocols that make up its name, *Transmission Control Protocol (TCP)* and *Internet Protocol (IP)*, are considered the most important. IP is the protocol that functions primarily at the OSI Network Layer (Layer 3) to provide addressing and routing. TCP is the main Transport Layer (Layer 4) protocol that is responsible for establishing connections and the reliable data transport between devices.

IP is responsible for addressing packets and sending them on the correct route to the destination, while TCP is responsible for reliable packet transmission.

TCP/IP uses its own four-layer architecture that includes Network Interface, Internet, Transport, and Application layers. Figure 4-4 shows how these layers correspond to the OSI reference model. The TCP/IP architecture gives a framework for the dozens of various protocols that comprise the suite. It also includes several high-level applications that are part of TCP/IP.

OSI model	TCP/IP model
7 Application	
6 Presentation	Application
5 Session	
4 Transport	(Host-to-Host) Transport
3 Network	Internet
2 Data Link	Network Interface
1 Physical	(Hardware)

Figure 4-4 OSI model vs. TCP/IP model
© Cengage Learning 2013

The Physical Layer is omitted in the TCP/IP model. This is because TCP/IP views the Network Interface Layer as the point where the connection between the TCP/IP protocol and the networking hardware occurs.

NOTE

Some of the basic TCP/IP protocols are Domain Name System (DNS), Dynamic Host Configuration Protocol (DHCP) and File Transfer Protocol (FTP).

There are many good resources available online regarding TCP/IP and its suite of protocols. The IBM Redbooks provide tutorials and technical overviews; see www.redbooks.ibm.com/redbooks/pdfs/gg243376.pdf.

TIP

Domain Name System (DNS) The **Domain Name System (DNS)** is a TCP/IP protocol that resolves (maps) an IP address (such as *69.32.133.79*) to its equivalent symbolic name (*www.cengage.com*). The DNS is a database, organized as a hierarchy or tree, of the name of each site on the Internet and its corresponding IP address. To store the entire database of names and IP addresses in one location would present several problems. First, it would cause a bottleneck and slow down the Internet with all users trying to access one copy of the database. Second, if something happened to this one database, then the entire Internet would be affected. Instead of being on only one server, the DNS database is divided and distributed to many different servers on the Internet, each of which is responsible for different areas of the Internet. The steps of resolving an IP address to a symbolic name, also called a DNS lookup, are as follows, illustrated in Figure 4-5:

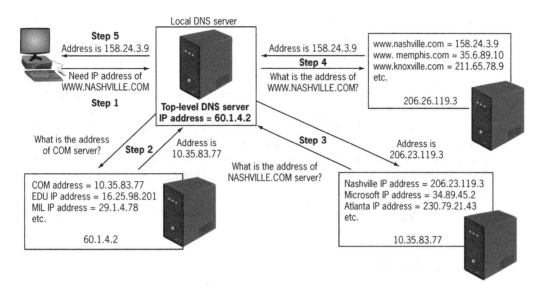

Figure 4-5 DNS lookup
© Cengage Learning 2013

Step 1. The request for the IP address of the site *www.nashville.com* goes from the user's computer to the local DNS server that is part of the LAN to which it is connected.

Step 2. The local DNS server does not know the IP address of *www.nashville.com*; yet it does know the IP address of a DNS server that contains the top-level domains and their IP numbers. A request is sent to this top-level domain DNS server.

Step 3. This top-level DNS server sends back the IP address of the DNS server that contains information about addresses that end in .*COM*. The local DNS server then sends a request to this second DNS server, which contains the IP address of the DNS server that contains the information about *nashville.com*.

Step 4. After receiving back that information, the local DNS server contacts the third DNS server responsible for *nashville*, which looks up the IP address of *www.nashville.com*.

Step 5. This information is finally returned to the local DNS server, which sends it back to the user's computer.

Dynamic Host Configuration Protocol (DHCP) Each device on a computer network must have a unique name or number. Because no two devices share the same name or number, packets can be transmitted through the network addressed to the device that has that unique identifier. Computers on a TCP/IP network use a logical address. This logical address, called an *IP address*, is assigned to each host computer. An IP address is made up of four bytes (called octets), each of which contain eight bits (a total of 32 bits in length). Each octet is a number from 1 to 254. IP addresses indicate the number of the computer network and the number of the host on that network. IP addresses are also broken down into groups called classes. There are five classes of IP addresses, Class A through Class E. Each class uses a different combination of octets to indicate the number of the computer network and the number of the host. The IP protocol is responsible for the addressing of packets.

Assigning IP addresses to each device can be done in one of two ways. The numbers can be assigned manually by having a computer technician go to each network device and enter the IP address, called a **static IP address**, which is an IP address that does not change. On a large network, this can be a very time-consuming process. Another way to assign IP addresses is to have them automatically distributed using a protocol in the TCP/IP suite known as the **Dynamic Host Configuration Protocol (DHCP)**. When a computer attaches to the network, it requests an IP address from a DHCP server. An IP address is then leased to that host. Once the computer is off the network, or its lease expires, that IP address becomes free and can be given to another computer.

Several Web sites contain animations that illustrate how the TCP/IP protocols work. One source is www.net-seal.net/animations.php.

File Transfer Protocol (FTP) Prior to the development of the Web and *HTTP (Hypertext Transfer Protocol,* the protocol used for transferring Web pages), the Internet was primarily used for transferring files from one device to another. As you learned in Chapter 2, the *File Transfer Protocol (FTP)* is a popular method by which computer files can be transferred from one system to another over the Internet or other computer network. FTP links to an FTP server in much the same way that HTTP links to a Web server.

There are several different methods for using FTP on a local host computer:

- *From a command prompt*—FTP commands can by typed at an operating system prompt, such as *ls* (list files), *get* (retrieve a file from the server), and *put* (transfer a file to the server).
- *Using a Web browser*—Instead of prefacing a URL with the protocol *http://*, the FTP protocol is entered with a preface of *ftp://*.
- *Using an FTP client*—A separate FTP client application can be installed that displays files on the local host as well as the remote server, as shown in Figure 4-6. These files can be dragged and dropped between devices.

FTP servers can be configured to allow unauthenticated users to transfer files, known as anonymous FTP (also called blind FTP).

Wireless Protocols Wireless data communications are replacing the need to be tethered by a cable to a network to surf the Web, check e-mail, or access inventory records. Wireless communication has made mobility possible to a degree never before possible or rarely even imagined; users can access the same resources standing on a street corner or walking across a college campus as they can while sitting at a desk. Although wireless voice communication started the revolution in the 1990s, wireless data communications have been the driving force in the twenty-first century.

Figure 4-6 FTP client software
© Cengage Learning 2013

Wireless data networks are found nearly everywhere. Travelers can access wireless networks while waiting in airports, traveling on airplanes and trains, and working in their hotel room. Businesses have found that employees who have wireless access to data during meetings and in conference rooms can significantly increase their productivity. Free wireless Internet connections are available in restaurants across the country, and, in some arenas and stadiums, fans can even order concessions wirelessly and have them delivered to their seats.

One of the reasons *wireless local area networks (WLANs)* have been so successful is because from the outset these networks were based on a set of standards. WLAN standards are set by the Institute of Electrical and Electronics Engineers (IEEE). There currently is one wireless LAN standard, IEEE 802.11-2007, and one significant amendment, 802.11n-2009.

The Web site of the IEEE is www.ieee.org.

IEEE 802.11-2007 Since the late 1990s, the IEEE has approved four standards for wireless LANs—IEEE 802.11, 802.11b, 802.11a, and 802.11g—along with several amendments (such as IEEE 802.11d, IEEE 802.11h, and so on). In order to reduce the confusion of this "alphabet soup" of standards and amendments, in 2007, the IEEE combined the standards and amendments into a single standard officially known as IEEE 802.11-2007. Here is a brief history of the 802.11, 802.11b, 802.11a, and 802.11g standards that are now combined in the 802.11-2007 standard.

In 1990, the IEEE began to develop a standard for WLANs operating at 1 and 2 megabits (million bits) per second (Mbps). Several different proposals were initially recommended before a draft was developed, yet this draft went through seven different revisions that took seven years to complete. In 1997, the IEEE approved the final draft known as *IEEE 802.11*. The IEEE 802.11 standard specified that wireless transmissions could take place in one of two ways. The first is through using *infrared light*. However, because of the limitations of infrared light, almost all IEEE 802.11 networks instead choose to use *radio waves*. Unlike infrared transmissions, radio waves can penetrate through objects like walls and allow the wireless user to be mobile. In addition, radio waves travel longer distances and can be used indoors as well as outdoors. Finally, radio waves can travel at much higher speeds than infrared transmissions. The use of radio waves in transmissions has become the preferred method for wireless LANs.

Although a speed of 2 Mbps was considered adequate when work on the 802.11 standard was begun in 1990, by the time it was completed in 1997, a 2 Mbps wireless network proved to be too slow. The IEEE body revisited the 802.11 standard shortly after it was released to determine what changes could be made to increase the speed. In 1999, a new *IEEE 802.11b* amendment was added to the standard, which added two higher speeds, 5.5 Mbps and 11 Mbps, to the original 802.11 standard of 1 Mbps and 2 Mbps. The 802.11b standard supports wireless devices that are up to 350 feet (107 meters) apart.

At the same time the IEEE created the 802.11b standard, it also issued another standard with even higher speeds. The *IEEE 802.11a* standard specifies a maximum rated speed of 54 Mbps and also supports 48, 36, 24, 18, 12, 9, and 6 Mbps transmissions, although it uses a different set of radio wave frequencies than 802.11b. Although the 802.11a standard achieves higher speed, the trade-off is that devices cannot be as far apart as with the 802.11b standard. A wireless network that follows the 802.11a standard may generally have devices that are no more than 100 feet (30 meters) apart.

A resource for information about wireless networks is the WiFi Alliance. Their Web site is www.wi-fi.org. The IEEE wireless networking standards are popularly known as *WiFi*.

The success of the IEEE 802.11b standard prompted the IEEE to reexamine the 802.11b and 802.11a standards to determine if a third intermediate standard could be developed. This "best of both worlds" approach would preserve the stable and widely accepted features of 802.11b but increase the data transfer rates to those similar to 802.11a. The IEEE formed a group to explore this possibility and by late 2001 a draft standard was proposed known as *IEEE 802.11g*. This standard was formally ratified in 2003. The 802.11g standard supports a maximum data speed of 54, with lesser speeds of 48, 36, 24, 18, 12, 9, and 6 Mbps. The standard also specifies that devices operate in the same radio frequency as IEEE 802.11b and not the frequency used by 802.11a. This gives the 802.11g standard the ability to support devices that are farther apart with higher speeds. Like 802.11b, 802.11g can support devices that are up to 350 feet (107 meters) apart.

IEEE 802.11n-2009 In September of 2004, the IEEE started work on a dramatically new WLAN standard that would significantly increase the speed, range, and reliability of wireless local area networks. Known as *IEEE 802.11n-2009* (or more popularly as 802.11n), it was intended to usher in the next generation of WLAN technology. The final 802.11n standard was ratified in 2009, exactly five years to the day after the IEEE started its work.

The 802.11n standard has four significant improvements over previous standards:

- *Speed*—Up to 600 Mbps data rate
- *Coverage area*—Doubles the indoor range and triples the outdoor range
- *Interference*—Uses different frequencies to reduce interference
- *Security*—Requires the strongest level of wireless security

The IEEE initially evaluated 62 different proposals for the wireless technology that would form the basis of 802.11n.

Remote Desktop Protocol (RDP) A proprietary Microsoft protocol known as **Remote Desktop Protocol (RDP)** allows a user to access another remote computer over a network and perform tasks on it as if they were sitting at the remote computer. It provides remote display and input capabilities over network connections for Windows-based applications running on a server. RDP is designed to support different types of networks and protocols.

Basic Network Setup

3.5 Compare and contrast basic client networks and tools.

3.6 Setup basic network devices and apply basic configuration settings.

3.9 Classify different server types, environments, features, and limitations.

When setting up a network, there can be a variety of configurations, depending on the services that the network is to provide. Generally, a network setup involves understanding the connections to the network devices as well as knowing how to configure the network hardware.

Client Connections

Connecting a client computer to a network traditionally involved a "wired" link using a cable from the computer to the network. The hardware needed on the computer to send and receive data on a wired network is called a *network interface card (NIC)* or *client network adapter*. Early NICs were separate devices that had one edge connected to the computer's *bus* (the subsystem for transferring data between the system's components) expansion slot, while the other end had a connection that provided access for a cable connection, as illustrated in Figure 4-7. The cable connects the NIC to the network, thus establishing the link between the computer and the wired network.

Today, many desktop computers and all laptop computers typically have NIC components built directly into the motherboard so that only the RJ-45 connection is externally exposed.

Figure 4-7 NIC and cable
© ronstik/www.Shutterstock.com

Over the last decade, many wired connections have been replaced with wireless connections based on the IEEE 802.11 family of wireless networks. A *wireless client network interface card adapter* performs the same functions as a wired NIC with one major exception: there is no external RJ-45 cable connection. In its place is an antenna (sometimes embedded into the adapter) to send and receive signals through the airwaves. For desktop computers, early wireless NICs plugged into an internal expansion slot inside the computer much like a NIC. These have generally been replaced with external wireless NICs that plug into the Universal Serial Bus (USB) port, as illustrated in Figure 4-8.

As wireless networks have become the standard for network communication, more desktop computers are shipping with wireless NICs as standard equipment, along with a wired NIC. This allows the desktop device to connect to either a wired network or to a wireless network.

Network Hardware

Client computers are connected to different types of network hardware devices. These devices include Internet modems, routers, and wireless access points. The client computers must be properly configured so that they can function on the network with such devices.

Internet Modem A modem (*modulator-dem*odulator) was originally a device that changed a continuous *analog* signal into a discrete *digital* signal (and vice versa). A modem allows for a digital computer to use an analog telephone signal, for example. However, as more and more telephone and cable TV connections have converted from analog to digital,

Figure 4-8 USB wireless NIC
© Oleksiy Mark/www.Shutterstock.com

the meaning of "modem" has become more general, meaning a device that allows computers or other devices to connect remotely to other networks. A modem used for connecting computers and networks to the Internet is sometimes called an **Internet modem** or *broadband* modem. An Internet modem is illustrated in Figure 4-9.

Figure 4-9 Internet modem
© David Philips/www.Shutterstock.com

There typically is little configuration that must be performed on the Internet modem itself. To set up an Internet modem, the device should be turned off. A cable or telephone line is first connected to the modem (the port may be designated as *CATV* for a cable connection or *DSL* for a telephone connection). Then an Ethernet patch cable (with an RJ-45 connection) is connected to the Ethernet interface external hardware port. Figure 4-10 illustrates an Ethernet cable and a port.

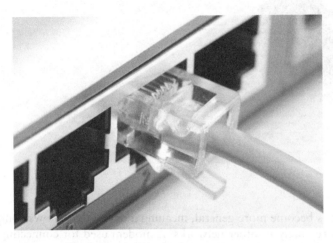

Figure 4-10 Ethernet cable and port
© Ugorenkov Aleksandr/www.Shutterstock.com

Router When connecting the router to an Internet modem, the router should be turned off. The Ethernet patch cable from the Internet modem should then be connected to the router. The router's external hardware port may be labeled *WAN, Uplink,* or *Internet.* For a wired network, another Ethernet patch cable from the router is then inserted into an available external hardware port (usually there are 4–6 hardware ports labeled *LAN* or simply numbered) and to the NIC on the computer. Then the Internet modem should be turned on. After the Internet modem is functioning (less than 1 minute) the router can be turned on.

Routers are generally preconfigured to act as a DHCP server to manage the automatic distribution of IP addresses. To determine if the router is configured as a DHCP server, the router setup utility must be accessed. This is done by opening a Web browser and entering *192.168.1.1* or *192.168.0.1* into the address bar of the browser and then entering the router's username and password (these can be found in the user manual or documentation). Once connected to the router setup utility, the setting *DHCP Server* should be set to *Enable.*

Routers can also be configured to support port forwarding. On a computer, *software ports* (not to be confused with physical interfaces on the rear of the computer that are also called "ports" such as USB or serial ports) are numbered software connections that a computer uses to identify different types of network traffic. For example, port 20 is commonly used for FTP transfers. For security reasons, software ports on a router are closed so that traffic cannot flow through them. In some instances it may be necessary to assign an unused software port number to a service that is associated with a software application that runs on the computer. This is known as **port forwarding.**

Port forwarding is often used for multiuser online gaming applications that are hosted on the local computer so that they are not blocked. However, virtually any application that requires a direct network link can use port forwarding.

To configure port forwarding, the router's setup utility is accessed and the *Port Forwarding* screen is opened. The available services that can be forwarded are listed along with the software port numbers. A *Server IP Address* can be added so that other computers can access this service. This is illustrated in Figure 4-11.

Port Forwarding / Port Triggering

Please select the service type
- Port Forwarding
- Port Triggering

Service Name	Server IP Address			
FTP	192 . 168 . 1 .	Add		
FTP				
HTTP	Server Name	Start Port	End Port	Server IP Address
ICUII				
IP_Phone				
NetMeeting	Edit Service	Delete Service		
News				
PPTP	Add Custom Service			
QuakeII/III				
Real-Audio				
Telnet				

Figure 4-11 Port forwarding
© Cengage Learning 2013

Wireless Access Point In a network that uses wireless technology, there are two ways in which the wireless clients can communicate. The first is called **ad hoc** mode, in which the devices send and receive network traffic only between themselves (such as between two laptop computers). However, this does not give access to any devices outside the wireless network or to the Internet. The second method is called **infrastructure** mode, which does provide the ability to access remote computers and the Internet.

Due to its limitations, ad hoc mode is rarely used.

When using infrastructure mode, a wireless **access point** (**AP**) must be part of the network. An AP is a device that receives all wireless signals and serves as a bridge between the wireless and wired networks. It has two basic functions. First, it acts as the "base station" for the wireless network. All wireless devices with a wireless NIC transmit to the AP, which in turn redirects the signal, if necessary, to other wireless devices. The second function of an AP is to act as a bridge between the wireless and wired networks. The AP can be connected to the wired network by a cable, allowing all the wireless devices to access the wired network through the AP (and vice versa), as shown in Figure 4-12.

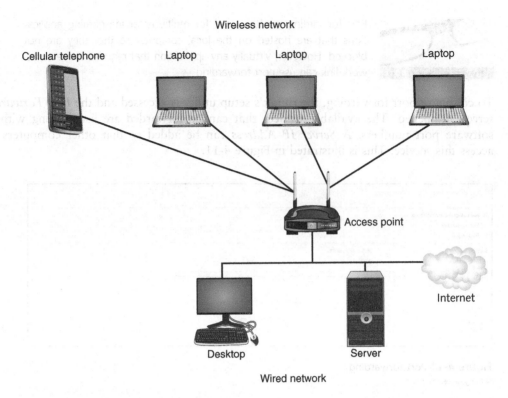

Figure 4-12 Infrastructure mode with AP
© Cengage Learning 2013

A single wireless hardware network device for small offices or home use typically combines multiple features into a single hardware device. These features often include those of an AP, router, DHCP server, and other features. Strictly speaking, these devices are *residential WLAN gateways* as they are the entry point from the Internet into the wireless network. However, most vendors instead choose to label their products as wireless broadband routers or simply *wireless routers*.

APs typically use antennas that radiate out the signal in all directions (called *omnidirectional antennas*). To provide the broadest area of coverage, APs should be located near the middle of the coverage area. Generally, the AP can be secured to the ceiling or high on a wall. It is recommended that APs should be mounted as high as possible for two reasons: there may be fewer obstructions for the radio frequency (RF) signal and to prevent thieves from stealing the device. In buildings with a false ceiling (also called a drop or suspended ceiling), there is a temptation to simply remove a ceiling tile, place the AP in the space above the ceiling, and then replace the tile. However, the air-handling space above drop ceilings is used to circulate and otherwise handle air in a building (these spaces are called *plenums*). Placing an access point in a plenum can be a hazard because if an electrical short in the AP were to cause a fire, it could generate smoke in the plenum that would be quickly circulated throughout the building. If it is necessary to place an AP in a plenum, it is important to place it within a special plenum-rated enclosure to meet fire safety code requirements.

Unlike wired networks that have network signals restricted to a cable that is in a wall or buried underground, wireless networks do not have these boundaries. An attacker can easily intercept an unencrypted wireless transmission and read its private contents, steal its passwords, or even change the message itself. In addition, attackers sitting in a car across the street with a radio frequency jammer can flood the network with wireless data and bring it to a crashing halt. Due to the nature of wireless transmissions, wireless networks have been vulnerable targets for attackers.

There are several security settings on APs that can be used to secure a wireless network:

- *Turn on WPA2*—*Wi-Fi Protected Access 2 (WPA2)* is the second generation of wireless security that addresses who can access a wireless network as well as provide encryption for all transmissions. Virtually all operating systems and wireless devices manufactured since 2005 support WPA2. The typical WPA2 security options on an AP are illustrated in Figure 4-13.

Security Options
- None
- WEP
- WPA-PSK [TKIP]
- WPA2-PSK [AES]
- WPA-PSK [TKIP] + WPA2-PSK [AES]
- WPA/WPA2 Enterprise

Figure 4-13 WPA2 settings
© Cengage Learning 2013

- *Disable SSID*—The **Service Set Identifier (SSID)** serves as the user-supplied wireless network name and can generally be any alphanumeric string from 2 to 32 characters. For a degree of protection, some wireless security sources encourage users to configure their APs to prevent the SSID from being beaconed out to any user who comes within range. Although this may seem to provide protection by not advertising the SSID, it only provides a weak degree of security and has several limitations. Enabling SSID broadcast on an AP is shown in Figure 4-14.

Figure 4-14 SSID settings
© Cengage Learning 2013

- *Center antenna placement*—For security purposes, the AP and its antenna should be positioned so that when possible, a minimal amount of signal reaches beyond the security perimeter of the building or campus.

- *Reduce power levels*—Another security feature on some APs is the ability to adjust the level of power at which the WLAN transmits. On devices with that feature, the power can be adjusted so that less of the signal leaves the premises and reaches outsiders.

- *Create guest network*—Many organizations segment traffic for security purposes by creating two wireless networks: the first is for employee access, in which employees can see the company's files and databases through the network, while a second is for guest access, limited only to the Internet or files stored for all users. Employees can configure their wireless network interface card client adapters to use the SSID *Employee* while guests use the SSID *Guest*. When the devices associate to the same access point, they automatically become part of their respective wireless network. Guest network settings are illustrated in Figure 4-15.

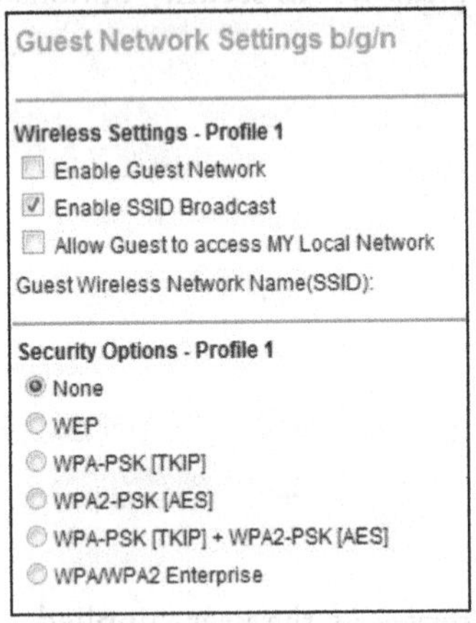

Guest Network Settings b/g/n

Wireless Settings - Profile 1
☐ Enable Guest Network
☑ Enable SSID Broadcast
☐ Allow Guest to access MY Local Network
Guest Wireless Network Name(SSID):

Security Options - Profile 1
◉ None
○ WEP
○ WPA-PSK [TKIP]
○ WPA2-PSK [AES]
○ WPA-PSK [TKIP] + WPA2-PSK [AES]
○ WPA/WPA2 Enterprise

Figure 4-15 Guest network settings
© Cengage Learning 2013

Network Troubleshooting

3.1 Identify commonly used IT terms and technologies.

3.5 Compare and contrast basic client networks and tools.

3.7 Given a scenario, troubleshoot and solve common network problems.

Troubleshooting a network is a necessary skill for healthcare IT technicians. Troubleshooting often involves diagnosing connectivity problems and IP settings.

Connectivity Problems

By some estimates, almost half of all network problems are the result of cabling or network devices. When a network fails to properly function, it is important to take a systematic approach to problem solving. This approach always involves examining the obvious solutions first before drilling down into the more technically advanced areas.

If a network loses its connectivity to the Internet, first check that the network devices, like the routers or APs, are receiving power. A tripped electrical circuit, a loose power cord, or even an accidental unplugging of a device can all result in a loss of connectivity. Another obvious step is that the entity responsible for providing Internet access, known as the Internet Service Provider (ISP), may be experiencing network problems. This problem is beyond the ability of the healthcare IT technician to solve; instead, the ISP must identify and fix the connectivity problem.

If all internal network devices are checked and are properly functioning, then you can use the command-line utility **ping** to check for connectivity outside the organization. Ping is designed to help determine if another computer can be reached. If sending a ping command to two or more Web sites (such as *ping www.cengage.com*) results in the message *100% packet loss*, then it may be an indication the connectivity problem is with the ISP. To determine if that is the case, the command-line utility **tracert** can be used, which displays the route (path) that a packet travels. Sending a tracert command to a Web site (such as *tracert www.cengage.com*) can show where the transmission was stopped and if that device belonged to the ISP, as illustrated in Figure 4-16.

```
C:\Windows\system32\cmd.exe                                      _  □  X

C:\Users\Dr. Mark Ciampa>tracert www.cengage.com

Tracing route to cengage.com [69.32.133.79]
over a maximum of 30 hops:

  1     1 ms    <1 ms    <1 ms  192.168.1.1
  2    24 ms    26 ms     25 ms  adsl-74-240-207-1.bna.bellsouth.net [74.240.207.
1]
  3    28 ms    27 ms     28 ms  70.159.210.49
  4    27 ms    27 ms     28 ms  70.159.210.51
  5    26 ms    27 ms     26 ms  70.159.210.137
  6    27 ms    28 ms     27 ms  12.81.32.118
  7    26 ms    26 ms     25 ms  12.81.32.109
  8    25 ms    26 ms     26 ms  74.175.192.162
  9    38 ms    38 ms     39 ms  cr1.nsvtn.ip.att.net [12.122.148.14]
 10    36 ms    38 ms     39 ms  cr2.attga.ip.att.net [12.122.28.105]
 11    33 ms    34 ms    173 ms  12.122.140.213
 12    33 ms    34 ms     34 ms  12.249.190.6
 13    55 ms    57 ms     52 ms  cnc1-ar3-xe-0-0-0-0.us.twtelecom.net [66.192.244
.202]
 14    53 ms    54 ms     53 ms  69.32.144.42
 15    62 ms    57 ms     57 ms  tluser.thomsonlearning.com [69.32.128.159]
 16     *        *         *     Request timed out.
 17    57 ms    57 ms     56 ms  academic.cengage.com [69.32.133.79]

Trace complete.

C:\Users\Dr. Mark Ciampa>
```

Figure 4-16 Tracert output
© Cengage Learning 2013

To access the command line in Microsoft Windows, click the Start button, type CMD, and press Enter.

Another source of connectivity problems is the network cabling to the devices. Coaxial and twisted-pair cables have a copper wire at the center that conducts an electrical signal. In contrast, a **fiber-optic** cable uses a very thin cylinder of glass at its center instead of copper. Fiber-optic cables send light impulses instead of transmitting electrical signals. For any type of cabling, make sure the cable is not crimped, broken, or torn loose from its connectors.

Interference (also called *noise*) is caused when a strong external signal interferes with the signal being transmitted. Although fiber-optic cables are immune to interference, cables using copper wires are susceptible to outside interference. *Radio frequency interference (RFI)* refers to interference that is caused by broadcast signals from a radio or television transmitter. *Electromagnetic interference (EMI)* may be caused by a variety of sources. A motor or another source of intense electrical activity can create an electromagnetic signal that interferes with a data signal. EMI can also be caused by cellular phones, Citizen's Band and police radios, small office or household appliances, fluorescent lights, and loose electrical connections. The solution is often to identify the source of the interference and either move it away from the cabling or provide additional shielding.

Wireless networks likewise can experience signal issues. A common misconception is that an RF signal that goes out from an antenna is a single signal that takes a direct straight path to the receiver. However, this is incorrect in two ways. First, there is not just one RF signal that reaches the receiver. Along with the primary signal, multiple "copies" of that signal may reach the receiver, all at different times. This is known as *multipath*. Second, because the signals radiate out in many directions, they may not always take a straight path to the receiver. The signal may bounce off walls and other objects in the area. The way in which the signal travels is known as *wave propagation*. The incorrect and correct views of wave propagation and multipath are illustrated in Figure 4-17.

Radio waves have several different behaviors, depending on the objects and even the materials that the wave encounters. These behaviors can interfere with wireless signals, and are listed in Table 4-2.

If you suspect your wireless network is having problems because of interference, the solution is to move the AP or the source of the interference.

IP Settings

Another common cause of network problems is incorrect IP settings, such as an incorrect IP address or the same IP address assigned to two devices. To help identify this problem, the Windows command-line utility **ipconfig/all** can be used. This command will list all of the IP settings for the device, such as the IP address, if DHCP is enabled, the address of the DHCP server, the address of the router, and other information.

Network Technologies for EHR/EMR

3.10 Compare and contrast EHR/EMR technologies and how each is implemented.

Determining which network technology is most appropriate for managing electronic health records (EHR) and electronic medical records (EMR) is not an easy task. There are a wide variety of variables that must be accounted for, including existing hardware and software, future expansion, new laws and regulations, costs, and so on. Today, there are two broad categories of decisions that must be made regarding network technologies used for EHR/EMR. These are cloud versus local network and installed applications versus remote access.

Incorrect

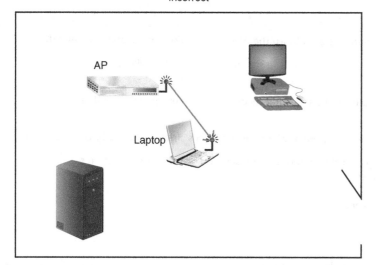

Correct

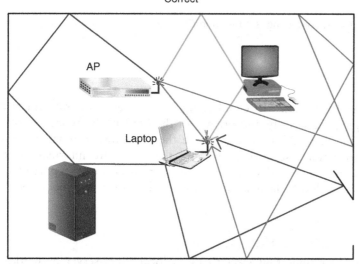

Figure 4-17 Incorrect and correct wave propagation and multipath
© Cengage Learning 2013

Cloud Computing vs. Local Network

With the growing popularity of cloud computing, it is being positioned as a viable alternative
to a locally hosted client-server network. Cloud computing can significantly reduce hardware,
software, and personnel costs. First, no servers, network equipment, and software must be
purchased, installed, and maintained; the only hardware needed is a basic computer with an
Internet connection. Second, because cloud computing is a "pay-per-use" model in which customers pay only for the computing resources that they need at any given time, as EHR/EMR
needs increase or decrease, cloud computing resources can be quickly and automatically be

Type of Interference	Description	Examples
Absorption	Certain types of materials can absorb the RF signal	Concrete, wood, and asphalt
Reflection	Signal is "bounced back" by large and smooth objects	Walls, buildings, metal roofs, and elevator shafts
Scattering	Signal is "bounced back" by small objects or rough surfaces	Foliage, rocks, and sand
Refraction	Signal moves through different atmospheric conditions	Bright sunshine to cold damp air
Diffraction	Caused by an object in the path of the transmission with rough surfaces	Automobile and tires

Table 4-2 **Wireless signal interference**
© Cengage Learning 2013

scaled up or down. Finally, because cloud computing is managed and maintained by the cloud computing organization, there is no need for highly skilled network system administrators.

Cloud computing is covered in Chapter 3.

However, a significant disadvantage to cloud computing is that a separate entity becomes responsible for managing the security and privacy of the EHR/EMR. What security protections are in place in the "cloud"? How tightly are they monitored? What happens if the cloud computing organization's security is lax and the healthcare information is stolen? Who is liable? Due to the security risks, many healthcare providers are keeping their records in-house and installing a local client-server network that they can be responsible for protecting.

Installed Applications vs. Remote Access

For the healthcare organizations that elect to use a local client-server network, another decision must be made. Should the software applications be installed on the local client computers, or should a remote access approach, in which the applications are installed on servers and then executed through desktop clients, be used instead? A remote access configuration results in a significant cost and time savings in installing, configuring, managing and maintaining the applications, which now can be done centrally on a smaller number of servers instead of on every desktop client. And because the processing is carried out on the server instead of the desktop, older desktop computers can be used as clients, reducing the need to purchase the latest high-performance desktops for users. However, not all applications may run efficiently in a remote access setting, especially specialized healthcare applications. In this case, installing the applications locally may be a better solution.

Chapter Summary

- The Open Systems Interconnection (OSI) reference model is a conceptual representation of how a computer prepares data for transmission and how it receives data from the network, based on a series of seven layers. Each layer provides specific services and shares with the layers above and below it. Standard network devices can be classified by the OSI layer at which they function. The most common network devices are switches and routers. A hub is an older network device that performed some of the functions of a switch. A router, operating at the Network Layer (Layer 3), is a network device that can forward packets across computer networks. When a router receives an incoming packet, it reads the destination address and then, using information in its routing table, sends the packet to the next network toward its destination. A domain controller is a server that manages the security-related elements on the network for the user.

- Servers play a crucial role in a client-server computing environment. There are several different types of services and servers. A print server is a server exclusively dedicated to managing the printing functions across the network, while a file server can be responsible for managing file services. A database server provides services to a database of stored data. An application server can be used to centrally store applications remotely on a server that are then accessible and run across the network on the client computer.

- Network load balancing is a technology that can help to evenly distribute work across a network. Requests that are received can be allocated across multiple devices such as servers. To the user, this distribution is transparent and appears as if a single server is providing the resources. There are several different technologies available that can provide enhanced storage capabilities for documents. One is storage virtualization, which hides the physical resources of storage (such as a specific hard drive) from the user. All storage devices are "pooled" and appear as a large repository of storage.

- Computer networks also have protocols, or rules for communication. These protocols are essential for proper communication to take place between network devices. The most common protocol suite used today for local area networks (LANs) as well as the Internet is Transmission Control Protocol/Internet Protocol (TCP/IP). TCP/IP is not one single protocol; instead, it is several protocols that all function together. Domain Name System (DNS) is a TCP/IP protocol that resolves (maps) an IP address to its equivalent symbolic name. A method for assigning the IP addresses is to have them automatically distributed using a protocol in the TCP/IP suite known as the Dynamic Host Configuration Protocol (DHCP). When a computer attaches to the network, it requests an IP address from a DHCP server. An IP address is then leased to that host. Once the computer is off the network, or its lease expires, that IP address becomes free and can be given to another computer. Transferring files is most commonly performed using the File Transfer Protocol (FTP). FTP is used to connect to an FTP server, much in the same way that HTTP links to a Web server.

- Wireless local area networks (WLANs) have been successful because from the outset they have been based on standards set by the Institute of Electrical and Electronics Engineers (IEEE). Since the late 1990s, the IEEE has approved four standards for wireless LANs (IEEE 802.11, 802.11b, 802.11a, and 802.11g). In 2007, the IEEE combined the standards and amendments into a single standard officially known as IEEE 802.11-2007. In 2009, the IEEE ratified a new WLAN standard known as IEEE 2801.11n-2009 (or just 802.11n) that significantly increased the speed, range, and reliability of wireless local area networks. A proprietary protocol developed by Microsoft is known as Remote Desktop Protocol (RDP). RDP allows a user to access another remote computer over a network and perform tasks on it as if they were sitting at the remote computer.

- When setting up a network, there are a variety of configurations, depending on the services that the network is to provide. Connecting a client computer to a network traditionally involved a "wired" link using a cable from the computer to the network. Over the last decade, wired connections have been increasingly replaced with wireless connections based on the IEEE 802.11 family of wireless network standards.

- There are different network hardware devices to which client computers are connected and properly configured so that they can function on the network. An Internet modem allows computers or other devices to connect to the Internet. When connecting a router to an Internet modem, the router should be turned off. The Ethernet patch cable from the Internet modem should then be connected to the router. Routers are generally pre-configured to act as a DHCP server to manage the automatic distribution of IP addresses. Routers can also be configured to support port forwarding.

- Most wireless LANs use a wireless access point (AP). APs typically use antennas that radiate out the signal in all directions. To provide the broadest area of coverage, APs should be located near the middle of the coverage area. Generally, the AP can be secured to the ceiling or high on a wall. Due to the nature of wireless transmissions, wireless networks have been vulnerable targets for attackers. There are several security settings that can be used to secure a wireless network.

- Troubleshooting a network is a necessary skill for healthcare IT technicians. If a network loses its connectivity to the Internet, first make sure that the network devices, like the routers or APs, are receiving power. Another obvious step is to check that the entity responsible for providing Internet access, known as the Internet Service Provider (ISP), is not experiencing network problems. Interference is caused when a strong external signal interferes with the signal being transmitted. Although fiber-optic cables are immune to interference, cables using copper wires are susceptible to outside interference. Wireless networks likewise can experience signal issues. Another common cause of network problems is incorrect IP settings, such as an incorrect or duplicate IP address.

- Determining which network technology is most appropriate for managing electronic health records (EHR) and electronic medical records (EMR) is not an easy task. There are a wide variety of variables that must be accounted for. Cloud computing can significantly reduce hardware, software, and personnel costs. However, a significant disadvantage to cloud computing is that a separate entity becomes responsible for managing the security and privacy of the EHR/EMR records. A remote access configuration results in a significant cost and time savings in installing, configuring, managing, and maintaining the applications, which now can be done centrally on a smaller number of servers instead of on every desktop client. However, not all applications run efficiently in a remote access setting. In this case, installing the applications locally may be a better solution.

Key Terms

access point (AP)   A device that receives all wireless signals and serves as a bridge between the wireless and wired networks.

ad hoc   A wireless mode in which devices send and receive network traffic only between themselves.

application server   A server that centrally stores applications (such as a multiuser version of a word processor) that are accessible and run across the network on client computers, instead of installing the software separately on each client.

application services   Processes that run software for network clients and thus enable clients to share processing power across a network.

database server   A server that provides services to a database of stored data.

domain controller   A server that manages the security-related elements on the network for the user.

Domain Name System (DNS)   A TCP/IP protocol that resolves (maps) an IP address with its equivalent symbolic name.

Dynamic Host Configuration Protocol (DHCP)   A protocol that automatically assigns IP addresses.

fiber optic   A cable that uses a very thin cylinder of glass at its center instead of copper.

infrastructure   A wireless mode in which devices communicate with an access point.

interference   (also called noise) External signals that interfere with the signal being transmitted.

Internet modem   A device used for connecting computers and networks to the Internet.

Internet Service Provider (ISP)   A company that provides access to the Internet.

ipconfig/all   A command that lists all of the IP settings for a device on Windows operating systems.

modem   A device that changes a continuous analog signal into a discrete digital signal (and vice versa).

operating system and application interoperability   Allows for applications to run on either the network's operating system or on the local client.

ping   A command that can determine if another computer can be reached.

port forwarding   Assigning an unused software port number to a service that is associated with a software application that runs on the computer.

print server   A server exclusively dedicated to managing the printing functions across the network.

Remote Desktop Protocol (RDP)   A proprietary Microsoft protocol that allows a user to access another remote computer over a network and perform tasks on it as if they were sitting at the remote computer.

router   A network device that can forward packets across computer networks.

Service Set Identifier (SSID)   A user-supplied wireless network name that can generally be any alphanumeric string from 2 to 32 characters.

static IP address An IP address that does not change.

switch A device that connects network segments together.

tracert A command that displays the route (path) that a packet travels.

Transmission Control Protocol/Internet Protocol (TCP/IP) The most common protocol suite used today for local area networks (LANs) as well as the Internet.

Healthcare IT Acronyms

Table 4-3 contains healthcare IT acronyms that were introduced in this chapter. Many of these terms are listed in the CompTIA Healthcare IT Technician exam objectives, and most are also defined in the Key Terms section of this chapter. For a complete list of the healthcare IT acronyms used in this book, see Appendix C.

Acronym	Full Name
AP	access point
DHCP	Dynamic Host Configuration Protocol
DNS	Domain Name System or Domain Name Service
DSL	Digital Subscriber Line
EMI	electromagnetic interference
FTP	File Transfer Protocol
HTTP	Hypertext Transfer Protocol
IP	Internet Protocol
LAN	local area network
MAC	Media Access Control
NIC	network interface card
RDP	Remote Desktop Protocol
RF	radio frequency
RFI	radio frequency interference
SSID	service set identifier
STP	shielded twisted pair
TCP/IP	Transmission Control Protocol/Internet Protocol
WIFI	wireless fidelity
WLAN	wireless local area network
WPA2	WiFi Protected Access 2

Table 4-3 CompTIA Healthcare IT Technician acronyms introduced in this chapter
© Cengage Learning 2013

Review Questions

1. The Open Systems Interconnection (OSI) reference model contains _____ layers.

    a. six
    b. seven
    c. eight
    d. nine

2. The most common type of computer networking is called _____.

    a. cloud computing
    b. mainframe computing
    c. client-server computing
    d. terminal services computing

3. A hub cannot _____.

    a. read the source and destination of the frames
    b. use twisted-pair copper cables
    c. create a single network segment
    d. regenerate the electrical signals

4. A switch examines the _____ address included in frames to know where to send the frame.

    a. IP address
    b. Media access control (MAC) address
    c. Server Resource (SR)
    d. core

5. _____ switches reside at the top of the hierarchy of a network and carry traffic between switches.

    a. Core
    b. Workgroup
    c. Smart
    d. Dumb

6. A _____ forwards packets across computer networks.

    a. hub
    b. switch
    c. router
    d. brouter

7. Which of the following is false regarding a domain controller?

   a. It is found in a Microsoft Windows network.

   b. It is a server.

   c. It manages the security-related elements on the network.

   d. It replaces a network domain.

8. _____ services allow users to share user-created documents.

   a. File

   b. Document

   c. Synchronizing

   d. Graphical user

9. Load balancing _____.

   a. can evenly distribute work across a network

   b. requires a Microsoft domain

   c. is no longer used in networks

   d. requires a network of at least 100 computers

10. _____ hides the physical resources of storage from the user.

    a. A transplant hard drive

    b. Secret data storage (SDS)

    c. Hard drive hiding

    d. Storage virtualization

11. The rules for communication for computer networks are called _____.

    a. standards

    b. protocols

    c. canons

    d. practices

12. Which of the following is not true regarding Transmission Control Protocol/Internet Protocol (TCP/IP)?

    a. It is the most common protocol suite used today for local area networks (LANs) as well as the Internet.

    b. It is not one single protocol.

    c. It is called a protocol suite.

    d. The two major protocols are RDP and XLORV.

13. The _____ protocol resolves an IP address (like 207.46.19.254) to a symbolic name (like www.cengage.com).

    a. Domain Name System (DNS)

    b. Remote Desktop Protocol (RDP)

    c. Domain Resolution Protocol (DRP)

    d. Transmission Control Protocol (TCP)

14. Which is the preferred method for assigning IP addresses to a large number of clients?

    a. Substitute using MAC addresses instead.

    b. Create a static domain.

    c. Use static IP addresses.

    d. Use Dynamic Host Configuration Protocol (DHCP).

15. Each of the following is a method for using FTP on a local host computer except: _____.

    a. from a command prompt

    b. using an FTP client application

    c. using a Web browser

    d. using an integrated hub/switch device

16. The wireless standard that supports the fastest transmission rates is IEEE _____.

    a. 802.11a

    b. 802.11b

    c. 802.11g

    d. 802.11n

17. Each of the following is true regarding Remote Desktop Protocol (RDP) except: _____.

    a. it is a proprietary protocol developed by Microsoft

    b. it has been replaced by DHCP

    c. it allows a user to access another remote computer over a network

    d. it can support different types of networks and protocols

18. Which type of connection is found on a network interface card (NIC) to connect it to a wired network?

    a. RJ-45

    b. SCSI-13

    c. MTB

    d. CD

19. Which of the following is not true regarding modems?

   a. They change a continuous analog signal into a discrete digital signal (and vice versa).

   b. They allow a digital computer to use an analog telephone or TV connection to connect remotely to other networks.

   c. When used for connecting to the Internet, these devices are sometimes called an Internet modem.

   d. "Modem" stands for Multiuser Orthogonal Detection Emulator.

20. The wireless mode that requires an access point (AP) is _____.

   a. ad hoc mode

   b. infrastructure mode

   c. remote mode

   d. WNIC mode

Case Projects

CASE PROJECTS

Case Project 4-1: Open Systems Interconnection (OSI) Reference Model

Draw a diagram of the Open Systems Interconnection (OSI) reference model. Label each of the layers and what function each performs.

Case Project 4-2: Switches

Use the Internet to research switches. Identify three vendors that sell 8-port switches and review the technical specifications of the devices. What speeds do they support? What are their features? How much do they cost? Summarize your findings in a one-page paper.

Case Project 4-3: Domain Controllers

Use the Internet to research domain controllers. Find information regarding how they are used, what advantages they present, and what are their disadvantages. Write a one-page paper on your research.

Case Project 4-4: Storage Management

Besides storage virtualization, there are other types of storage management solutions. These include storage area networks, network-attached storage, and IP SAN. Use the Internet to research one of these technologies. What is its advantage? What is its disadvantage? Could it be used in a healthcare setting? Why or why not? Write a one-page paper on your research.

Case Project 4-5: Dynamic Host Configuration Protocol (DHCP)

Research Dynamic Host Configuration Protocol (DHCP). What functions does a DHCP server provide? What options are available, such as how long does a lease last? How difficult are they are to manage? Write a one-page paper on your research.

Case Project 4-6: FTP Client

Identify three FTP clients that are available for download. Create a table that lists and compares their features. Which would you recommend? Why? Write a one-page paper on your findings.

Healthcare IT: Challenges and Opportunities—Revisited

Refer to the Superior Care Health Group (SCHG) scenario related in the chapter opening section entitled "Healthcare IT: Challenges and Opportunities." Assume you are in Abby's position as the consultant.

For this case, complete the following:

1. Think outside the box. What additional changes would you make to the office staff's suggestion about using iPads for securing and recording patient information and examinations? For example, what if a cell phone application were distributed to patients so that they could complete the information before visiting the office? Would that improve the health care? What about a Web site through which patients could chat with a nurse practitioner regarding an illness? What other ideas would you have?

2. Keeping EHR/EMR data secure is an ongoing challenge. Braden asks Abby if the iPad system he has proposed would keep patient information secure. How would you respond? Develop a brief slide presentation that addresses security in wireless transmissions. The presentation should be at least seven slides in length.

3. What type of network would you suggest for SCHG? Create a one-page memo that compares the different network options along with your recommendation for SCHG.

References

1. Nicole A. Baker, "The securities enforcement manual: tactics and strategies." Accessed Oct. 10, 2011, http://books.google.com/books?id=XdBN7IRt0NcC&pg=PA125&lpg=PA 125&dq=Coleman+Holdings+v.+Morgan+Stanley+(Florida+Cir.+Ct.+2005)&source=bl& ots=6z9ZUFPxCm&sig=zF4MSI15cjbWmKdhqjYDW1I4f6o&hl=en&ei=8Z6TTuHaKcW 4tge4z8iHBw&sa=X&oi=book_result&ct=result&resnum=10&ved=0CGQQ6AEwCQ#v= onepage&q=Coleman%20Holdings%20v.%20Morgan%20Stanley%20(Florida%20Cir.% 20Ct.%202005)&f=false.

chapter 5

Medical Business Operations

After completing this chapter, you should be able to do the following:

- Define frequently used healthcare terms

- Identify and describe the functions of certain healthcare departments

- Describe the uses for clinical software

- List and describe the steps in the clinical process or environment

- Identify and describe the functions of various medical devices

Healthcare IT: Challenges and Opportunities

Recently, the Superior Care Health Group (SCHG) has been experiencing a large percentage of billing claim rejections from various third-party payers. Although there are many reasons for the claim rejections, the main problem is inaccurate billing codes, specifically those known as ICD-10 codes.

The office manager, Braden Thomas, who is new to SCHG, suspects that the problem is with the group's old billing software. When an office associate is given medical chart information to code, the software only provides a list of potential ICD-10 codes when the physician's diagnosis is keyed into the system. It is up to the office associate to make the determination between diagnosis codes that are very similar and difficult to differentiate. Braden knows that newer software can make the code differentiation more automatic and accurate, but has no idea where to start with such a project.

How can Braden address these issues? Where should he start his research?

For many people, health care is about healing, caring, and comfort. The thought of health care as a business seems foreign, even unpleasant. However, consider the following statistics:[1]

- According to the Bureau of Labor Statistics (BLS), health care is one of the largest industries in the United States, with 14.2 million wage and salary workers.

- The BLS forecasts that health care will create over 3 million new jobs between 2008 and 2018.

- One of the fastest growing areas until 2018 will be home healthcare services.

Given the size of the industry and its growth, health care is not only business, it is big business, and its growth is accelerating.

The purpose of this chapter is to review the various aspects of medical business operations. In doing so, you will cover terminology, functional departments within various organizations, clinical process and software applications, and typical medical devices.

According to the BLS, the average wage for nonsupervisory workers in the healthcare industry as a whole in 2008 was $20.28/hour. Hospitals were higher at $23.99/hour.

Medical Terminology

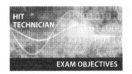

4.1 Identify commonly used medical terms and devices (clinical terms).

As with other industries, health care has very specialized terminology and numerous acronyms. Therefore, it is important for anyone considering employment in the field to become familiar with common terminology, especially in the functional area in which they intend to work.

Imaging

In the healthcare environment, **imaging** is often called *radiology* and usually refers to the use of technologies that provide a visual representation of internal body structures to help diagnose and treat medical disorders. In some cases, these techniques can eliminate the need to take *biopsies* or conduct surgical procedures.

There are many different types of imaging, or *radiographic,* technologies. However, the following list is representative of the major types:

- *X-ray*—One of the earlier types of health imaging technologies employed the use of x-rays to cast static shadows of internal body structures on photographic film. More modern machines use laser scanners to digitize the image. Figure 5-1 shows a modern example of an x-ray machine.

- *CT scan*—X-ray images can be digitized and processed by a computer using special computer software algorithms that covert the data into radiographic image slices of the body. This process is called **computed tomography (CT)** or **computerized axial tomography (CAT)** and is used mainly for diagnostic purposes.

- *Fluoroscopy*—While standard x-ray machines can be used to show static images of internal body structures, if the shadows cast by the body structure are projected onto a fluorescent screen, then real-time, moving x-ray images can be shown. These devices are known as *fluoroscopes.*

- *Magnetic resonance imaging (MRI)*—Instead of using radiation as do x-rays, MRI uses very strong magnetic fields to visualize internal body structures. One of the advantages to this process is that certain viewpoints are more easily obtained than with other imaging techniques.

- *Ultrasound*—A diagnostic tool that does not use x-rays, ultrasound uses high-frequency sound waves to image soft-tissue structures like organs. While ultrasound does not provide the detail of other radiologic imaging devices, it lacks the downside of *ionizing radiation* exposure.

- *Nuclear medicine*—If certain *radiopharmaceuticals* (radioactive substances that are not toxic in small doses) are administered to patients, they behave in different ways in different body organs. These differences can be measured by devices known as gamma cameras to detect problems with certain physiologic functions.

As computers and other digital technologies are combined with radiographic techniques, new ways of imaging are developed. One newer technique combines radiology with digital telecommunications in such a way as to instantly transmit radiographic images from one location to another. Thus, if a doctor specializing in a certain disorder is not available at the patient's location, the diagnostics imaging information can be instantly reviewed by the specialist, even around the world.

Another interesting and newer imaging technique is *capsule endoscopy*. In this technique, a small capsule that contains a camera, light source, and digital storage is swallowed. Later, images of the entire gastrointestinal tract can be reviewed in high resolution.

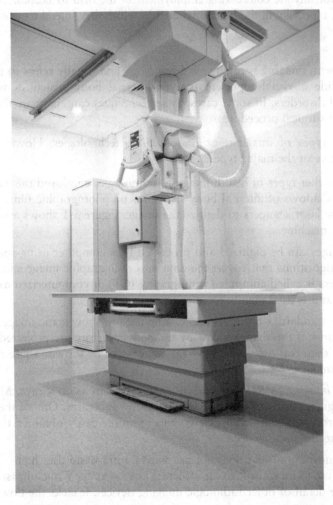

Figure 5-1 Modern x-ray machine
© Tyler Olson/www.Shutterstock.com

Primary Care Physician

There are over 20 physician specialties in medicine. A **primary care physician** (PCP) is a doctor who diagnoses and treats patients in three of these specialties: *family* or *general practice* (GP), *internal medicine*, or *pediatrics*. Family or GP refers to a specialty wherein a physician treats a broad range of ailments that would typically be found in a family. Thus, these physicians are frequently the first to see patients with chronic disorders, regardless of origin.

Internists practice internal medicine, which is a specialty that concentrates on treatment and diagnosis of representative adult diseases, especially diseases that involve multiple systems. Much like GPs, internists typically treat patients with chronic disorders.

Pediatrics (PEDS) is the specialized diagnosis and treatment of children. Pediatricians usually diagnose and treat children until age 18.

One of the advantages of using a PCP is that if patients see a PCP on a regular basis, the PCP can develop a health baseline that helps detect potential health problems before they become more severe. An example would be the early detection of high blood pressure before it causes organ damage.

Stat

In many aspects of health care there is always the potential for life-threatening situations. For example, a hospital emergency room (ER) frequently receives patients with acute conditions that may be life threatening or need immediate treatment. In an effort to expedite diagnosis or treatment or other activities, the word **stat** was derived from the Latin word *statim*, which means "immediately." Thus, instead of asking for something in a hurry, it is asked for stat. For example: "Get these results to ER, stat!"

Acuity

Acuity is a measure of the degree of patient disease or injury. However, it can refer to multiple properties of patient disease or injury such as severity, time sensitivity, physical effects, or psychological suffering. For example, a patient suffering from a heart attack (myocardial infarction) may have a high acuity when measured by time sensitivity, but lower acuity when measured by psychological suffering. Generally, a high-acuity patient is "less healthy" than a low-acuity patient.

Code Blue

When a life-threatening situation occurs in a healthcare setting, it is imperative that the right staff is present to treat the patient in distress. In larger hospitals, the right staff could be several floors away. To solve this problem, many hospitals have an emergency code system wherein certain code words or phrases can be announced over the public address (PA) system. **Code Blue** is such an emergency code, and commonly means that a patient is in respiratory or cardiac distress and needs immediate help. For example, to call a "code" for a patient in the ER, the announcement would be similar to the following: "Code Blue, ER, Code Blue, ER!"

Trauma Levels

In the context of health care, the word *trauma* means a physical wound or injury to the body, sometimes caused by accidents, sometimes caused by violence. Patients who suffer from trauma are commonly treated at hospital ERs. Problems occur because not every ER is equipped to respond to every type of trauma. For example, a small rural ER may not have the staff or equipment to treat patients with severe wounds or burns. To address this difficult issue, different ERs are equipped to address differing levels of trauma and then certified as a **trauma center** of a certain level. Table 5-1 illustrates the various levels and their characteristics.

Resources	Level 1	Level 2	Level 3	Level 4	Level 5
Surgeons (24x7)	Yes	Yes	Note 1	Note 3	No
ER physicians (24x7)	Yes	Yes	Note 2	Note 4	Note 4
ER (24x7)	Yes	Yes	Yes	Yes	No
Anesthesiologists (24x7)	Yes	Yes	Note 1	Note 3	No
Research	Yes	No	No	No	No
Trauma nurse	No	No	No	Yes	Yes
Transfers to...	N/A	L1	L1, L2	L1, L2	L1, L2

Notes:
1. Can provide surgery to most trauma patients on emergency basis, but may not cover all specialties
2. Can provide emergency treatment, but may not cover all specialties
3. May or may not provide surgery to most trauma patients on emergency basis, but may not cover all specialties
4. ER physicians may not be on staff, but should be available on patient's arrival.

Table 5-1 Trauma center levels and resources
© Cengage Learning 2013

Each state has a different number of trauma centers. The American College of Surgeons maintains a verified list by state at http://www.facs.org/trauma/verified.html.

Controlled Substances

The *Controlled Substances Act (CSA)* of 1970 established governmental control of certain drugs and/or chemicals, which are known as **controlled substances** (Figure 5-2). This resulted in a classification scheme that categorizes these drugs and chemicals into five levels or schedules.

The CSA legislation is important to healthcare providers because many drugs that are routinely used in the healthcare environment are also found on the CSA schedules. As a result, they must be managed in a specific manner. The levels include the following:

- *Schedule 1*—These substances have high potential for abuse, but no currently accepted medical use. Examples include marijuana, peyote, and LSD.

- *Schedule 2*—These substances can cause psychological or physical dependence and have high risk for abuse. Examples include morphine, opium, oxycodone, methamphetamine, and cocaine.

- *Schedule 3*—These substances have less potential for abuse than Schedule 1 or Schedule 2 substances. Examples include combination products containing less than 15 milligrams of hydrocodone per dosage and anabolic steroids such as oxandrolone.

- *Schedule 4*—These substances have less potential for abuse than Schedule 3. Examples include diazepam, alprazolam, and propoxyphene.

- *Schedule 5*—These substances have less potential for abuse than Schedule 4. Examples include cough and cold preparations containing limited quantities of certain narcotics such as Robitussin AC® and Phenergan with Codeine®.

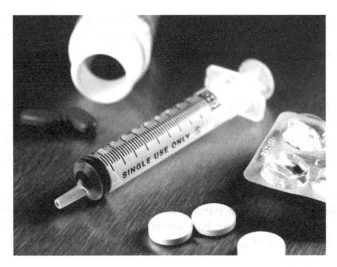

Figure 5-2 Controlled substances
© Kitch Bain/www.Shutterstock.com

Healthcare providers that use controlled substances frequently have well-defined policies and procedures that address their management and use. Policy components may address aspects such as availability of locked storage, authorization of staff to access substances, substance use protocol, and substance audits.

Controlled substance use and management is taken very seriously in most hospitals. There are numerous reports of healthcare professionals stealing controlled substance medications instead of giving them to patients. The result is invariably loss of the job, and frequently criminal prosecution.

Electronic Medical Record

When a patient is treated by a healthcare provider, the provider commonly records various aspects of the patient's diagnosis and treatment. This record is called the patient's *medical record* or *medical chart*. Examples of what would be contained in the medical record could include the patient's original complaint; test results such as blood pressure, x-ray evaluations, laboratory results; diagnosis; and treatment, including medications or referrals to other healthcare professionals.

An *electronic medical record (EMR)* is similar to a paper medical record with a few exceptions:

- Because the EMR is electronic, it is not limited to physical storage. As a result, review of the EMR does not have to be accomplished at the point of creation. The EMR can be viewed by authorized individuals anywhere in the world.

- The EMR can be interfaced to other electronic systems so that various laboratory or radiologic results can be instantly updated.

- While increased access to patient data via the EMR is usually helpful, controlling access can be more difficult than with a traditional medical record. This can create privacy issues.

The future of EMR use seems to be one of increasing usage. However, even though some governmental organizations report an EMR adoption rate that approaches 50 percent, it is also reported that their current functionality is not satisfactory.[2]

Electronic Health Record

An *electronic health record (EHR)* is very similar to an EMR, but much broader. For example, in addition to medical treatment and diagnoses of the EMR, it would be advantageous to also add demographics, weight trends, billing information, and all historical medical information. This type of electronic medical dossier would give healthcare providers the widest possible perspective on a patient.

One problem with the idea of an EHR for all patients is the potential for abuse. If the information were made available to unauthorized parties, it could create complications for the patient. For example, if an insurance company had access to a patient's EHR, could they deny the patient insurance on the basis of certain disease precursors?

Medical Departments

As organizations, hospitals usually divide functionality into departments. The number and types of departments depend greatly on hospital type and size and can be characterized in multiple ways. For example, some departments directly provide patient care. Others provide support services. Some only treat high-acuity patients, others only outpatients.

Ambulatory/Day Surgery

Various surgical procedures can be accomplished without the patient needing an overnight stay. While these can be limited to eye, ear, nose, throat, and extremity procedures in healthy patients, other procedures normally done on an inpatient basis are moving to outpatient treatment as medical technology improves.

Outpatient surgeries are known as **ambulatory surgery**, day surgery, or same-day-surgery. These surgical procedures are frequently done in hospital outpatient surgical centers, but stand-alone healthcare facilities known as *ambulatory surgical centers (ASC)* specialize in this type of surgery. The word ambulatory refers to walking, so ambulatory surgery refers to surgery on patients who are able to "walk"or be wheeled—away. By definition, ambulatory surgery is done on an outpatient basis.

Behavioral Health

Psychiatry is the study and treatment of mental disorders. **Behavioral health** is an area of *psychiatry* that studies the relationship between behavior and the inpatient's overall well-being. Thus, a Behavioral Health department may be staffed with psychiatrists or other mental health professionals.

Cardiac Care Units

A hospital that provides treatment to patients with heart disease will likely have a **Cardiac Care Unit (CCU)**. This department may be physically separate from other areas of the hospital and have controlled access. It may also have its own staff, including CCU nurses, medical assistants, and others. The CCU beds are commonly reserved for patients who require specialized cardiac monitoring; the patient's *electrocardiogram (EKG)* is monitored on a central console at the bedside. In some hospitals, cardiac patients are also treated in *intensive care units (ICUs)*.

Cardiovascular

A hospital that provides treatment to patients with heart disease may also have a **Cardiovascular department**. Such departments address advanced cardiac specialties like *electrophysiology*, heart failure, and heart transplantation. Cardiovascular departments mainly serve inpatients due to high patient acuity.

Dermatology

The hospital department where skin diseases like dermatitis, hives, and psoriasis are treated is called Dermatology. Due to low patient acuity, not all hospitals have dermatology departments. However, hospitals that do have dermatology departments usually treat patients on an outpatient basis.

Ears, Nose, and Throat

Otolaryngology is the medical study of the **ears, nose, and throat** (ENT). This includes subspecialties such as the following:

- Facial plastic surgery
- Head and neck
- *Laryngology* (voice)
- *Neuro-otology* (middle/inner ear, base of skull)
- *Otology* (ear)
- *Rhinology* (sinuses)

Because many ENT maladies are not acute in nature, much ENT work is performed on an outpatient basis.

Emergency Room

Emergency rooms (ER) receive, either by ambulance or by other means, patients with acute conditions that may be life threatening or need immediate treatment. Because every ER is not equipped to respond to every type of trauma, different ERs are equipped to address differing levels of trauma and then certified as to that level. However, most ERs are capable of stabilizing patients for transport to a certified trauma center if necessary.

Intensive Care Unit

Patients with life-threatening diseases or trauma frequently need specialized care. This can include intensive monitoring using specialized electronic monitoring equipment. In some cases, the patient's breathing must be supported through mechanical devices known as ventilators. In comatose patients, feeding tubes are used to maintain the proper dietary nutrition levels. **Intensive Care Units** (ICUs) maintain the equipment, systems, and staffing to support these inpatients. Some ICUs also care for cardiac patients, but usually this is accomplished in the CCU. Intensive care monitoring is illustrated in Figure 5-3.

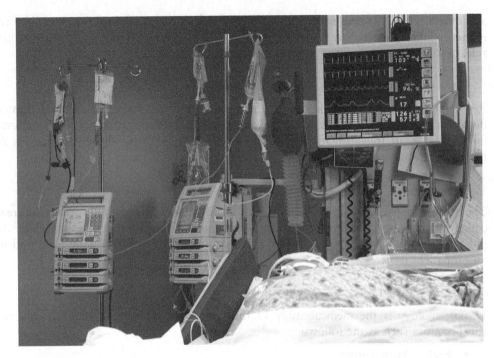

Figure 5-3 Intensive care monitoring
© Edwin Verin/www.Shutterstock.com

Laboratory

Laboratories are departments that provide various chemical, microbial, microscopic, and other studies for the purpose of diagnosing and treating disease or injury. In small hospitals, only basic capabilities like hematology (blood analysis), urinalysis (urine analysis), and microbiology (analysis for pathogenic organisms) may exist. Other needed studies may be outsourced to laboratories outside the hospital. Larger hospitals frequently have more robust laboratory capabilities and outsource less frequently.

Medical/Surgical

The **Medical/Surgical (Med/Surg) department** primarily cares for adult patients before and after surgery. However, it also sees patients after an illness or injury or those on medication who simply need nursing care. It is frequently one of the largest medical departments with relatively low patient acuity.

Nuclear Medicine

Nuclear medicine is a medical imaging technology that uses the radioactive decay of radio-pharmaceuticals in the diagnosis and treatment of disease. Nuclear medicine patients commonly have low acuity. As a result, these patients are treated as outpatients.

Obstetrics/Gynecology

Gynecology is the study of the female reproductive system. As a matter of practice, many if not most gynecologists (doctors who specialize in gynecology) also specialize in **obstetrics**, which is the area of medicine specifically concerned with pregnancy, childbirth, and post-birth issues. As a result, the two functions are frequently combined into one department (called OB/GYN).

In addition to the traditional OB/GYN department, other departments related to OB/GYN may be found in some hospitals. These include:

- *Family birth center*—A **family birth center (FBC)** can be a department within a hospital or a stand-alone organization. In either case, FBCs strive to provide a family-oriented approach to childbirth, making the process less clinical. Some FBCs are also called **stork units**.

- *Labor and delivery*—The physical area where patients in labor are cared for until and during childbirth is called *Labor and Delivery (L&D)*. It may be a subunit of an OB/GYN department.

- *Neonatal Intensive Care Unit*—In the event a newborn needs acute care, specialized staff and equipment are commonly required. Therefore, some hospitals have a **neonatal intensive care unit (NICU)** to address these needs.

OB/GYN patients may or may not be high acuity, but are usually always inpatients.

Occupational Therapy

Occupational therapy (OT) strives to help people complete tasks of daily living. For example, this may include helping people recovering from injury to regain work-related skills. It may also include helping people with disabilities accomplish self-care tasks. Some hospitals have occupational therapy departments, but occupational therapy is frequently conducted on an outpatient basis.

Oncology

The study of tumors (cancer) is called **oncology (ONC)**. Cancer patients frequently undergo various diagnostic procedures such as *biopsies* (removal of tissue specimens from the body), imaging, and blood tests. They also are treated with a range of therapies, including the use of drugs, called *chemotherapy*; the use of radiation, called *radiotherapy*; and *hormone therapy*, particularly in the case of breast and prostate cancer. The ONC department addresses these specific needs on both an inpatient and outpatient basis.

ONC patients are generally low acuity, and diagnosed and treated on an outpatient basis. However, in some cases where the patient's disease has advanced, inpatient ONC care can occur.

Operating Room

Surgery is the medical specialty in which physicians *operate* (invasively cut tissues) on patients to intervene with disease or trauma. The **operating room (OR)** is the department where surgical operations are conducted. In a surgical operation (or procedure) the patient's body is penetrated or opened to allow access for the purpose of assessing or correcting a disease or injury. Surgery can also be affiliated with a recovery room (see the Post-Anesthesia Care Unit section), where post surgical patients are moved directly after surgery until anesthesia wears off. A typical OR is illustrated in Figure 5-4.

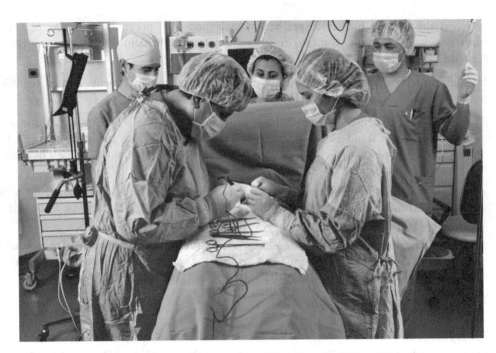

Figure 5-4 Operating room
© Levent Konuk/www.Shutterstock.com

Ophthalmology

Ophthalmology is the medical science of the human eye. **Ophthalmology departments** maintain the staff and equipment necessary to diagnose and treat various eye conditions, including *cataracts*, *glaucoma*, and *retinal disorders*. Ophthalmology patients are commonly seen on an outpatient basis.

Pediatrics

Because infants, children, and adolescents have specialized needs, they are generally not treated within the general inpatient population. Instead, special departments called *pediatrics (PEDS)* are maintained with staff appropriate for the children's age, size, and disease or trauma type.

PEDS patients may be medium or high acuity, and are usually treated on an inpatient basis. Low-acuity PEDS patients are commonly treated by a GP or pediatrician.

Physical Therapy

In some cases, patients may lose *range of motion (ROM)* due to illness or injury. In these cases, ROM may be restored through the use of ROM exercises such as balance training, gait training, and others. Many hospitals maintain **physical therapy (PT) departments** for the diagnosis and treatment of inpatients, but they may be also used for outpatients who need ongoing treatment.

Plastic Surgery

The medical specialty that is concerned with the alteration or reconstruction of the human body is called **plastic surgery**. Although sometimes used for cosmetic purposes, reconstructive techniques are the most widely used. While much plastic surgery is accomplished in a doctor's office, many hospitals have outpatient clinics for the same purpose.

Post-Anesthesia Care Unit

Patients recovering from the use of any type of *anesthesia* require a period of recovery due to the potential for post-anesthesia events such as respiratory arrest. Accordingly, hospitals regularly have a department called a **Post-Anesthesia Care Unit (PACU)** wherein inpatients can recover while being monitored before a typical transfer to a Med/Surg unit. PACUs are also sometimes called recovery rooms.

Radiology

A **radiology (x-ray) department** provides imaging equipment that may use x-rays, ultrasound, or nuclear isotopes as a method to detect and diagnose disease or injury.

Respiratory

If a patient is having problems breathing, they may be treated by staff from the **respiratory therapy (RT)** department. These treatments may consist of medications like *bronchodilators*, *pulmonary rehabilitation*, and *mechanical ventilation*. While some respiratory therapy (for example, simple pulmonary rehabilitation techniques) is accomplished on an outpatient basis, other therapies, like ventilation, must be accomplished for inpatients only.

Transitional/Progressive Care Unit

In some cases, CCU and ICU patients who are making progress may not need the full resources of the CCU or ICU. However, they still need around-the-clock monitoring in the event of an acute episode. For these cases, some hospitals have a **Transitional Care Unit (TCU)** or **Progressive Care Unit (PCU)** that continues monitoring but without the same staffing levels as an ICU or CCU.

Clinical Software

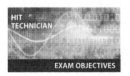

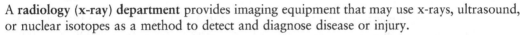

4.1 Identify commonly used medical terms and devices (clinical software and modules).

Software contains the logic that makes computers do what they do. Software is a set of instructions that helps hardware process data into information. Together, hardware and software are used to manage and manipulate both data and information. **Clinical software** is used to manage and manipulate data and information in the clinical environment. This can be in a hospital, a doctor's office, or a clinic.

Patient Tracking

In many hospitals, doctor's offices, or clinics, the flow of patients can become overwhelming to office staff, especially at peak flow times. To help better manage patients and the practice,

patient tracking software is frequently employed. Some of the benefits of such software include:

- The ability to track services provided
- Management of patient demographics
- Management of patient visit history, including services performed, time, and diagnosis
- Tracking patient-specific illnesses like allergies

Many patient-tracking systems can also be interfaced to other clinical software packages such as scheduling, medical records, and lab systems.

Scheduling

While some medical offices may only see a dozen patients per day, other practices may see hundreds of patients per day. With large numbers of patients, scheduling becomes increasingly more difficult. **Scheduling software** addresses this problem by helping manage the patient scheduling process through automation. Some of the major benefits of patient scheduling software are the ability to quickly scan for open appointments; track patient cancellations, no-shows, and reschedules; and track patient visits as to when they arrive, check in, and depart.

Order Entry

Computerized physician order entry (CPOE) is the use of electronic systems to store and transmit physician-generated orders to other healthcare professionals in departments such as pharmacy, laboratory, or radiology. Advantages of CPOE include:

- Instant availability of the patient's medical history and current results provides evidence-based clinical guidelines, which support treatment decisions.
- Instant availability of the patient's medical history and drug interactions provides another layer of safety to prevent drug interactions.
- Orders are standardized across the organization
- Statistical reports help improve resource management.
- Linking diagnoses to the order improves billing management.

Despite the benefits, CPOE systems are highly complex and may take years to completely implement.

Billing/Coding/Auditing

As opposed to being paid for service by the person receiving the service, healthcare organizations are frequently paid by third-party payers like insurance companies or the government. As a result, the healthcare organization may not receive the billed amount. Moreover, the entire billing process can be difficult. For example, many insurance companies have strict policies regarding claim submission. If the claim is not valid, it will be rejected and have to be resubmitted, which constrains healthcare organizations' financial resources. **Billing software** helps manage the billing process using technology like insurance claim validation. In some cases, insurance claims can be validated by *software decision engines* and then submitted to the appropriate payer.

Third-party payers also may require that claims for patient services use the International Statistical Classification of Diseases and Related Health Problems Codes (ICD-9) for services rendered. This means that each patient diagnosis must be described using a predefined list of over 13,000 codes.

ICD-10 stands for International Statistical Classification of Diseases and Related Health Problems, 10th Revision, sometimes shortened to International Classification of Diseases-10. ICD-10 is a complete revision of the diagnosis code set and increases the number of codes to about 68,000.

Incorrect coding can result in a rejected claim, which has to be recoded, and then resubmitted. Coding software is used to help clinical staff, professional coders, and others generate complete and accurate coding using ICD and other codes before claim submission. Table 5-2 illustrates various diagnoses and their ICD-9 and comparable ICD-10 codes.

ICD-9 Diagnosis	ICD-9 Code	ICD-10 Diagnosis	ICD-10 Code
Decubitus (ulcer)	707.00	Pressure ulcer of unspecified site, unspecified stage	L89.90
Derangement, ankle (internal)	718.97	Joint derangement, unspecified	M24.9
Derangement, collateral ligament	717.82	Chronic instability of knee, unspecified knee	M23.50
Derangement, gastrointestinal	536.9	Disease of stomach and duodenum, unspecified	K31.9
Derangement, joint	718.90	Joint derangement, unspecified	M24.9

Table 5-2   **ICD-9 and ICD-10 code examples**
© Cengage Learning 2013

To help ensure that a practice's medical records are accurate and that claims reflect actual diagnoses and treatments, third-party payers, including the government, may have the option to audit those records. **Audit software** uses computer algorithms to automatically check that the correct *Current Procedural Terminology (CPT)* and ICD codes are used. Moreover, the software can use historical data for trending and analysis to predict and improve future practice performance.

Practice Management

Practice management software (PMS) integrates medical software functionalities for day-to-day operations of a medical practice into one integrated system. Functions supported can include:

- Patient tracking
- Scheduling
- Computerized physician order entry
- Billing
- Coding
- Audit

For a complete integration of the practice, PMS is often interfaced with *electronic medical records* (EMR) systems.

The Clinical Environment

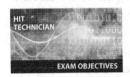

4.2 Explain aspects of a typical clinical environment.

Each healthcare environment, whether it is a hospital or physician's office, implements a certain workflow. That is, a sequence of operations must occur for the patient to be examined, diagnosed, and treated. These operations are generally known as the clinical process or **clinical environment**. While the clinical process may vary based on environment, certain general features may be found in all processes. These include registration, consultation, examination, CPOE, dictation/transcription, and referrals or consults.

Registration

Usually, before the patient can be seen by medical staff, they must be registered or admitted. In **registration**, the initial clinical workflow step, the patient's demographic data (contact information, billing information, next of kin, current medications, and other information pertinent to the patient's general condition) are collected.

Consultation

It is important for medical staff to know what problems the patient is experiencing. This may give them insight into the illness and help them make a better diagnosis. **Consultation** (also known as medical history) questions may include information such as pain levels, location, and intensity. It may also include a brief history of activity so as to determine if behavior or certain actions contributed to the illness.

Examination

In addition to the patient's personal reflection of their problem, their physical status is also important. Thus, patients are usually physically examined to determine if there are any *macroscopic* (seen by the eye) irregularities like swelling, rashes, or other external expressions of illness, disease, or trauma.

The patient's vital signs may also be taken. These include:

- Body temperature (degrees Fahrenheit or Celsius)
- Blood pressure (millimeters of mercury)
- Pulse rate (heart rate, beats per minute)
- Respiratory rate (breaths per minute)

Depending on the patient's primary complaint, other body systems may be further explored during the initial **examination** to determine if there are any macroscopic (seen by the eye) irregularities like swelling, rashes, or other external expressions of illness, disease, or trauma.

Normally, the initial examination is performed by a nurse or other medical professional, but it could be by a physician. However, once the initial examination is completed, the patient is usually examined in more detail by a physician.

Physician Order Entry

After examination, the physician may need to run tests or order treatments. **Physician order entry** is the process of storing and transmitting diagnostic or treatment orders to other healthcare professionals in departments such as pharmacy, laboratory, or radiology. This may be accomplished using several methods, including the use of handwritten or typed paper orders; verbal orders, or, as described earlier in this chapter, an electronic order entry system (CPOE).

One aspect of CPOE that changes the way physicians enter orders is the use of **digital signatures**. Digital signatures are encrypted messages that are analogous to handwritten signatures but allow for electronic transmission and storage.

Dictation/Transcription

In cases where physicians give verbal orders, they may do so using a **dictation** system. This is usually a centralized voice-recording system that is shared amongst various physicians, all dictating orders at different times. A **transcription** is then created by a transcriptionist who transcribes the verbal orders to an electronic, paper, or film format. In the electronic format, the data can be directly interfaced to the EMR. A film format must be manually filed, either in a paper format or, in some cases, using *microfiche* (a small piece of photographic film).

Referrals/Consults

When the results from the ordered tests or treatments are available, the physician may complete a diagnosis. Sometimes, the physician may give the patient a **referral**, or send them, to other healthcare professionals for further diagnosis or treatment. If the physician is unclear about the diagnosis, he or she may **consult**, or communicate, with other physicians or specialists for additional information or ideas about a patient's diagnosis or treatment.

Medical Devices

4.1 Identify commonly used medical terms and devices (interfaces and devices).

Medical devices are used to diagnose and treat patients using physical and chemical means. Diagnostically, medical devices can measure heat, conductivity, and electrical waves. For treatment, they commonly emit various types of energy.

The *Food and Drug Administration (FDA)* regulates the manufacture and distribution of medical devices in the United States. It defines a medical device as an "instrument, apparatus, implement, machine, contrivance, implant, in vitro reagent, or other similar or related article, including a component part, or accessory which is:

- recognized in the official National Formulary, or the United States Pharmacopoeia, or any supplement to them,
- intended for use in the diagnosis of disease or other conditions, or in the cure, mitigation, treatment, or prevention of disease, in man or other animals, or

- intended to affect the structure or any function of the body of man or other animals, and which does not achieve any of its primary intended purposes through chemical action within or on the body of man or other animals and which is not dependent upon being metabolized for the achievement of any of its primary intended purposes."[3]

Medical devices can be as simple as a *stethoscope* (a mechanical device for listening to internal body sounds), or they can be highly complex, like a *computerized axial tomography scanner (CAT scanner)*.

Computerized Axial Tomography Scanner

Tomography is an imaging technique in which image sections or slices are created by using a penetrating wave. *Computerized axial tomography* (CAT or CT) is an x-ray system wherein the tomography is created by computer processing. CAT scans have several advantages over traditional radiography. For example, because of their inherent high-contrast resolution, very small differences between tissues that differ in density are distinguishable.

CAT scanners are large and complex, sometimes filling one or more rooms. Figure 5-5 shows an example of a CAT scan cross section of a human torso.

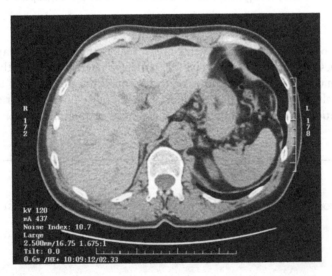

Figure 5-5 CAT scan of a human torso
© Hank Frentz/www.Shutterstock.com

Electrocardiogram Machine

Because the heart is electrically active, it generates an electrical signal that can be monitored. By positioning electrodes on the chest, an **electrocardiogram** (**EKG** or **ECG**) machine can display or print an electrocardiogram, which is a two-dimensional representation of electrical heart activity. Trained health professionals can "read" this two-dimensional representation of electrical heart activity as part of the diagnostic process for detecting heart disease or abnormality.

EKG machines are commonly small and transported by hand or by a small utility cart.

Electroencephalograph Machine

Part of brain activity is the *ionic* current flows within the brain's neurons. These electrical signals can be monitored using an **electroencephalograph** (**EEG**) machine. Trained health professionals can "read" this two-dimensional representation of electrical brain function to determine disorders such as coma, epilepsy, and brain death.

EEG machines are usually portable and may be transported by a utility cart.

Glucose Monitor

Diabetes mellitus is a disease in which the patient has high blood glucose as a result of one of two causes; either their bodies do not produce enough insulin, or their cells do not respond to the insulin that is produced. In either case, they must measure their blood glucose levels frequently. A **glucose monitor** is a portable electronic device that directly reads the level of glucose in the blood just seconds after a small sample is measured.

Magnetic Resonance Imaging

Instead of using x-ray radiation, it is possible to use **Magnetic Resonance Imaging** (**MRI**), which uses very strong magnetic fields to visualize internal body structures. One of the advantages to this process is that certain viewpoints are more easily obtained than with other imaging techniques. Another advantage is that the detail shown of internal body structures is greater than with traditional techniques. MRI machines are large and complex, usually filling a room.

Figure 5-6 illustrates an MRI scan of a human brain.

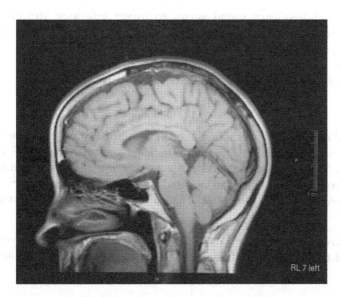

Figure 5-6 Human brain scan from an MRI machine
© Donna Beeler/www.Shutterstock.com

Portable X-ray Machine

An x-ray machine is a device that uses x-rays to cast static shadows of internal body structures on photographic film or an image sensor. However, these devices tend to be very large and can easily fill an entire room. A problem occurs when some patients are so sick they cannot easily be transported to the Radiology department where x-ray imaging is normally done. As a result, smaller, **portable x-ray machines** that can be moved to the patient were developed. Although they have less capability, the machines are portable (although still very heavy), which makes patient transport unnecessary.

Positron Emission Tomography

If certain radiopharmaceuticals are administered to patients, they behave in different ways in different body organs. In the case of **Positron Emission Tomography (PET)** scans, a positron-emitting radiopharmaceutical emits gamma rays, which can be reconstructed by the PET scanner into a three-dimensional image of tracer concentration, thereby providing highly detailed imaging of internal body structures. This technology is commonly used for the following diagnostic applications:

- Cardiology
- Musculoskeletal imaging
- Neuroimaging
- Oncology
- Pharmacology

PET scanners are large and complex, filling one or more rooms.

Ultrasound

Ultrasound machines use high-frequency sound waves to image soft-tissue structures like various organs. They do not use ionizing radiation, so they tend to be small and relatively inexpensive. However, image quality is not nearly as detailed as with x-ray or other technologies. Typical applications for ultrasound imaging include testing for fetal health during pregnancy, evaluating blood flow to the brain, and diagnosis of heart abnormalities.

Vascular/Nuclear Stress Test

A cardiac stress test is used to clinically determine the heart's response to physical stress. This can be done by having the patient walk on a treadmill or ride a stationary bicycle. If certain radiopharmaceuticals are administered to the patient, a *gamma camera* (a device that creates two-dimensional images from gamma rays) can be used to capture detailed images of the blood flow in the heart during a cardiac stress test. This is known as a **nuclear stress test** or **vascular stress test**.

While gamma cameras are not especially large, nuclear stress tests can involve other equipment like EKGs and treadmills or stationary bicycles. As a result, they are not very portable.

Vitals Cuff

To assess the status of a patient's condition, a baseline of standard measurements is regularly established. Each measurement can be taken with specific type of medical device. These commonly include the following:

- *Body temperature*—While historically measured with a mercury thermometer, newer technologies include digital infrared thermometers.

- *Blood pressure (BP)*—The most frequent blood pressure measurement method is with a blood pressure cuff. The cuff may have an analog dial or digital display. In the former case, the operator has to calculate the patient's blood pressure. In the latter case, both *systolic* (pressure from heart contraction) and *diastolic* (pressure at heart rest) pressures are displayed.

- *Pulse rate*—The rate that the human heart beats is measured in *beats per minute (BPM)*. It is commonly measured by taking the patient's pulse, which is done by feeling an artery's pulsation, which is caused by the beating heart.

- *Respiratory rate*—The number of breaths per minute is called the *respiratory rate (RR)*. Generally, the most accurate RR is measured with a stethoscope, but listening to breath sounds alone is also common.

Vital signs (or vitals) are frequently measured at one time during initial examination. Current technology is integrating the entire vital sign process, which results in a **vitals cuff**. This device measures two or more vital signs at one time for continuous monitoring without staff intervention.

Vitals cuffs are generally small, handheld devices that can be positioned on a bedside stand or IV pole.

Medical Interfaces

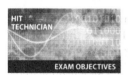

4.3 Identify and label different components of medical interfaces.

For information to be shared between systems, whether electronic or manual, there must be a common language or dialect that supports the system **interface**. In health care, there are many of these interfaces, and they provide standards by which health information can be exchanged. A nonexhaustive list of medical interfaces follows:

- *Health Level Seven (HL7)*—**Health Level Seven (HL7)** is a not-for-profit standards organization that develops frameworks and associated standards that support the exchange of electronic health information. Examples of HL7 standards include Clinical Document Architecture (CDA), Structured Product Labeling, and Clinical Context Object Workgroup.

- *e-prescribing*—The ability of a prescriber (healthcare professional who is authorized to order medications for patients) to electronically transmit an accurate prescription to a pharmacy from the point-of-care is called **e-prescribing**.

- *Continuity of Care Document*—An extension of the HL7 CDA, the **Continuity of Care Document (CCD)** specification is based on *XML markup standards* (an encoding mechanism that makes documents machine readable) for encoding patient summary clinical documents for exchange between systems.

- *Continuity of Care Record*—A **Continuity of Care Record (CCR)** is a standard based on XML that defines a patient health summary. The summary may contain information such as patient demographics, insurance information, medications, and care plan.

- *International Statistical Classification of Diseases and Related Health Problems, 10th Revision (ICD-10).* The **International Statistical Classification of Diseases and Related Health Problems, 10th Revision (ICD-10)** is a standard taxonomy for the classification of diseases, causes, social conditions, and other pertinent data, as retained by the *World Health Organization (WHO).* ICD-10 supersedes ICD-9 and provides five times more codes, significantly increasing diagnosis specificity.

- *Current Procedural Terminology (CPT)*—CPT is a coding scheme that describes various medical, surgical, and diagnostic services to facilitate uniform information communication regarding medical services.

- *Systematized Nomenclature of Medicine (Snomed)*—The **Systematized Nomenclature of Medicine (Snomed)** is a taxonomy that provides for the classification of disease. Its nomenclature includes 11 axes (or properties) of disease. These include topography, morphology, and function, in addition to others.

- *National Drug Code ID (NDCID)*—The **National Drug Code ID (NDCID)** is a 10-digit, 3-segment unique numeric code that identifies each medication listed in Section 510 of the U.S. federal Food, Drug, and Cosmetic Act.

- *Picture archiving and communication system (PACS)*—A system for providing storage and access to medical images from multiple source types is called **picture archiving and communication system (PACS)**. PACS eliminates manual storage requirements by encoding images using the Digital Imaging and Communications in Medicine (DICOM) format.

- *Evaluation and Management Coding (E/M codes)*—**Evaluation and Management Coding (E/M coding)** is a coding system for billing based on CPT codes that physicians must use with private insurance, Medicare, and Medicaid programs.

Health system interfaces are usually managed by a standards organization. These groups manage the process of developing, coordinating, and disseminating the standards such that health information can be exchanged, even in a changing technological environment.

Chapter 6 covers medical interfaces in more detail. It also includes common problems and systematic approaches to determining problem sources.

Chapter Summary

- As with other industries, health care has very specialized terminology and numerous acronyms. Therefore, it is important for anyone considering employment in the field to become familiar with common terminology, especially in the functional area in which they intend to work. For example, in the functional area of radiology alone, x-ray, CT scan, fluoroscopy, MRI, ultrasound, and nuclear medicine all represent regularly used imaging technologies.

- Hospitals usually have different medical departments. The number and types of departments depend greatly on hospital type and size and can be characterized in multiple ways. For example, some departments directly provide patient care. Others provide support services. Some only treat high-acuity patients, while others only treat outpatients.

- Software contains the logic that makes computers do what they do. Software is a set of instructions that helps hardware process data into information. Together, hardware and software are used to manage and manipulate both data and information. Clinical software is used to manage and manipulate data and information in the clinical environment. This can be in a hospital, a doctor's office, or a clinic.

- Each healthcare environment, whether it is a hospital or physician's office, implements a certain workflow. That is, a sequence of operations must occur for the patient to be examined, diagnosed, and treated. These operations are generally known as the clinical process or clinical environment. While the clinical environment may vary, certain general features may be found in all operations. These include registration, consultation, examination, physician order entry, dictation/transcription, and referrals or consults.

- Medical devices are used to diagnose and treat patients using physical and chemical means. Medical devices frequently measure heat, conductivity, or electrical waves. For treatment, they commonly emit various types of energy. The Food and Drug Administration regulates the manufacture and distribution of medical devices in the United States. In some cases, these devices must communicate.

- For information to be shared between devices or other systems, whether electronic or manual, there must be a common language or dialect that supports the system interface. In health care, there are many of these interfaces, and they provide standards by which health information can be exchanged.

Key Terms

acuity   A measure of the degree of patient disease or injury.

ambulatory surgery   Surgical procedures that can be accomplished without the patient needing an overnight stay.

audit software   Software that uses computer algorithms to automatically check that the correct Current Procedural Terminology (CPT) is used.

behavioral health   An area of psychiatry that studies the relationship between behavior and the patient's overall well-being.

billing software   Software that helps manage the billing process using technology like insurance claim validation.

cardiac care unit (CCU)   Hospital unit commonly reserved for patients who require specialized cardiac monitoring; the patient's electrocardiogram (EKG) is usually monitored on a central console at the bedside.

Cardiovascular department   A hospital department that addresses advanced cardiac specialties like electrophysiology, heart failure, and heart transplantation.

clinical environment   Sequence of operations that must occur for the patient to be examined, diagnosed, and treated.

clinical software   Used to manage and manipulate data and information in the clinical environment. This can be in a hospital, a doctor's office, or a clinic.

Code Blue   An emergency code, generally announced over a public address (PA) system in a hospital, that means a patient is in respiratory or cardiac distress and needs immediate help.

coding software   Used to help clinical staff, professional coders, and others generate complete and accurate coding using ICD and other codes before claim submission.

computed tomography (CT) or **computerized axial tomography (CAT)**   An x-ray system wherein the tomography is digitized and processed by a computer using special computer software algorithms that convert the data into radiographic image slices of the body.

computerized physician order entry (CPOE)   The use of electronic systems to store and transmit physician-generated orders to other healthcare professionals in departments such as pharmacy, laboratory, or radiology.

consult   When a physician communicates with other physicians or specialists for additional information or ideas about a patient's diagnosis or treatment.

consultation   Questions asked of a patient as part of the clinical process. May include information such as pain levels, location, and intensity. May also include a brief history of activity so as to determine if behavior or certain actions contributed to the illness (also known as medical history).

Continuity of Care Document (CCD)   An extension of the HL7 Clinical Document Architecture (CDA) based on XML markup standards for encoding patient summary clinical documents for exchange between systems.

Continuity of Care Record (CCR)   A standard based on XML that defines a patient health summary.

controlled substance   A drug or chemical substance controlled by the U.S. Controlled Substances Act (CSA) of 1970.

Current Procedural Terminology (CPT)   A coding scheme that describes various medical, surgical, and diagnostic services to facilitate uniform information communication regarding medical services.

Dermatology department   The hospital department where skin diseases are treated.

dictation   When a physician uses a centralized voice-recording system to give verbal orders. The recording system may be shared by various other physicians.

digital signatures   Encrypted messages that are analogous to handwritten signatures, but allow for electronic transmission and storage.

ears, nose, and throat (ENT)   The area of medical study that addresses facial plastic surgery, the head and neck, laryngology (voice), neuro-otology (middle/inner ear, base of skull), otology (ear), and rhinology (sinuses).

electrocardiogram (EKG or **ECG)**   A two-dimensional representation of electrical heart activity used to determine disorders such as undesirable heart rhythms (dysrhythmias).

electroencephalograph (EEG)   A two-dimensional representation of electrical brain function used to determine disorders such as coma, epilepsy, and brain death.

e-prescribing   The ability of a prescriber (healthcare professional who is authorized to order medications for patients) to electronically transmit an accurate prescription to a pharmacy from the point-of-care.

Evaluation and Management Coding (E/M coding) A coding system for billing based on CPT codes that physicians must use with private insurance, Medicare, and Medicaid programs.

examination Part of the clinical process, a physical examination to determine if there are any macroscopic (seen by the eye) irregularities like swelling, rashes, or other external expressions of illness, disease, or trauma.

family birth center (FBC) A department within a hospital or a stand-alone organization that strives to provide a family-oriented approach to childbirth.

glucose monitor A portable electronic device that directly reads the level of glucose in the blood just seconds after a small sample is measured.

gynecology The study of the female reproductive system.

Health Level Seven (HL7) A not-for-profit standards organization that develops frameworks and associated standards that support the exchange of electronic health information.

imaging The use of technologies that provide a visual representation of internal body structures to help diagnose and treat medical disorders.

Intensive Care Unit (ICU) Hospital unit reserved for patients with life-threatening diseases or trauma who need specialized care.

interface A common language or dialect that supports system communication and interaction with other systems.

International Statistical Classification of Diseases and Related Health Problems, 10th Revision (ICD-10) A standard taxonomy for the classification of diseases, causes, social conditions, and other pertinent data, as retained by the World Health Organization (WHO).

laboratory Department that provides various chemical, microbial, microscopic, and other studies for the purpose of diagnosing and treating disease or injury.

Magnetic Resonance Imaging (MRI) An imaging technology that uses very strong magnetic fields to visualize internal body structures.

medical devices Used to diagnose and treat patients by the use of physical and chemical means.

Medical/Surgical (Med/Surg) department A hospital department that primarily cares for adult patients before and after surgery.

National Drug Code ID (NDCID) A 10-digit, 3-segment unique numeric code that identifies each medication listed in Section 510 of the U.S. Federal Food, Drug, and Cosmetic Act.

neonatal intensive care units (NICU) A department for the care of newborns who need acute care in addition to specialized staff and equipment.

nuclear medicine Medical imaging technology that uses the radioactive decay of radiopharmaceuticals in the diagnosis and treatment of disease.

nuclear stress test The use of a gamma camera (a device that creates two-dimensional images from gamma rays) to capture detailed images of the blood flow in the heart during a cardiac stress test (also called a *vascular stress test*).

obstetrics Area of medicine concerned with pregnancy, childbirth, and post-birth issues.

occupational therapy (OT) An organizational department that helps people complete tasks of daily living.

oncology (ONC) The ONC department addresses the specific needs of cancer patients on both an inpatient and outpatient basis.

operating room (OR) The department where surgical operations are conducted.

ophthalmology department Department with staff and equipment necessary to diagnose and treat various eye conditions, including cataracts, glaucoma, and retinal disorders.

patient tracking software Used to help better manage patients and the practice by providing the ability to track services provided; by helping better manage patient demographics; by managing patient visit history, including services performed, time, and diagnosis; and by tracking patient-specific illnesses like allergies.

physical therapy (PT) Department for the diagnosis and treatment of range-of-motion issues due to illness or injury.

physician order entry The process of storing and transmitting diagnostic or treatment orders to other healthcare professionals in departments such as pharmacy, laboratory, or radiology.

picture archiving and communication system (PACS) A system for providing storage and access to medical images from multiple source types thereby eliminating manual storage requirements.

plastic surgery The medical specialty that is concerned with the alteration or reconstruction of the human body.

portable x-ray machine A smaller version of an x-ray machine that can be moved to the patient.

positron emission tomography (PET) A device in which the gamma rays emitted by positron-emitting radiopharmaceuticals (tracers) can be reconstructed into a three-dimensional image of tracer concentration, thereby providing highly detailed imaging of internal body structures.

Post-Anesthesia Care Unit (PACU) Department for patients recovering from the use of any type of anesthesia due to the potential for post-anesthesia events such as respiratory arrest. PACUs are sometimes called recovery rooms.

practice management software (PMS) Integrates medical software functionalities for day-to-day operations of a medical practice into one integrated system.

primary care physician (PCP) A doctor who diagnoses and treats patients in one of three specialties: family or general practice (GP), internal medicine, or pediatrics.

Progressive Care Unit (PCU) Used for transition of CCU and ICU patients who are making progress and may not need the full resources of the CCU or ICU (also called *Transitional Care Unit [TCU]*).

radiology (x-ray) department Department that provides imaging equipment that uses x-rays, ultrasound, or nuclear isotopes to detect and diagnose disease or injury.

referral Sending a patient to other healthcare professionals for further diagnosis or treatment.

registration A workflow step in which the patient's demographic data (contact information, billing information, next of kin, current medications, and other information pertinent to the patient's general condition) is collected.

respiratory therapy (RT) RT treats many respiratory conditions using resources such as bronchodilators, pulmonary rehabilitation, and mechanical ventilation.

scheduling software Software that helps manage the patient-scheduling process.

Systematized Nomenclature of Medicine (Snomed)   A taxonomy that provides for the classification of disease. Its nomenclature includes 11 axes (or properties) of disease.

stat   Derived from the Latin word, *statim*, meaning "immediately," stat means to expedite diagnosis, treatment, or other activities.

Stork unit   See *family birth center*.

transcription   The conversion of verbal physician orders to an electronic, paper, or film format.

Transitional Care Unit (TCU)   Used for transition of CCU and ICU patients who are making progress and may not need the full resources of the CCU or ICU (also called *Progressive Care Unit [PCU]*).

trauma center   An ER that is equipped and certified to address differing levels of trauma.

ultrasound   Machines that use high-frequency sound waves to image soft-tissue structures like various organs.

vascular stress test   The use of a gamma camera (a device that creates two-dimensional images from gamma rays) to capture detailed images of the blood flow in the heart during a cardiac stress test (also called a *nuclear stress test*).

vitals cuff   A device that measures two or more vital signs at one time for continuous monitoring without staff intervention.

Healthcare IT Acronyms

Table 5-3 contains healthcare IT acronyms that were introduced in this chapter. Many of these terms are listed in the CompTIA Healthcare IT Technician exam objectives, and most are also defined in the Key Terms section of this chapter. For a complete list of the healthcare IT acronyms in this book, see Appendix C.

Acronym	Full Name
ASC	ambulatory surgical center
BP	blood pressure
CAT	computerized axial tomography
CCD	Continuity of Care Document
CCR	Continuity of Care Record
CCU	Cardiac Care Unit
CPOE	computerized physician order entry
CPT	Current Procedural Terminology
CT	computed tomography
ECG or EKG	electrocardiogram
EEG	electroencephalograph

Table 5-3 **Healthcare IT acronyms used in this chapter** *(continues)*

Acronym	Full Name
E/M coding	Evaluation and Management Coding
ENT	ears, nose, and throat
FBC	family birth center or family birthing center
FDA	Food and Drug Administration
GP	general practice or general practitioner
HL7	Health Level Seven
ICD	International Classification of Diseases
ICU	Intensive Care Unit
L&D	Labor and Delivery
MRI	Magnetic Resonance Imaging
NDCID	National Drug Code ID
NICU	Neonatal Intensive Care Unit
OB/GYN	obstetrics/gynecology
ONC	Oncology
OR	operating room
OT	occupational therapy
PACS	picture archiving and communication system
PACU	Post-Anesthesia Care Unit
PCP	primary care physician
PCU	Progressive Care Unit
PEDS	Pediatrics
PET	positron emission tomography
PMS	practice management software
PT	physical therapy
RT	respiratory therapy
SNOMED	Systematized Nomenclature for Medicine
TCU	Transitional Care Unit

Table 5-3 Healthcare IT acronyms used in this chapter (*continued*)
© Cengage Learning 2013

Review Questions

1. Which of the following is true about medical imaging?
   a. No medical imaging technology is portable.
   b. It is accomplished using radiographic techniques.
   c. It is used to treat disease or injury.
   d. The images produced must be managed using manual storage techniques.

2. A PCP can include _____.
   a. those who practice internal medicine
   b. those with acute disease or disability
   c. cardiac surgeons
   d. practical nurses

3. A(n) _____ is an example of a hospital department that treats patients with high acuity.
   a. CCU
   b. PT
   c. ENT
   d. Dermatology department

4. In a hospital, if one hears, "Code Blue, CCU, Code Blue, CCU," over the PA system, what does it mean?
   a. Housekeeping is needed in CCU.
   b. All staff should report to CCU, stat.
   c. CCU beds are full and patients need to be directed to the Blue wing.
   d. A patient in CCU is likely in respiratory or cardiac distress and needs immediate help.

5. Hospitals in rural areas may not have _____.
   a. level-1 ERs
   b. an ambulance entrance
   c. any staff
   d. proper lighting

6. Which level of controlled substance will not likely be found in most hospitals?
   a. Schedule 1
   b. Schedule 2
   c. Schedule 3
   d. Schedule 4

7. An EMR is like a paper medical record, except _____.

    a. it must be manually indexed

    b. it has less storage capacity

    c. it can be more easily managed by people with little or no training

    d. it can be interfaced to other electronic systems

8. The types of patients seen by ASCs are usually _____.

    a. female with high acuity

    b. male with low acuity

    c. inpatients

    d. outpatients

9. In what department would a patient on a ventilator likely be treated?

    a. ONC

    b. ICU

    c. PT

    d. Radiology

10. The department where the family-oriented approach to childbirth is practiced is called _____.

    a. FBC

    b. OB/GYN

    c. NICU

    d. None of the above

11. To better manage patient demographics in many hospitals, doctor's offices, or clinics, _____ is frequently employed.

    a. CPT coding software

    b. patient tracking software

    c. communication software

    d. scheduling software

12. Standardizing orders across the organization is an advantage of what?

    a. Coding taxonomies

    b. Patient tracking software

    c. CPOE

    d. CAT scans

13. A third-party payer rejected a patient bill for a decubitus (ulcer) because the ICD-9 code submitted was 707.10. Was the payer correct in rejecting the bill?

    a. No, if the patient's insurance covers decubitus ulcers

    b. No, if the patient really had a decubitus ulcer

    c. Yes, because the ICD-9 code should have been 707.00.

    d. None of the above

14. Consultations are examples of _____.

    a. doctor-to-doctor interaction

    b. a stage in the sequence of operation in the clinical process or environment

    c. the endpoint in the sequence of operation in the clinical process or environment

    d. none of the above

15. After giving verbal orders via dictation, the orders are then _____.

    a. transcribed

    b. relayed to radiology

    c. included in informal care procedures

    d. transmitted to a third-party payer

16. A machine that displays or prints an EKG is called a(n) _____.

    a. EEG machine

    b. BP machine

    c. stethoscope

    d. EKG machine

17. To create a three-dimensional image of an internal body structure using gamma rays, one could use a(n) _____.

    a. PET scanner

    b. CAT scanner

    c. EKG machine

    d. none of the above

18. Vital signs include _____.

    a. body temperature, intracranial pressure, and respiratory rate

    b. blood pressure, pulse rate, respiratory rate, and body weight

    c. blood pressure, pulse rate, respiratory rate, and intracranial pressure

    d. body temperature, blood pressure, pulse rate, and respiratory rate

19. A common language or dialect that supports the ability of systems to exchange health information is called a(n) _____.

    a. PHI system

    b. telecommunication system

    c. interface

    d. computer program

20. An international standard taxonomy for the classification of diseases is _____.

    a. CPT

    b. HL7

    c. NDCID

    d. ICD-10

Case Projects

Case Project 5-1: Medical Terminology

Use the Internet as a research resource. Search for a list of common medical terms, and then identify 10 terms not found in this chapter. List and define each.

Case Project 5-2: Medical Departments

Visit your local hospital and ask for a list of their medical departments. Pick one department and ask for an interview with the department head. Write a two-page paper that outlines the function of the department, the type of patients they treat, and technology they use.

Case Project 5-3: Clinical Software

Clinical software is used to manage and manipulate data and information in the clinical environment. Research various medical practice management software suppliers. Create a table that compares the features of at least three packages.

Case Project 5-4: Clinical Environment (Process)

A sequence of operations must occur for the patient to be examined, diagnosed, and treated. These operations are generally known as the clinical process or clinical environment. Develop a scenario of a patient with a broken left arm. Describe in one page the experiences the patient may encounter during each stage of the process.

Case Project 5-5: Interfaces

Research ICD-9 and ICD-10 codes. Write a one-page paper that describes their similarities and differences.

Case Project 5-6: PHI Best Practices II

Use the Internet or other sources and conduct research on HL7 and CCD. Write a one-page paper that describes how they are related and how they are used.

Healthcare IT: Challenges and Opportunities—Revisited

Refer to the Superior Care Health Group (SCHG) scenario as related in the chapter opening section on "Healthcare IT: Challenges and Opportunities." Assume you are in Braden's position and are doing the research to mitigate SCHG's coding errors.

For this case, complete the following:

1. What does Braden need to do to find new medical coding software? Develop a one-page discussion.

2. In his research, Braden determines that some newer coding software uses algorithms to generate the codes. This process is either statistics based or rule based. What is the difference? Why would Braden want to use one or the other at SCHG? Develop a one-page discussion.

3. Braden also discovered that coding software tends to work better in settings like a hospital ER, outpatient surgery, or radiology department. Why is this? Does this preclude SCHG from using newer coding software? Develop a one-page discussion.

References

1. "Career Guide to Industries," *Bureaus of Labor Statistics. February 2, 2010, accessed October 21, 2011, http://www.bls.gov/oco/cg/cgs035.htm.*

2. "Electronic Medical Record/Electronic Health Record Systems of Office-based Physicians: United States, 2009 and Preliminary 2010 State Estimates." *Centers for Disease Control and Prevention. December 8, 2010, accessed October 26, 2011, http://www.cdc.gov/nchs/data/hestat/emr_ehr_09/emr_ehr_09.htm.*

3. "Is The Product A Medical Device?" *U.S. Food and Drug Administration. March 1, 2010, accessed October 31, 2011, http://www.fda.gov/MedicalDevices/DeviceRegulation andGuidance/Overview/ClassifyYourDevice/ucm051512.htm.*

Document Imaging and Problem Solving

After completing this chapter, you should be able to do the following:

- Describe frequently used healthcare image file types and their characteristics

- Identify medical interface components

- Explain the interface diagnosis process

- Describe the clinical software troubleshooting process

- Explain the need for and use of change control in the clinical environment.

Healthcare IT: Challenges and Opportunities

The Superior Care Health Group (SCHG) recently installed a new system for electronically sending patient prescriptions to pharmacies. This new e-prescribing system was working well until recently. Now the system is displaying errors periodically. When this occurs, the prescribing doctor has to call the prescription in to the pharmacy, which takes much more time.

The new office manager, Braden Thomas, is responsible for maintaining the system. Braden found an error-log file in the system. These errors are perplexing and contain cryptic messages such as the following:

SCRIPT error #3407, incorrect PVD format
PProc error #3212, Schedule 1 not allowed
PProc error #3245, not in formulary

After spending several hours changing various system configuration settings, the problems started getting worse. He finally realized that he doesn't know enough about troubleshooting the system to correct the problems. Even worse, he doesn't know who to contact to solve the problem other than the sales associate who sold SCHG the system. When he called that number, he was sent to voice mail. Meanwhile, the group's doctors are expressing displeasure with his ability to manage the system.

In a recent study, it was determined that less than 2 percent of hospitals surveyed employed a comprehensive electronic health record (EHR) system.[1] One reason for this may be the challenges associated with the integration of new technologies. For example, many of today's x-ray machines still produce images on cellulose or polyester film. In order to transfer this information into an electronic system, the film image has to be digitized, or the x-ray machine has to be modified to output digital images. In either case, there is an added cost in terms of time and resources.

Another example of transition challenges includes interfacing dissimilar systems. In order for information to be shared between systems, whether electronic or manual, there must be a common format, language, or dialect that supports the information exchange (interface). In health care, there are many of these interfaces, and they provide standard methods by which health information can be exchanged. They can also be very complicated, confusing, and the source of numerous operational problems.

The purpose of this chapter is to review the various aspects of document imaging, interfacing, and problem solving. In doing so, you will learn about file types and their characteristics, scanning and indexing, medical interface components, how to diagnose interface problems, how to troubleshoot clinical software problems, the concept of change control, and why it is needed.

Document Imaging

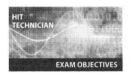

4.5 Explain the basics of document imaging.

When images are created in an electronic format, either natively (the device or system output is digital) or through conversion (the device or system output is physical and then converted to digital), they must be organized into a standardized format for storage. Because computers use data file storage techniques for data storage, images are commonly stored in **image files**. These files are composed of *pixels* (very small picture elements), *bitmap* data, vector (geometric) data, or some combination of these.

File Types

Digital image data is frequently stored in computer-readable data files, called image files. Because there are many different applications for image files, there are also many different types of image files. Image file types can be categorized by characteristics such as quality, size, resolution, and compression.

Characteristics

Image *quality* refers to how well the image file maintains the fidelity of the source image. For example, if a source image (a traditional x-ray, for example) and an image stored in an image file are viewed side by side, they will look the same if the image file-type quality is high. If the image file-type quality is low, there will be noticeable differences, depending on the image file type.

If a given image is stored in different image file types, the **file size**, the number of *bytes* (units of data) needed to store data in a given file, will be different. File size can be a factor in choosing which file type is used because in some applications file size is a constraint.

Some images, such as those that are physically large or are very detailed, create very large files. **Compression,** a technique to reduce to size of a digital image file, can be used.

Image **resolution** refers to the number of pixels (smallest image element) in an image. This is typically measured by multiplying the number of pixels high by the number of pixels wide. For example, a digital camera with a resolution of 2048 × 1536 pixels is said to have a resolution of 3 megapixels (actually, 3,145,728 pixels). File types with higher resolution (more *bits*) can store images with higher resolution.

A *bit* (from binary digit) is the smallest unit of computer storage. A *byte* commonly consists of eight bits. Computer file sizes are frequently measured in bytes.

Although there are a dozen or more image file types, the following four are ordinarily used in health care:

- *Graphics Interchange Format (GIF)*—The **Graphics Interchange Format (GIF)** format is best used for images with few distinct colors because it has low resolution and can only represent 256 unique colors. GIFs should not be used for photographic images.

- *Joint Photographic Experts Group (JPG or JPEG)*—The **Joint Photographic Experts Group (JPG or JPEG)** format is widely used for image storage when small size is needed and image quality degradation is not a problem. A typical application would be images presented on a Web site page.

- *Portable Document Format (PDF)*—This file format was created by Adobe Systems in 1993, but was released to the public domain in 2001. The **Portable Document Format (PDF)** format was created for representing documents that can be used with almost any type of software, hardware, or operating systems. As such, it is not truly an image format, but instead is a standardized system for capturing text, image, and document formatting information. However, it is possible to create a *PDF Image Only*, which is a non-searchable image of the page.

- *Tagged Image File Format (TIFF)*. Frequently used in commercial applications, **Tagged Image File Format (TIFF or TIF)** files are frequently used in commercial image applications because they are widely supported by most computer operating systems, including Linux, Mac, and Windows. TIFF files maintain excellent image quality, but at the expense of larger file sizes.

Some compression techniques decrease image quality, and are said to be *lossy*. Others also reduce file size, but do not impact image quality. These are said to be *lossless*. Many of today's file types are lossless even when compressed, which means image quality remains high.

TIFF files are frequently used in healthcare imaging because image quality can be very important in terms of patient diagnostic procedures. Table 6-1 summarizes the characteristics of TIFF and the other major image file types.

File Format	Quality	File Size	Resolution	Compression
GIF	Low	Small	8 bits	Lossless for few colors
JPG	Medium	Small	24 bits	Lossy and lossless
PDF	High	Large	64 bits	Lossy and lossless
TIFF	High	Large	64 bits	Lossy and lossless

Table 6-1 Image file formats and characteristics
© Cengage Learning 2013

There are additional image file characteristics that may apply in certain applications. For a complete summary, see http://www.library.cornell.edu/preservation/tutorial/presentation/table7-1.html.

Scanning and Indexing

Storing image data in image data files is the leading step in creating an electronic document storage and retrieval system. However, a typical hospital can create hundreds or thousands of electronic images per day. For instance, at registration, patient identification and insurance status is frequently captured by **scanning** identification and insurance cards for each patient admitted. Scanning is the process of converting data printed on paper-based (or other flat) media into electronic format by using a device called a *scanner*. Figure 6-1 illustrates a typical desktop scanner.

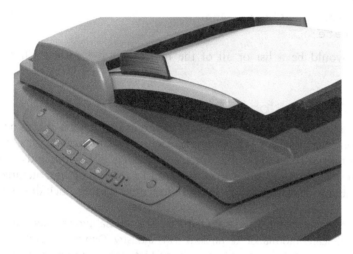

Figure 6-1 Desktop scanner
© Konstantin Shevtsov/www.Shutterstock.com

Regardless of the type of data scanned, the electronic file is part of the patient's health record, which means they are also considered protected health information (PHI). Consequently, their storage and retrieval must be managed in a prescribed manner. As a result, a very important step is to ensure the images are labeled with the appropriate patient information. This is called adding image *metadata*.

Metadata is data used to describe image attributes such as creation date, patient ID number, diagnostic results, and other information. For example, if a patient receives an MRI scan, the following metadata could be included in the image data file, or in addition to the image data file:

```
Title of Image = "Sagittal MRI of Left Knee"
Technician = "Emily J. Wesley"
Patient = "Cheryl Ann"
Date = "10/02/12"
Keywords = "T₁-weighted"
Format = "image/tiff"
Source = "Superior Care Health Group"
```

The metadata included in or with the image file will vary greatly, depending on the application, how the data is used, and regulatory requirements.

The process of saving structured or unstructured data for future retrieval and use is called **storage**. Assuming a *database* (an organized collection of digital data) was used for storage of the metadata shown in the previous example, the metadata elements could be used to create indexes. An **index** is a data structure that allows for fast **retrieval** (the process of locating saved data) of information. For example, if metadata element Patient was an index, images for patients could quickly be retrieved using the patient name. Using *Structured Query Language (SQL)*, a language used to retrieve database data, this could be accomplished as follows:

```
SELECT *
      FROM Images
      WHERE Patient = 'Cheryl Ann'
      ORDER BY Date;
```

The result of this code would be a list of all of the images for the patient Cheryl Ann, ordered by date.

Optical Character Recognition (OCR) and Structured Data

Data can be classified as structured or unstructured. **Structured data** is data that is arranged in a defined manner. Using the previous SQL example, each metadata element was stored in the database in a certain format so as to be able to retrieve it using SQL commands. **Unstructured data** is data that has no predefined arrangement. Examples of unstructured data include bitmap images, audio files (such as MP3), and most types of text (including e-mail).

The management of unstructured data is a colossal problem for the healthcare information technology (HIT) industry. One reason is that unstructured data cannot be transformed into actionable information the way structured data can. One solution is to convert unstructured data to structured data, but that would be a massive activity.

Some unstructured data occurs in the form of text printed on paper. Converting this to an electronic format requires creating (photographing) an image of the text. However, an electronic image of a document that contains text is just that—an image. As such, the document cannot be edited or searched. One method by which this problem can be avoided is called **optical character recognition (OCR)**. OCR is the process in which scanned images of handwritten or printed text are translated into computer readable text. This converts the image file into a data file containing the text, which can then be edited, searched, or printed, as with any normal computer-generated, word processor text.

Medical Interface Components

4.3 Identify and label different components of medical interfaces.

In order for information to be shared between systems, whether electronic or manual, there must be a common format, language, or dialect that supports the system interface. In health care, there are many of these interfaces, and they provide standard ways in which health information can be exchanged.

Sharing information between systems
© AcaG/www.Shutterstock.com

Health Level Seven

Health Level Seven (HL7) is a not-for-profit, accredited standards development organization that develops standard languages that define how electronic messages sent between health-care providers are formatted.

HL7 messages can be very complex and can appear unintelligible. One reason is the vast number of message types that providers need to exchange. Another is the variability in **provider types,** or the categories of healthcare suppliers who use electronic interfaces. For example, providers can be inpatient, nursing home, or day care and need to communicate with other providers, billing agents, or pay-to entities. All of this variation adds to the message complexity.

An HL7 message is composed of groups of message elements called segments that are presented in a defined sequence. These segments (or groups of segments) can be optional, required, and/or repeatable. This provides a basic message structure as shown in the following example:

```
MSH   Message Header segment
EVN   Event Type segment
PID   Patient Identification segment
[PD1] Patient Additional Demographic segment
[PV1] Patient Visit segment
```

In this message example, a Message Header segment, Event Type segment, and Patient Identification segment are required for the message. A Patient Additional Demographic segment and Patient Visit segment are optional

To demonstrate the contents of each message segment, consider a message with the purpose of recording a patient admission. The HL7 message type would be ADT (admit, discharge, transfer) and would be used with the code A01, which means admission. A typical admission message could be as follows:

```
MSH|^~\&|SCHG|SCHG|STR1|STR2|100459126753||ADT^A01|1463560660718C
000.1.|P|2.3|||AL|NE

EVN|A01|100459126753|||10432

PID|||000273546^^^^U|000273546^^^M^D~7273546726^^^M^N~03C2735467^
^^^X~03P2735462^^^^X~UV01-1134^^^^X~U00-127346^^^^X~D01-
2s297^^^^X~A01-12345^^^^Y~N98-
4033^^^^X|ANN^CHERYL^^^MRS|134222204|F|||77 Sunset
Strip^Smith^AASDSSA^^CF4 0TE||0101 465
76234|||2|||61253256719|||||||||||00000000

PD1||

PV1||
```

Thus, because a message sender and receiver both know how an HL7 ADT A01 would be formatted, both of their systems would be able to process the message automatically.

In health care, several HL7 message types are commonly used. The following subset is representative:

- ACK—general acknowledgement
- ADT—admit, discharge, transfer
- BAR—add/change billing account
- DFT—detailed financial transaction

Each message type has subtypes. For example, in the case of the ADT admission message, subtypes could include:

- A01—patient admit
- A02—patient transfer
- A03—patient discharge
- A04—patient registration

Each message subtype has a standard group of segments, or **standard contents**. In the case of the ADT A01 message, a group subset includes:

- MSH—message header
- SFT—software segment
- EVN—event type
- PID—patient identification

Technicians working with HL7 interfaces regularly come in contact with certain segments because some segments are commonly used in more than one message type. Table 6-2 summarizes seven commonly used HL7 segments.

Description	Code	Notes
Patient allergy information segment	AL1	The **AL1 segment** is used to transmit patient allergy information.
Billing segment	BLG	The **BLG segment** is used to provide billing information on the ordered service.
Insurance information segment	IN1	The **IN1 segment** is used to provide insurance policy coverage information for private health insurers.
Message header segment	MSH	The **MSH segment** defines the message's source, purpose, destination, and *syntax* specifics such as *delimiters* (separator characters) and character sets.
Observation request segment	OBR	The **OBR segment** defines information about an exam, diagnostic study/observation, or other assessment that is specific to an order.
Patient identification segment	PID	The **PID segment** is used to uniquely identify the patient.
Schedule activity information segment	SCH	The **SCH segment** contains patient scheduling information.

Table 6-2   **Common HL7 message segments**
© Cengage Learning 2013

E-Prescribing

The ability of a *prescriber* (healthcare professional who is authorized to order medications for patients) to electronically transmit accurate prescription information to a pharmacy from the point of care is called **e-prescribing**. E-prescribing can lower the cost of medication transactions and also help to better manage traditional medication administration problems. Because medications may be prescribed at any point of the patient's care, medication discrepancies can occur from one care setting to another. Thus, there is a need to *reconcile* the medication delivery. **Medication reconciliation** is the process of avoiding medication inconsistencies across care settings. This can be accomplished by reviewing the patient's complete medication schedule in one care setting and then comparing it with the treatment in a new care setting. This is often accomplished by integrating a medication reconciliation process within an EMR.

Another potential problem with patient medication administration is verifying that the right medications are administered to the right patient. **Bedside medication verification (BMV)** is commonly accomplished by using *barcodes* and a *barcode scanner* to verify that the right medications are administered to the right patient. A barcode is a two-dimensional representation of data that can be read by a machine through the use of a barcode scanner. In the BMV process, the medication intended for a patient has a barcode label that identifies the contents and intended patient. The patient also has a barcode, usually on a bracelet. Before the medication is administered, the medication is scanned using a handheld barcode scanner. Then, the patient is also scanned. The BMV system can then verify that the medication and patient combination is correct. Figure 6-2 illustrates a typical barcode.

Figure 6-2 Barcode
© Pastushenko Taras/www.Shutterstock.com

Drug allergy interactions (DAI), or the effects of certain drugs, when used individually or together, can also present concerns when administering medication. For example, it is possible that certain drugs, when used individually or together, can cause *allergic reactions* (undesirable activation of the immune system) in some patients. Accordingly, it is helpful to keep an accurate database of a patient's allergy list. This is accomplished using a CPOE system, patient tracking software, or other clinical systems.

Medical practices also have to consider the business aspects of medication administration. In some cases, a medication prescribed by a provider will not be reimbursed by a third-party payer like an insurance company. If this is the situation, it is said that the medication was not in the insurance company's *formulary*. A formulary is a list of medicines. **Formulary checking** is a process in which an e-prescribing system helps ensure that the medications prescribed are covered by the patients' insurance formularies.

Billing

Because most healthcare billing is based on a third-party payer system, bills are not usually sent to patients, but to insurance companies or governmental entities. When a provider converts to an electronic system, medical information from the provider's EMR/EHR system is used to create an electronic version of the bill. Thus, instead of the EMR/EHR receiving information, it is transmitting information using what is known as **outbound communication**. This means that the information is not staying within the organization (clinic, hospital, or private practice), but is being sent outside the organization.

As with other electronic messages, outbound messages also require a common format, language, or dialect that supports the message interface between the local system and the outbound system. Several HL7 **billing segments** are used for billing interface purposes. These are summarized as follows:

- PID—patient information
- PV1—visit information
- FT1—financial transaction
- IN1—insurance information
- IN2—additional insurance information
- IN3—additional insurance information, certification
- GT1—guarantor
- AUT—authorization information

As with other message types, each segment can be optional, required, and/or repeatable.

With thousands of providers sending millions of claims to payers, the ability of some payers to develop an infrastructure capable of managing the volume can be challenging. One solution is an intermediary service called a billing **clearinghouse**. A clearinghouse validates the claims to ensure they are error free. When the claim meets this standard, it is securely transmitted to the specified payer over a secure connection in order to meet HIPAA standards.

Diagnosing Interface Problems

4.4 Determine common interface problems and escalate when necessary.

All medical system interfaces can be complex. A vast number of systems and devices are trying to communicate with each other, and some of them were not necessarily designed to do so. Others may not follow the desired message standard or protocol. Even the lack of data quality can negatively impact the interface capability of certain systems. All of these problems add to the overall interface complexity.

When problems do arise, a timely resolution requires a *systematic approach* to determining the source of a problem. This is ordinarily called *troubleshooting* and can be distilled into four steps:

1. *Identification*—The system malfunction(s) or symptoms are identified.
2. *Generation*—Based on existing knowledge, research, or previous experience, generate a list of possible causes.
3. *Determination*—After additional data collection, frequently based on a process of elimination, determine the cause(s) of the problem.
4. *Confirmation*—Test and confirm that the solution has solved the problem.

This process can be applied to all medical interface problems with only slight variation.

HL7 Message Problems

One common problem that can occur with HL7 messages and other message types is **improperly formatted patient demographics**. For example, assume a PID segment as follows:

```
PID|||123-4T-6789||ANN^CHERYL^L^^^^L|SMITH|13650720|F|||690
HAPPYVILLE DR.^
```

Note that the patient's *Social Security number (SSN)* is 123-4T-5678, when it should be 123-45-6789. Problems like this are usually caught or prevented by the originating system, but this is not always the case.

Communication link errors are problems generated as a result of a failure in a fax, network, or Internet connection and can also cause minor data anomalies. This is especially true in geographic areas where the communication infrastructure is older, or where severe weather frequently interrupts power and other technological infrastructure.

In some cases, the software that is used to interpret HL7 messages can be misconfigured. For example, there may be an unintentionally **deactivated node**, message thread, or other HL7 object. This type of problem could allow an incorrect SSN of 123-4T-5678.

E-Prescribing Problems

Inaccurate patient demographics can also be a problem with e-prescribing systems. In many cases, this can occur at the patient level. During consultation (medical history), patients may be asked questions that include a brief history of medication allergies or reactions. Patients may not always respond honestly, or they respond with inaccurate information based on memory.

In terms of system interfaces, improperly formatted patient demographics can also be an issue. To illustrate, consider the HL7 message type RDE - Pharmacy Encoded Order. The segments included are as follows:

- MSH—message header
- PID—patient identification
- AL1—allergy
- PV1—patient visit
- ORC—common order
- RXE—pharmacy encoded
- RXR—pharmacy order route
- RXC—pharmacy order component

Because it is clear that the PID segment is included in this message, the same potential for improperly formatted patient demographics can occur with a medication order as with any other electronic message.

While HL7 messages can be used to order medications, the *National Council for Prescription Drug Programs (NCPDP)* developed the national standard for e-prescribing. Their goal was to create and encourage data interchange standards for pharmacies. One NCPDP message type that can be problematic is the SCRIPT Standard Implementation. This message is composed of segments that are identified by a three-character identifier. Segments are subdivided into smaller, logical components called **fields**, which are designated by a plus (+) symbol. Each field may have additional components, which are separated by a colon (:). Those may further have subcomponents separated by slashes (/). An example of a SCRIPT message is as follows:

```
UNA:+./*
UIB+UNOA:++1234567+++88888888:C:PASSWORDA+56897:P+199812:83333
UIH+SCRIPT:8:1:NEWRX+11732+++1998711:83333
PVD+P1+77121:D3+++++SCHG PHARMACY++615543656:TE
PVD+PC+6666666:B+++SMITH:SAM++++615543656:TE
PTT++19541225+JON:EMMY+F+3878845665:SY
DRU+P:LIPITOR 20MG::::24:ME+EA:7:38+:1 QD -TAKE ONE TABLET ONE
TIMES A DAY +85:199811:12*ZDS:3:84++R:1
UIT+1892+6
UIZ++1
```

Note that any errors in the formatting of this message may cause the message to be flagged as not translatable.

As with other message types, communication link errors as a result of fax, network, or Internet problems can also sometimes cause minor data anomalies in e-prescribing messages.

Another error that can occur with e-prescribing is a **deactivated medication**. This is a medication that is no longer contained in the pharmacy's formulary and therefore cannot be filled. In some cases, a pharmacy may not be able to accept messages for certain controlled substances based on local laws and regulations.

Billing Problems

As with other messages, billing messages can also have improperly formatted patient demographics and communication link errors. However, an additional potential problem with billing is an improperly formatted superbill. A **superbill** is a form used by providers to quickly list a patient's procedures and diagnosis for reimbursement. It is commonly adapted for a specific provider and is composed of patient demographic data, common CPT procedure codes, and common ICD diagnostic codes. Errors in the superbill may cause other errors in the billing process and delay reimbursement. For instance, a superbill with a diagnostic code for acute bronchitis and a liver profile exam could be rejected because the procedure does not fit the diagnosis. Figure 6-3 illustrates a typical superbill.

Some billing software can be configured to perform differently by changing the user configuration options available on hardware and software called **configuration settings**. As an illustration, consider the following settings:

- Bill patient for missed copays?
- Display diagnosis description?
- Display procedure description?
- Rendering provider?
- Scheduling provider?
- Service location?
- Supervising provider?

While some configuration settings like displaying a diagnosis description may only be cosmetic, others like provider data are fundamental for accurate data transmission. Therefore, when troubleshooting billing interface problems, software configuration issues should be on the list of possible causes.

CODE	MOD	DESCRIPTION	CODE	MOD	DESCRIPTION	CODE	MOD	DESCRIPTION
		OFFICE VISITS - NEW PATIENTS	10060		I&D ABSCESS/CYST, SIMPLE			**TRAYS (ADD TO SURGICAL PROCEDURES)**
99201		LEVEL 1, BRIEF; 10 min	10061*		I&D ABSCESS, COMPL. OR MULT.	02094		TRAY, SMALL W/ANESTHESIA
99202		LEVEL 2, LIMITED: 20 min	11200		SKIN TAG REMOVAL, UP TO 15	02097		SUTURE TRAY W/ANESTHESIA
99203		LEVEL 3, EXPANDED; 30 min	11201		SKIN TAG REMOVAL, EA ADDL 10	02098		TRAY, MEDIUM W/SPEC. ROOM(SIG)
99204		LEVEL 4, COMPREHENSIVE; 45 min	17000		DEST.BEN LESION,ANY METHD, 1st	02095		TRAY, LARGE + RM + SPEC. EQUIP
99205		LEVEL 5, COMPREHENSIVE; 60 min	17003		2nd THROUGH 14th LESIONS EA			**SUPPLIES**
99025		NEW PT. INITIAL VISIT W/*PROC.	17004		DEST BEN LES. ANY METH. > 15	02113		CANVAS KNEE BRACE
		PREVENTIVE EXAM - NEW PATIENTS	93000		EKG, COMPLETE	02010		CANVAS WRIST SUPPORT
99381		PREVENTIVE MEDICINE < 1 YEAR	93005		EKG, TRACING ONLY	02112		ELASTIC ANKLE WRAP
99382		PREVENTIVE MEDICINE, 1 - 4	20550		INJ TENDON/LIGAMENT/CYST/TRIGGER PT	02018		ELASTIC ANKLET
99383		PREVENTIVE MEDICINE, 5-11	20600*		INJECT.SMALL JT/BURSA/CYST	02579		FINGER SPLING
99384		PREVENTIVE MEDICINE, 12-17	20605*		INJECT. INT. JOINT/BURSA/CYST	02129		RIB BELT
99385		PREVENTIVE MEDICINE, 18-39	20610*		INJECT.MAJOR JOINT/BURSA/CYST	02255		SLING
99386		PREVENTIVE MEDICINE, 40-64	94150		VITAL CAPACITY; SEPARATE PROC	02488		STERI-STRIPS
99387		PREVENTIVE MEDICINE, 65+	69210		REMOVAL IMPACTED CERUMEN	02033		SUTURE REMOVAL KIT
		OFFICE VISITS - EST. PATIENTS	45330		SIGMOIDOSCOPY; FLEXIBLE	02011		TENNIS ELBOW SUPPORT
99211		LEVEL 1, BRIEF: 5 min	94010		SPIROMETRY W/GRAPHIC RECORD	02084		UNIVERSAL THUMB SPLINT
99212		LEVEL 2, LIMITED: 10 min			**DIAGNOSTICS**	OTHER: SPECIFY		
99213		LEVEL 3, EXPANDED: 15 min	87220		KOH			
99214		LEVEL 4, COMPREHENSIVE: 25 min	82270		OCCULT BLOOD			
99215		LEVEL 5, COMPREHENSIVE: 40min	Q0091		PAP SMEAR HANDLING			
		PREVENTIVE EXAM - EST. PATIENTS	86580		PPD			**CASTS/SPLINTS**
99391		PREVENTIVE MEDICINE < 1 YEAR	81000		URINALYSIS, ROUTINE	29065		LONG ARM CAST
99392		PREVENTIVE MEDICINE, 1 - 4	87210		WET MOUNT	29075		SHORT ARM CAST
99393		PREVENTIVE MEDICINE, 5-11	86588		QUICK STREP	29105		LONG ARM SPLINT
99394		PREVENTIVE MEDICINE, 12-17			**INJECTIONS** UNITS	29125		SHORT ARM SPLINT
99395		PREVENTIVE MEDICINE, 18-39	90782		SUB Q OR IM INJECTION OF MED	29405		SHORT LEG CAST
99396		PREVENTIVE MEDICINE, 40-64	J3420		B-12 ; up to 1000 mcg	29515		SHORT LEG SPLINT
99397		PREVENTIVE MEDICINE, 65+	J0702		CELESTONE SOLUSPAN 1cc	02220		CAST MATERIAL, PLASTER, ARM
		INITIAL NURSING FACILITY CARE	J2175		DEMEROL PER 100mg	02221		CAST MATERIAL, PLASTER, LEG
99301		LEVEL 1 , ANNUAL ASSESSMENT	J1460		GAMMA GLOBULIN; IM 1cc	02222		CAST MATERIAL, FIBERG, ARM
99302		LEVEL 2, NEW PROBLEM	J2000		LIDOCAINE	02223		CAST MATERIAL, FIBERG, LEG
99303		LEVEL 3, INITIAL ADMIT TO NH	J2550		PHENERGAN UP TO 50 mg			
		SUBSEQUENT NURSING FACILITY CARE	J0696		ROCEPHIN 250 mg X____ UNITS			
99311		LEVEL 1, STABLE NH VISIT	J3030		IMITREX 6mg X____ UNITS			
99312		LEVEL 2, MINOR PROBLEM	J1055		DEPO-PROVERA 150mg (CONTRACEPTIVE)			**FRACTURE MANAGEMENT:**
99313		LEVEL 3, MAJOR PROBLEM	J1070		DEPO-TESTOSTERONE 100mg			INITIAL _____
		PROCEDURES	J1080		DEPO-TESTOSTERONE 200mg			_____
94640		AIRWAY INHALATION TREATMENT	J9215		INTERFERON .05cc			_____
46600		ANOSCOPY;DIAGNOSTIC	J3301		KENALOG, PER 10mg			FOLLOW-UP 99024 (NO CHARGE VISIT) V54.8
92551		AUDIOMETRY AIR ONLY						

Figure 6-3 Superbill
© Courtesy of Don Self & Associates, www.donself.com

Medical Device Problems

As with messaging, there can be numerous problems and issues with medical device interfaces. In more than one instance, hours of troubleshooting were used just to determine that a subsystem or device was turned off and had no electrical **power**. Consequently, checking for power should be one of the first items on the list of possible problem causes.

Other power problems can cause medical device interface issues. *Brownouts* or voltage *sags* are temporary decreases in power line voltage caused by the start-up power demands of many electrical devices. They may result in medical device or interface components not operating accurately.

Less common power problems include *blackouts* (total loss of power), *spikes* (very short duration voltage increases), *surges* (short duration voltage increases), and *electrical noise* (unwanted high frequency energy). All power problems can be improved by using an *uninterruptible power supply (UPS)* on the device or central power system. Other devices also help stabilize power provided to sensitive electronic equipment. Table 6-3 summarizes less common power problems and potential solutions.

Problem Type	Description	Potential Solution
Blackout	A total loss of power	Uninterruptible power supply (UPS)
Spikes	Very short duration voltage increases	Surge arrestor at main breaker panel or surge suppressor at the equipment
Surges	Short duration voltage increases	Surge arrestor at main breaker panel or surge suppressor at the equipment
Noise	Unwanted high frequency energy	EMI/RF line filter or shield the source

Table 6-3 **Less common power problems**
© Cengage Learning 2013

Closely related to power problems are device **network and communication problems.** Network failure is a common reason for data corruption and can be caused by damaged *network media*, deteriorating *network interface cards* (NICs), or *server* crashes. In some cases, network and communication errors can occur even if nothing is broken, but there is excess network traffic, or a server is unable to service its load. These problems normally generate network **input/output (I/O) errors.**

Some medical devices can be configured to perform differently by adjusting their configuration settings. These settings may be user configurable or require the attention of specialized staff. Examples of network configuration settings for a typical electrocardiograph (EKG) machine are as follows:

- Network type
- Use Dynamic Host Configuration Protocol (DHCP)?
- Use wireless networking?
- Use network security?
- Type of network security
- Use Point-to-Point Protocol (PPP)?

If any of these settings are configured incorrectly, the device may not be able to communicate with the EMR/EHR.

Troubleshooting Clinical Software Problems

HIT TECHNICIAN
EXAM OBJECTIVES

4.6 Given a scenario, determine common clinical software problems.

Clinical software is a broad term. For example, it can refer to software for managing clinical drug trials and clinical outcomes management. However, in the context of HIT, it commonly refers to one or more of the following:

- Auditing systems
- Billing systems
- Coding systems
- CPOE systems
- EMR/EHR systems
- Lab information system (LIS)
- Patient care planning systems
- Pharmacy information system (PIS)
- Patient tracking systems
- Patient scheduling systems
- Radiology information system (RIS)
- Workflow management systems

Each of these systems is complex, but when they are used together as an integrated system, their complexity increases exponentially. Therefore, having a defined plan for troubleshooting is imperative for the HIT professional.

Locate the Affected Modules or Fields

Recall that troubleshooting is the process of addressing problems using a systematic approach to determining the source of a problem. The troubleshooting process is often distilled into four steps:

1. The system malfunctions or symptoms are identified.
2. A list of possible causes is generated based on existing knowledge, research, or previous experience.
3. After additional data collection, and frequently based on a process of elimination, the causes of the problem are determined.
4. A solution is tested to confirm the problem has been solved.

In the case of troubleshooting clinical software, the first step may be difficult. Software systems like EMR/EHR are extremely complex and may contain many software **modules** (subunits that are a part of larger medical software systems) that could be introducing problems. For example, an incorrect SSN of 123-4T-5678 that is causing a billing claim to be rejected could be the result of a database configuration error. However, numerous layers of software could be between the actual database and a report that shows the error. In these cases, a common approach is to divide the problem into smaller *domains* (areas of concern or interest) and work backward in the system from where the problem appears. Thus, the billing data that was transmitted to the third-party payer or clearinghouse should be examined to rule out communication link errors. If this source data has the error, then the problem domain should be moved backward to the next subsystem. If the source data does not have the error, communication link errors are suspect. This process continues until the source of the problem is determined.

Determine Data Types

Using the previous example, if the problem is determined not to be a communication link error, it could be a **data type** error, a data classification based on data properties like text, numeric, and binary. Because database and/or software applications know what type of data is expected, it is highly unlikely that the wrong type of data will be passed through the system unless it was configured to do so. To illustrate, when collecting data during patient admission, the system will have an SSN entry **field** (a computer screen data entry area) as part of a patient demographic collection computer screen. The software (or underlying database) is expecting the SSN to be entered using a certain format and with certain characters. Thus, if the operator tries to enter 123-4T-5678, the system will disallow the entry because that is not a valid SSN due to the inclusion of the 'T' character. However, in some systems it is possible to configure various aspects of data entry, including formats and data types. In this case, a manual configuration change may have allowed the incorrect SSN. Consequently, configurations must always be considered as a source of software problems.

Escalate When Necessary

In the case where a software problem cannot be determined through normal troubleshooting methods, it may have to be *escalated*. This means that the problem is reported to either an in-house or outside technical support group.

If the organization is large, like a hospital, it may have IT staff that can address certain software problems, especially if the IT department produced the software. Even if that is not the case, the in-house IT staff may have specialized training such that they can address certain problems. Therefore, as part of the **problem escalation process**, appropriate personnel such as in-house support groups are usually contacted first. If an in-house group is not available, or the in-house group cannot solve the problem, the problem is usually escalated to an outside **technical support** group, which is a group of technicians trained to support the use of certain hardware and software.

An outside technical support group may be part of the software vendor's organization, or the software vendor may contract the service out to a third party. In some cases, the technical support services may be contracted to third party in another country.

Technical support groups often organize their support into levels or tiers, called **tiered support**, so as to provide the best support in the most efficient manner. Using this scheme, the initial call to a support group will encounter Tier 1 support, which collects customer information and provides the most basic level of support. If the problem cannot be resolved at this level, it is escalated to Tier 2, which provides more in-depth support from staff with more experience and knowledge. If the problem cannot be resolved at this level, it is escalated to Tier 3. In many organizations, this is the highest level of support, and may involve staff capable of working directly with the software designers.

One problem with tiered support is that it may take hours or days to reach the right level for problem resolution. Another concern is that, in some cases, the technical support services may be contracted to a third party in another country. This can create a language barrier, making a situation that is already difficult to communicate even more difficult. Table 6-4 summarizes support tier functionality.

Tier Level	Description
Tier 1	Collects customer information, provides very basic support for simplest problems
Tier 2	More in-depth support from staff with more experience and knowledge
Tier 3	Usually the highest level of support; may involve staff capable of working directly with the software designers
Tier 4	In rare cases, provides direct access to software designers

Table 6-4 Tiered technical support
© Cengage Learning 2013

Change Control

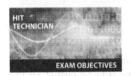

4.7 Describe change control best practices and its system-wide effects.

When clinical software modules are used together as an integrated system, their complexity increases exponentially. Another dimension that increases complexity even more is the fact that software regularly changes over time. This is because of new requirements and changes to existing requirements, especially in a highly regulated industry. Moreover, the software may have to be changed to correct errors (also known as *bugs*), or to improve its performance.

Imagine a clinical software system with 10 modules. If the LIS module is updated, what impact will that have on the EMR? The problem is compounded especially if the modules are provided by different vendors, making it difficult to coordinate software updates.

Procedural Systematic Customization

To help better manage clinical software changes, a **change control** system is needed. This system should represent a process that provides a procedural method for **systematic software customization**. In other words, a routine process should be developed to address the needs of software change throughout an organization. This includes adapting to change, controlling change, and implementing change. Generally, the specifics required include:

- Change compliance reporting
- Defining specific activities that will occur during a change process
- Delineating the testing and cutover process
- Developing a change schedule
- Identifying impacts of change
- Specifying roles for staff with regard to change control

Even though many organizations implement change control, some still use paper-based tools, spreadsheets, and e-mail to manage the change process. While manual tools can be somewhat effective, automated change management tools are available that should be considered by large organizations.

Governance Board

As software applications increase in importance to the organization, increasing numbers of people are affected by software changes. This increases the risk and cost of failure. Consequently, there is a general need to align the entire organization around objectives, strategies, tools, and methods that minimize change failures. This approach is called *governance*, and basically means that more organizational members will be involved in the software change process. One way this occurs is through a **change management governance board (CMGB)**, whose responsibility is to work together to approve changes that may result in critical service interruption.

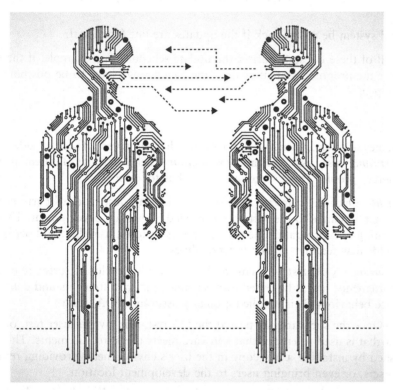

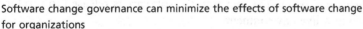

Software change governance can minimize the effects of software change for organizations
© VLADGRIN/www.Shutterstock.com

System Patching and Updates

A software change can be a patch or an update. A **patch** refers to a specific software problem fix for a security, usability, or performance issue. Patches are usually considered small changes, and may be issued on a frequent basis. **Updates** are usually larger changes than patches, and while they can address software security, usability, or performance issues, they can also add features or functionality. Updates are usually issued less frequently than patches.

Change Scheduling

Scheduling software changes in a large hospital for systems that are highly integrated can be challenging. To make matters worse, some clinical software systems are used around the clock, every day of the year. Therefore, the change scheduling process must take into consideration several important questions:

- Is there a backup system?
- Can collected data be recovered during the system downtime?
- Will the downtime impact any life support systems?
- Were all impacted departments notified, and did they approve the proposed schedule?
- Can the old system be rolled back if the updates are not functional?

The answers to all of these questions affect the update schedule. For example, if there is no backup system for the proposed system change, the change may have to be postponed until one can be developed.

Change-Control Environments

There are four stages or environments in the software change process. These include *development, quality assurance test, user test,* and *production.* Each stage has different properties and involves different people. These stages are defined as follows:

- *Development*—Once the software developers (either in-house or third-party vendor) determine that a change to the software is needed, they start **development**. This involves writing new program code that addresses security, usability, and performance issues or adds new features and/or functionalities.
- *Quality assurance (QA) test*—To ensure that the newly developed software meets the stated requirements, it will be tested to meet functional requirements and defined performance behaviors. This is called a **quality assurance (QA) test.**
- *User test*—Once the software has passed the QA test, it is given a **user test,** or an assessment that is used to ensure that software meets users' requirements. This can be accomplished by installing a test copy in the user's environment, providing remote access to users, or even bringing users to the development location.
- *Production (live)*—Following the user test, the software is released to **production,** where it is used in a live environment.

Each of these steps may be subdivided into more detailed steps, or additional steps may be added. For example, once the user test is accomplished, it may be necessary to test how well the software interfaces with other systems. This is called *system integration testing.*

Chapter Summary

- When images are created in an electronic format, either natively (the device or system output is digital) or through conversion (the device or system output is physical and, then converted to digital), they must be organized into a standardized format for storage. Because computers use data file storage techniques, images are commonly stored in image files. These are composed of pixels (very small picture elements), bitmap data, vector (geometric) data, or some combination of these.

■ Storing image data in image files is the leading step in creating an electronic document storage and retrieval system. However, a typical hospital can create hundreds or thousands of electronic images per day. For instance, at registration, patient identification and insurance status is frequently captured by scanning identification and insurance cards for each patient admitted. Scanning is the process of converting data printed on paper-based (or other flat) media into an electronic format by using a device called a scanner.

■ Data can be classified as structured or unstructured. Structured data is arranged in a defined manner. Using SQL as an example, each metadata element was stored in the database in a certain format so as to be able to retrieve it using SQL commands. Unstructured data has no predefined arrangement. Examples of unstructured data include bitmap images, audio files (MP3), and most types of text (including e-mail). Some unstructured data occurs in the form of text printed on paper. Converting this to an electronic format requires creating (photographing) an image of the text. However, an electronic image of a document that contains text is just that—an image. As such, the document cannot be edited or searched. One method by which this problem can be circumvented is optical character recognition (OCR). OCR is the process in which scanned images of handwritten or printed text are translated into computer-readable text. This converts the image file into a data file containing the text, which can then be edited, searched, or printed, as with any normal computer-generated, word processor text.

■ In order for information to be shared between systems, whether electronic or manual, there must be a common format, language, or dialect that supports the system interface. In health care, there are many of these interfaces, and they provide standard ways in which health information can be exchanged. For example, Health Level Seven (HL7) is an accredited standards development organization that develops standard languages that define how electronic messages sent between healthcare providers are formatted. An HL7 message is composed of groups of message elements called segments that are presented in a defined sequence. These segments (or groups of segments) can be optional, required, and/or repeatable.

■ Troubleshooting is the process of addressing problems using a systematic approach to determine the source of a problem. The troubleshooting process is often distilled into four steps. In the first step, system malfunctions or symptoms are identified. Then, based on existing knowledge, research, or previous experience, a list of possible causes is generated. After additional data collection, and frequently based on a process of elimination, the causes of the problem are determined. In the last step, the solution is tested to confirm the problem has been solved. In the case of troubleshooting clinical software, the first step may be difficult. In these cases, a common approach is to divide the problem into smaller domains (areas of concern or interest) and work backwards in the system from where the problem appears. This process continues until the source of the problem is determined.

■ A dimension that increases the complexity of clinical software management is the fact that software regularly changes over time. This is the result of new requirements and changes to existing requirements, especially in a highly regulated industry. Moreover, the software may have to be changed to correct errors (also known as bugs), or to improve its performance. In order to manage these problems, a change control system is used.

Key Terms

AL1 segment An HL7 segment used to transmit patient allergy information.

bedside medication verification (BMV) Verification that the right medications are administered to the right patient by scanning barcodes at the bedside.

billing segments HL7 message units that are used for billing interface purposes.

BLG segment HL7 message unit used to provide billing information on the ordered service.

change control A process for addressing the needs of software change throughout an organization.

change management governance board (CMGB) An organizational group whose responsibility is to work together to approve changes that may result in critical service interruption.

clearinghouse An intermediary billing service that validates claims to ensure they are error free.

clinical software Computer programs that define EMR/HER, LIS, PIS, RIS, and other electronic healthcare systems.

communication link errors Problems that are generated as a result of failure in a fax, network, or Internet connection and that can cause minor data anomalies.

compression A technique used to reduce the size of a digital image file.

configuration settings User configuration options available on hardware and software.

data type A data classification based on data properties like text, numeric, and binary.

deactivated medication A common cause of e-prescribing message failure due to medication no longer being contained in the pharmacy's formulary; therefore, the prescription cannot be filled.

deactivated node A common cause of HL7 message failure due to configuration or other errors.

development Writing new program code that addresses security, usability, and performance issues or adds new features or functionality. The first stage of the software change process.

drug allergy interactions (DAI) The effect of certain drugs, when used individually or together, causing allergic reactions (activation of the immune system) in some patients.

e-prescribing The ability of a prescriber to electronically transmit accurate prescription information to a pharmacy from the point of care.

field A computer screen data entry area. Also, a component of an HL7 segment.

file size Numbers of bytes (units of data) needed to store data in a given file.

formulary checking A process in which an e-prescribing system helps ensure that the medications prescribed are covered by the patients' insurance formularies.

Graphics Interchange Format (GIF) Image format best used for images with few distinct colors because it has low resolution and can only represent 256 unique colors.

Health Level Seven (HL7) A not-for-profit, accredited standards development organization that develops standard languages that define how electronic messages sent between healthcare providers are formatted.

image files Files that are composed of pixels (very small picture elements), bitmap data, vector (geometric) data, or some combination of these.

improperly formatted patient demographics A common problem with HL7 and other message types.

IN1 segment HL7 message unit used to provide insurance policy coverage information for private health insurers.

index A data structure that allows for fast retrieval of information.

input/output (I/O) errors Errors that are the result of network and communication problems.

Joint Photographic Experts Group (JPG or **JPEG)** Format widely used for image storage when small size is needed and image quality degradation is not a problem.

medication reconciliation The process of avoiding medication inconsistencies across care settings.

metadata Data used to describe image attributes such as creation date, patient ID number, diagnostic results, and other information.

modules Software subunits that are part of larger medical software systems.

MSH segment HL7 message unit that defines the message's source, purpose, destination, and syntax specifics such as delimiters (separator characters) and character sets.

network and communication problems A common reason for data corruption. Can be caused by damaged network media, deteriorating network interface cards (NIC), or server crashes.

OBR segment HL7 message unit that defines information about an exam, diagnostic study/ observation, or other assessment that is specific to an order.

optical character recognition (OCR) The process in which scanned images of handwritten or printed text are translated into computer readable text.

outbound communication Billing information that is not staying within the organization (clinic, hospital, or private practice) but is being sent outside the organization.

patch A specific software problem fix for security, usability, or performance issues.

PID segment HL7 message unit used to uniquely identify the patient.

Portable Document Format (PDF) A file format created by Adobe for representing documents that can be used with almost any type of software, hardware, or operating system.

power (lack of) A common hardware problem is the unintentional lack of electricity.

problem escalation process A system by which hardware or software malfunctions can be addressed by appropriate personnel.

production The final step in the software change process wherein software is used in a live environment.

provider types Categories of healthcare suppliers who use electronic interfaces.

quality assurance (QA) test An assessment to ensure that software meets functional requirements and defined performance behaviors. The second stage of the software change process.

resolution The number of pixels (smallest image element) in an image. More pixels mean higher resolution.

retrieval The process of locating saved data.

scanning The process of converting data printed on paper-based (or other flat) media into an electronic format by using a device called a scanner.

SCH segment HL7 message unit that contains patient scheduling information.

standard contents Group of standard segments used frequently in an HL7 message subtype like MSH, SFT, EVN, and PID.

storage The process of saving structured or unstructured data for future retrieval and use.

structured data Data that is arranged in a defined manner.

superbill A form used by providers to quickly list a patient's procedures and diagnosis for reimbursement.

systematic software customization Another term for change control, but using procedural techniques.

Tagged Image File Format (TIFF or **TIF)** File format frequently used in commercial image applications because it is supported by most computer operating systems, including Linux, Mac, and Windows and provides good image quality. However, file size tends to be large.

technical support A group of technicians trained to support the use of certain hardware and software.

tiered support Technical support provided in service levels so as to provide the best support in the most efficient manner.

unstructured data Data that has no predefined arrangement.

update A software problem fix that may address security, usability, or performance issues but also adds features or functionality.

user test An assessment used to ensure that software meets users' requirements; the third stage of the software change process.

Healthcare IT Acronyms

Table 6-5 contains healthcare IT acronyms that were introduced in this chapter. Many of these terms are listed in the CompTIA Healthcare IT Technician exam objectives, and most are also defined in the Key Terms section of this chapter. For a complete list of the healthcare IT acronyms used in this book, see Appendix C.

Acronym	Full Name
BMV	bedside medication verification
DAI	drug allergy interactions
HL7	Health Level Seven
I/O	input/output
LIS	lab information system
OCR	optical character recognition
PIS	pharmacy information system
QA	quality assurance
RIS	radiology information system
SQL	Structured Query Language
SSN	Social Security number
UPS	uninterruptible power supply

Table 6-5 **Healthcare IT acronyms introduced in this chapter**
© Cengage Learning 2013

Review Questions

1. Which of the following is true about image files?

   a. They can contain bitmap or geometric data.

   b. They are produced only using radiographic techniques.

   c. They are used as treatments for disease or injury.

   d. They must be managed using manual storage techniques.

2. Image compression techniques that decrease image quality are said to be _____.

   a. poor

   b. above average

   c. lossy

   d. lossless

3. Because image quality can be very important to patients in terms of patient diagnostic procedures, _____ files are frequently used.

   a. GIF

   b. JPEG

   c. TIFF

   d. PDF

4. _____ describes image attributes such as creation date, patient ID number, diagnostic results, and other information.

   a. Text
   b. File type
   c. Data properties
   d. Metadata

5. A newspaper would be an example of _____.

   a. metadata
   b. structured data
   c. unstructured data
   d. none of the above

6. An HL7 message header segment would be labeled _____.

   a. MHS
   b. MSH
   c. HMS
   d. EMR

7. An HL7 observation request segment would be labeled _____.

   a. ORS
   b. OBS
   c. OBR
   d. OBE

8. _____ is the process of avoiding medication inconsistencies across care settings.

   a. Medication reconciliation
   b. Medication formulation
   c. Medication fixation
   d. Medication derivation

9. _____ are used in the BMV process.

   a. Flatbed scanners
   b. Barcode scanners
   c. Wi-Fi scanners
   d. Formulary scanners